THE
YOUNG VICTORIA

ALSO BY ALISON PLOWDEN

The House of Tudor
Marriage with my Kingdom
The Assassination of Elizabeth

THE
YOUNG VICTORIA
Alison Plowden

C. 1

STEIN AND DAY / *Publishers* / *New York*

B

VICTORIA

First published in the United States of America in 1983
Copyright © 1981 by Alison Plowden
All rights reserved
Printed in the United States of America

STEIN AND DAY/*Publishers*
Scarborough House
Briarcliff Manor, N.Y. 10510

Library of Congress Cataloging in Publication Data

Plowden, Alison.
   The young Victoria.

   Bibliography: p.
   Includes index.
   1.   Victoria, Queen of Great Britain, 1819–1901 —
Childhood and youth.   2.   Great Britain —Kings and
rulers —Biography.   I.   Title.
DA555.P55   1981   941.07′4′0924   [B]   80-5908
ISBN 0-8128-2766-X

Contents

Illustrations

Authors Note

In writing this book I have leant gratefully on the work and research of recent biographers of Queen Victoria, notably *Queen Victoria* (1819–1861), by the late Cecil Woodham-Smith (Hamish Hamilton, 1972) and *Victoria R.I.* by Elizabeth Longford (Weidenfeld and Nicolson, 1964). I would like to acknowledge the gracious permission of Her Majesty The Queen for the republication of material from the Royal Archives which is subject to copyright.

I am also grateful for permission to quote from the letters of the Dowager Duchess of Saxe-Coburg-Saalfeld, translated by Helen Cathcart, which appear in *Royal Bedside Book* by Helen Cathcart (W. H. Allen, 1969).

Other invaluable sources include *The Greville Memoirs*, edited by Lytton Strachey and Roger Fulford (Macmillan, 1938), *The Letters of Queen Victoria*, edited by A. C. Benson and Viscount Esher (1907) and *The Girlhood of Queen Victoria*, edited by Viscount Esher (1912) which contains selections from her early Journal.

THE
YOUNG VICTORIA

Prologue
A Nation Bleeds

It is with the most poignant grief we announce that H.R.H. the Princess Charlotte is NO MORE. This melancholy intelligence was at 7 o'clock this morning communicated to the Lord Mayor by Lord Sidmouth.

The Times, 6 November 1817

At Claremont House everything was ready for the happy event. The baby linen, chosen 'in the plainest style and the finest quality', had been carefully laid out by the monthly nurse Mrs Griffiths, 'a respectable woman in the habit of attending the first families in the country on similar occasions for the past thirty years'. Sir Richard Croft, the accoucheur, was already in residence. Dr Baillie, the family physician, and Dr Sims were standing by, while a bevy of important personages – Earl Bathurst, Secretary for War, Viscount Sidmouth, the Home Secretary, Mr Vansittart, Chancellor of the Exchequer, the Archbishop of Canterbury and the Bishop of London – had made their preparations to set out at a moment's notice in response to a summons from Claremont.

Outside these exalted circles, the people of England waited in eager anticipation of an announcement that the heiress presumptive to the throne had presented them with a much needed addition to the royal family – preferably a boy, whose arrival would, it was estimated, send the stock market up by at least six points. Princess Charlotte of Wales was only twenty-one.

She looked to be a fine, healthy young woman, if a trifle on the stout side, and she would, of course, be getting the best available medical attention at her lying-in. To the uninitiated there seemed no reason why anything should go wrong. So the nation waited hopefully, and went on waiting.

The Princess's doctors had calculated that she could expect to be confined at any time after 19 October, but it was not until the evening of Monday, 3 November that a message was sent round to the stables and the grooms were able to mount their ready-saddled horses and set out with the news that Her Royal Highness's labour had begun at last. During the early hours of Tuesday the distinguished gentlemen whose presence was required to attest the birth were being set down at the pillared and porticoed entrance of Claremont House and Dr Baillie came hurrying over from Virginia Water. But there was, apparently, no urgent need for haste even now. At midday Sir Richard Croft announced that matters were 'in every way in as much forwardness as he would desire it', but the Princess had still not been put to bed and was walking about her room on her husband's arm. At three o'clock another confident bulletin was issued, but that night Dr Sims, an expert in the use of instruments, was summoned from London, although he was not admitted to see the patient.

At 8.15 a.m. on Wednesday, 5 November, when Charlotte had been in labour for more than thirty-six hours, the bishops and Cabinet ministers keeping their weary vigil in the breakfast-room at Claremont were informed that considerable though very gradual progress had been made during the night, and the doctors hoped that the child would be born without artificial assistance. There was a strong prejudice against the use of forceps among the medical profession and, while in this case their use might have saved both mother and child, there was, at a time when antiseptic precautions were unknown, admittedly always a high mortality rate when instruments were used.

Wednesday dragged by interminably. The village of Esher, which lay on the edge of the Claremont estate, had filled up with journalists and sightseers and the Bear Inn was doing a roaring trade. At Claremont itself, the Princess, supported by her devoted husband, seemed to be bearing up well under her long, exhausting ordeal. Leopold of Saxe-Coburg had scarcely left her, holding her hand and sometimes lying down on the bed beside her. At nine o'clock that night the child was born. It was a boy, well-formed and unusually large, but it showed no signs of life. Hastily plunged into a bath of hot water, shaken and slapped and rubbed with salt and mustard, it stubbornly resisted all attempts to persuade it to take an interest in its surrounding. But the mother was still 'doing extremely well'. She had accepted the loss of her baby with stoicism, almost with indifference, and now, her amazing vitality and high spirits apparently unimpaired, she was chatting away to her attendants and sitting up eating toast and chicken broth. The witnesses dispersed thankfully to their homes and Prince Leopold went away to get some sleep. Even Richard Croft thought it safe to leave his patient to rest.

Soon after midnight Charlotte began to complain of nausea and ringing in her ears. Her pulse became rapid and although she had so far been able to keep her promise to Mrs Griffiths not to 'bawl or shriek', she was now obviously in great pain. Croft, hurriedly recalled by the nurse, found her very restless, breathing with difficulty and 'cold as any stone'. Frantically the doctors tried to warm her, plying her with hot wine and brandy until the unfortunate girl protested that they were making her tipsy, and placing hot water bottles and hot flannel on the abdomen — this despite the fact that the recognized method of arresting *post partum* haemorrhage was to use cold water. Presently 'terrible spasms' set in and at two-thirty in the morning of 6 November 1817 the Daughter of England, on whom so many hopes had rested, was dead, almost certainly as the result of a pulmonary embolism.

For Richard Croft, Charlotte's death marked the end of his professional career; he committed suicide three months later. For her husband, the penniless younger son of a small German duchy, it was a personal disaster from which he never fully recovered. Her father, the Prince Regent, was said to be prostrated, while the nation, stunned by the double tragedy at Claremont, reacted with an unprecedented demonstration of public mourning.

'It is but little to say', remarked *The Times* in a leading article on 7 November, 'that we never recollect so strong and general an expression and indication of sorrow.' In his autobiography Henry Brougham, the Whig politician who had known Charlotte well, was to remember vividly the feelings of deepest sorrow and most bitter disappointment which 'this most melancholy event produced throughout the kingdom'. 'It is scarcely possible to exaggerate', he wrote, 'and it is difficult for persons not living at the time to believe, how universal and how genuine those feelings were. It was really as if every household throughout Great Britain had lost a favourite child.' Countess Granville, in a letter to her sister Lady Georgiana Morpeth, felt 'quite unable to write upon any subject but one. We are all heart-sick at this terrible event. Poor Princess Charlotte . . .' Dorothea Lieven, wife of the Russian ambassador, told her brother that the charming Princess Charlotte, 'so richly endowed with happiness, beauty, and splendid hopes', had been cut off from the love of a whole people. 'It is impossible to find in the history of nations or families an event which had evoked such heartfelt mourning', she went on. 'One met in the streets people of every class in tears, the churches full at all hours, the shops shut for a fortnight (an eloquent testimony from a shop-keeping community), and everyone, from the highest to the lowest, in a state of despair which it is impossible to describe.'

> . . . Forth from the abyss a voice proceeds,
> A long, low, distant murmur of dread sound,
> Such as arises when a nation bleeds
> With some deep and immedicable wound . . .

Up and down the country, in cathedrals, in parish churches, chapels and synagogues, memorial services were held and memorial sermons preached, while every public building wore a suit of black drapery. 'It certainly does not belong to us to repine at the visitations of Providence . . .,' boomed *The Times*; 'but as the Almighty sometimes, for the most benevolent purposes, deals severe chastisements on mankind, there is nothing impious in grieving for that as a calamity, which appears and is felt to be such.'

On the day of the funeral, Sunday, 19 November, Mr Sutton, Solicitor General to the Prince Regent, wrote to his friend Lord Colchester:

This day has been the most extraordinary I ever witnessed in London. The crowds of attendants at morning service, if I may judge of other services by St Margaret's . . . the body of the church so full that there was not even standing room left unoccupied. The whole congregation, as far as I could see, in mourning. In the streets all the shops shut; even those ordinarily left open on Sundays, such as pastrycooks. And yet, with this cessation of all trade and business, the streets very thin of passengers. Altogether this melancholy event has produced an effect on this metropolis such as I believe none could have foreseen . . . I wish it may not be pushed to an extreme to become offensive, because artificial . . . The public press seems to me to have run raving mad upon the subject.

The Duke of Wellington's verdict on the 'melancholy event' was characteristically terse and to the point. 'I think it probable', he told his niece Priscilla Burghersh, 'that she [Princess Charlotte] would have behaved well, and her death is one of the most serious misfortunes the country has ever met with.' Up in Yorkshire, the Reverend Benjamin Newton, rector of the parish of Wath on the edge of the North Riding, noted in his diary that 'the loss of any other branch of the Royal Family would have cost less regret'. And Lady Charlotte Bury, formerly a lady-in-waiting to the Princess's raffish mama, confided to *her* diary her dread 'that this national calamity is the forerunner of many future woes. There is now no object of great interest to the English people, no one great rallying point, round which all parties are ready to join. . . . A greater public calamity could not have occurred to us; nor could it have happened at a more unfortunate moment.'

Chapter One
Hymen's War Terrific

The great and general question which everyone asked himself and asked his neighbour was how will this event operate on the succession to the Crown?

Lord Liverpool

Even before the coffins of Princess Charlotte and her baby had been ceremoniously lowered into the family vault at Windsor, and while the nation was still indulging in its funeral orgy, thoughtful persons were reflecting gloomily on the political and dynastic implications of the tragedy at Claremont which, as Lady Charlotte Bury observed, could scarcely have happened at a more unfortunate moment.

After twenty-two strenuous years of armed struggle against Napoleon, the victors of Trafalgar and Waterloo were suffering the customary pangs of post-war disillusion. Economic recession had brought acute economic distress. In the manufacturing districts the unemployed were starving. The ruined harvest of 1816 had sent food prices rocketing. Banks and businesses were failing at an alarming rate, and there was a spirit of revolution abroad menacing enough to agitate stronger nerves than Lady Charlotte's.

A dignified and popular monarchy would have provided an important stabilizing force, so the death of the only member of the royal family whose 'amiable and sensible deportment' had endeared her to the nation, and who alone had seemed to offer hope for the future, could reasonably be considered a calamity. Certainly not even the most committed royalist could now regard the future of the English monarchy with anything but the deepest despondency and the succession, as the Reverend Mr Newton remarked, had become 'a matter of no interest if not of regret'.

In 1817 King George III was seventy-nine years old and irreversibly insane – an old, mad, blind ghost with a long unkempt white beard immured with his keepers at Windsor Castle. But blame for the present regrettable state of the succession could hardly be laid at his door, for he and his ugly, indomitable little German wife had filled the royal nurseries to overflowing, raising a family of no fewer than fifteen children of whom twelve were still living. The uncomfortable (and rather astonishing) fact remained that, with the removal of Princess Charlotte, George III did not possess a single legitimate grandchild. His five surviving daughters were either spinsters or childless, and since the youngest was over forty there could be little to hope for from that direction. Nor did his sons, at first glance, look much more promising.

The Prince Regent was fifty-five and long since estranged from his wife. Years of self-indulgence had transformed the beautiful young man of Hoppner's portrait into a bloated, brandy-soaked disaster, 'a despiser of domestic ties, the companion of demi-reps'. In the circumstances, it did not seem at all likely that Prinny would ever father another heir to the throne.

His remaining brothers, unkindly described by the poet Shelley as 'the dregs of their dull race', were chiefly remarkable for debts, mistresses and scandals, and all were middle-aged. Nevertheless, it was on their shoulders that responsibility for the continuance of the House of Hanover now rested. Two were already married. Frederick, Duke of York, was fifty-four and best remembered for his alleged connivance in the corrupt traffic in army commissions conducted by his mistress Mary Ann Clarke; although, according to his friend, the diarist Charles Greville, he was the only one of the princes who possessed the feelings of an

English gentlemen. He had for twenty-five years been the unfaithful husband of a Prussian princess, an eccentric lady who seldom went to bed and lived surrounded by an unmanageable number of pet dogs, monkeys and parrots. They were childless. Ernest, Duke of Cumberland, the ogre of the family, a rabid reactionary popularly credited with a startling variety of crimes and vices, was forty-six and had recently married the widowed Princess of Solms-Braunfels, whose own reputation was none too fragrant. The Cumberlands had no living children, although a daughter had been born dead.

Augustus, Duke of Sussex, now forty-four, had had two unofficial wives, the first of whom had borne him a son and a daughter. But as neither union had been blessed by the King's consent, they were, under the provisions of the Royal Marriages Act, pronounced legally void and the children not in the line of succession.

Of the three bachelor princes, William, Duke of Clarence, was the eldest at fifty-two. Clarence had served in the navy in his youth (he had been a friend of Nelson's and was best man at his wedding), but had subsequently settled down to a life of irregular domestic bliss with the actress Dorothea Jordan who, in the intervals of fulfilling her theatrical engagements, had given birth to ten little FitzClarences. Edward, Duke of Kent, was fifty. He had made the army his career and also kept a mistress with whom he had lived contentedly for the past twenty-seven years. Last came Adolphus, Duke of Cambridge, at forty-three. Apart from being the youngest, he could claim to be the most eligible *parti*, since he was not in debt and had acquired no extra-marital encumbrances. He spent a good deal of his time practising the violin, wore a blond wig and talked too much, but was otherwise harmless.

The duty of these three brothers now lay plain before them. 'It will be the earnest prayer of the nation', declared the *Morning Chronicle*, 'that an early alliance of one of the unmarried Princes may forthwith be settled', and one after the other the unmarried Princes hastened to answer the call.

Agog are all, both old and young
Warm'd with desire to be prolific
And prompt with resolution strong
To fight in Hymen's war terrific,

jeered the satirist Peter Pindar, and the nation sniggered ungratefully at the spectacle of a queue of stout, balding royals jostling one another to the altar in the race to beget an heir.

The Duke of Cambridge was first off the mark, proposing to and being accepted by Augusta of Hesse-Cassel within a fortnight of his niece's death, but Clarence and Kent were not far behind. Clarence and Kent had, in fact, both been contemplating matrimony for quite some time, though as the result of financial rather than dynastic pressures. Both suffered from the family complaint of insolvency in an acute form, and marriage had always offered the best hope of persuading a skinflint Parliament to loosen the purse-strings.

The Duke of Clarence had parted from Mrs Jordan as long ago as 1811. 'Could you believe or the world believe that we never had for twenty years the *semblance* of a quarrel?' she wrote sadly to a friend. But 'money, money . . . or the *want* of it' had broken up the idyllic ménage at Bushey Park and, to the unconcealed amusement of the polite world, the Duke proceeded optimistically to pursue a string of English heiresses. Princess Anne of Denmark was suggested as a possible bride and so was the Tsar's sister, but neither lady could be tempted by the bluff, excitable William. Rebuffed, he returned to Bushey and the tribe of sons and daughters to whom he was deeply attached. Then, in the summer of 1818, it was announced that 'the Duke of Clarence is to be married after all' to yet another German princess, Adelaide of Saxe-Meiningen, and, if his past record was anything to go by, some addition to the royal house could surely be expected before long.

Meanwhile, his younger brother had also been giving serious thought to the future. Edward, Duke of Kent, had never been satisfied by the way the world had treated him. A humourless man, with inflated ideas of his own importance and no tact, he contrived to exude an air of righteous self-pity which infuriated the Prince Regent, who called him Simon Pure, and led his sisters to dub him Joseph Surface, after the arch-hypocrite in *The School for Scandal*. Charles Greville, who loathed him, described him as 'the greatest rascal that ever went unhung' and 'far the worst of the family', while the harsh tyranny of his discipline made him the most hated man in the army.

His military career had come to an abrupt end in 1803, when his brutal severity, his obsessive preoccupation with parades and 'bull', and – worst of all – his closure of the wine-shops, provoked a mutiny in the garrison at Gibraltar. The Duke was recalled to England under a cloud – an injustice which only increased his perennial sense of grievance – and for the next fourteen years was obliged to find an outlet for his restless energies by devoting himself to good works (he supported no fewer than fifty-three charitable bodies) and dabbling in radical politics, which did not endear him to his Tory brothers. A tireless busybody, he maintained 'an active and very extensive correspondence, which three or four private secretaries were scarcely able to master', with the unsurprising result that 'his name was never uttered without a sigh by the functionaries of every public office.'

But in spite of his unerring eye for the trivial, the Duke of Kent was not without intelligence, indeed some of his opinions were unexpectedly advanced. Generously endowed with the family gift of the gab, he was a fluent and graceful speaker, and in private life the Genghis Khan of the parade ground was capable of inspiring genuine affection. He got on particularly well with young people, and could be a charming host and an agreeable friend. His personal habits, too, compared favourably with those of the Regent and the Duke of York. He rose early, ate sparingly, disapproved of gambling and drunkenness, and took a complacent pride in his fine soldierly physique. But unhappily he followed the family tradition in having absolutely no conception of the value of money.

On his return from Gibraltar he had installed his mistress in a luxurious house at Knightsbridge, and bought himself a country retreat in the then rustic village of Ealing. At Castle Hill Lodge, a pleasant, rambling domain surrounded by forty acres of parkland, the Duke proceeded to indulge his mania for ordered perfection, going to endless pains to ensure that 'in this complicated machine of souls and bodies, the genius of attention, of cleanliness, and of smart appearance is the order of the day'. A system of bells in the porter's lodge brought six immaculately accoutred footmen (a resident hairdresser was employed to dress and powder their hair) drawn up at the front door to receive callers. Another servant was required to sit up all night ready to light the bedroom fires punctually at five a.m. and the household included a thirty-piece band which entertained the company at meal times. In the grounds a regiment of gardeners was poised to advance purposefully on the first fallen leaf, and the stables looked as if the occupants were permanently on the point of conveying their master to church in full state. The house itself had been equipped with an interesting selection of mechanical contrivances. There were coloured illuminations, musical clocks and cages of artificial singing birds, not to mention such eccentricities of plumbing as fountains and running streams concealed in the closets – a novelty which moved one startled guest to wonder if he had been transported to 'the fields Elysian'.

Housekeeping on this scale – and there was also the main-tenance of a London headquarters at Kensington Palace to be considered – might be gratifying to the ego, but it was costing its optimistic chatelain a staggering amount of money. By 1807 the Duke of Kent's debts had passed the £200,000 mark, and by 1815 his creditors were closing in. An appeal to the Regent met with a cold response, as did various ingenuous schemes for raising more cash to pay off the most pressing of his obligations, and it became unpleasantly clear that drastic measures would be necessary to avoid the ignominy of public bankruptcy. The Duke therefore handed over three-quarters of his income to a committee of trustees and prepared rather sadly to economize.

Since it was obviously impossible for a prince and a gentleman to manage in England on a mere £10,000 or so, he had to resign himself to a sojourn abroad and in the summer of 1816 departed for Brussels, where the cost of living was among the lowest in Europe. The Duke was probably quite sincere in his belief that he was carrying out 'the full spirit of my plan of economy and retrenchment'; but as his notions of economy included leasing a large mansion in the Place Royale, which he at once started to renovate and improve out of recognition and at considerable expense, his chances of becoming solvent again by his target date of 1821 did not look very bright.

Loyally sharing his Belgian exile was the comfortable middle-aged woman known in the family as 'Edward's French lady', and officially described as Madame de St Laurent. A certain aura of romantic mystery used to be attached to the Duke of Kent's mistress. It was said that she was a widow, a French-Canadian (the Duke had spent some of his army service in Canada), and that she came from an aristocratic Catholic background. It was also said that the Duke had married her and that they had several children, whose descendants were the rightful occupants of the English throne. Recent research, however, has revealed the more prosaic facts that Mademoiselle Julie de St Laurent, as she then called herself, was the daughter of a civil engineer from Besançon in eastern France and had been engaged or, perhaps more accurately, procured back in 1790 by a M. Fontiny to act as Prince Edward's hostess, to sing for him, to ornament his household and to share his bed. Julie proved to be good-tempered, pretty and clever, and what began as a purely business arrangement had ripened over the years into a tender and mutually rewarding domestic felicity.

They never married. If they had, it would not have been recognized under English law, nor is there any evidence to suggest that they had children. Certainly there seems no valid reason why the Duke should have concealed his progeny – George III's sons were never in the least coy about their bastards – but what he was currently doing his best to conceal from Madame de St Laurent was the fact that he had begun to look seriously for a wife as the only sure way out of his financial imbroglio, and that two possible candidates were already under consideration. One was the well-connected but plain Princess Katherine Amelia of Baden; the

other, Marie Louise Victoire, the recently widowed Princess of
Leiningen and a sister of Princess Charlotte's husband, Leopold of
Saxe-Coburg.

Charlotte had always been fond of her uncle Edward, who had
supported her sympathetically during the difficult days preceding
her marriage, and she and Leopold were now busy matchmaking
on his behalf. So, in the autumn of 1816, taking advantage of
Madame's absence on a visit to Paris, the Duke crossed into
Germany for a quick tour of inspection, having first had to borrow
the money for his journey. Princess Amelia turned out to be an old
maid of over forty and altogether 'odious', but at Amorbach, a
pleasant little place nestling in a deep, wooded valley, where he
arrived armed with a letter of recommendation from Princess
Charlotte, things looked very much more promising. The Duke of
Kent, in short, took an immediate fancy to the plump, personable
Victoire and her two handsome children, and wasted no time in
making his declaration.

But although he seems to have made quite a good impression,
the Princess of Leiningen refused to commit herself. Her life so far
had not been an easy one. Born in 1786, she had grown up in a
Germany ravaged by Napoleon's armies and where many of the
princely families, including her own and her late husband's, had
been impoverished and dispossessed. (Ironically enough, Victoire
had had far more first-hand experience of the unpleasant realities
of war than the martial Duke.) Her previous marriage at the age of
seventeen to a morose, embittered man twenty-three years her
senior and 'entirely devoted to the amusements of the chase' had
been lonely and depressing. Now, still a comparatively young
woman, she was free to please herself and naturally hesitated to
give up her home, her friends and her emancipation. At her
elbow, too, stood the slightly enigmatic figure of Captain
Schindler, Master of the Household and the Dowager Princess's
closest adviser, who had his own reasons for urging the unwisdom
of relinquishing an income of £5,000 a year and her 'enviable
independence' all for the sake of another middle-aged husband
whom she hardly knew by sight. There was another more serious

obstacle. Victoire loved her children, especially her son Charles, and was afraid that if she married an Englishman and left Amorbach for any length of time she might lose their guardianship and perhaps be permanently separated from them.

On the other hand, and in spite of his debts, the Duke of Kent would undeniably be a splendid match, offering her the entry into a wider, more exciting world as well as the glamorous, if remote, prospect of becoming a Queen Consort, perhaps even a Queen Mother. Victoire was horribly torn in two but the Duke, jolting back to Belgium in his 'travelling baroutsch', did not despair of the outcome. He knew he could rely on Prince Leopold and Charlotte (who had struck up an enthusiastic pen-friendship with her sister-in-law) to use their influence, and felt that time and reflection must surely work in his favour. Meanwhile, he was not ungrateful for an excuse to postpone the moment of decision and the inevitable upsetting interview with Madame de St Laurent.

Matters remained in a state of suspended animation for the next six months, although tentative and very discreet negotiations were proceeding between Brussels, the Leiningen residence at Amorbach, Claremont House and Victoire's family at Coburg. Then came the news of Charlotte's pregnancy. Obviously Leopold could not be expected to interest himself in his uncle-in-law's affairs until this was safely over, and again the Duke prepared to wait. But the events of 6 November 1817 effectively put an end to further procrastination. It was now his clear patriotic duty to get married. To stand aside, isolated in his Brussels backwater, while brother William and even brother Adolphus acquired wives and sired heirs to the throne would have been more than his busy, thrustful nature could bear. Besides, his activities had not been quite so discreet as he thought they were. On the day after Charlotte's death, the *Morning Chronicle* came out with a report, which it believed to be well founded, of 'the intended marriage of the truly amiable and excellent Duke of Kent with a Princess of the House of Saxe-Coburg, one of the sisters of Prince Leopold'. Most unfortunately, a copy of this newspaper fell into the hands of Madame de St Laurent, and a painful scene had ensued.

The Duke felt the need to unburden himself and chose to

confide his problems to Thomas Creevey, who had the ear of all the Whig politicians and who was also to be found economizing in Brussels. Mr Creevey, an avid collector of gossip, listened enthralled to the account of Madame de St Laurent going into strong convulsions at the breakfast-table, and of the Duke's own heart-searchings as he steeled himself to do his princely duty at the expense of his private inclinations and domestic comfort. His Royal Highness did not attempt to conceal the pangs it would occasion him to part with Madame. They had lived together for so long, they were of the same age and had been 'in all climates and in all difficulties together'. How would Mr Creevey feel, if he were obliged to separate from Mrs Creevey?

One thing Madame's protector was determined on. She must be suitably provided for. She came of a very good family and 'had never been an actress'. If she was to return to live among her friends, then it must be in such a state of independence as to command their respect. She would not require very much, but a certain number of servants and a carriage were essential – surely a modest enough request, bearing in mind that the Duke of Clarence, in a similar situation, was having the gall to demand the payment of all his debts, which were very great, plus 'a handsome provision for each of his ten natural children'.

As for himself, he was a man of no ambition and wished only to remain as he was, but since he would be marrying – if he married at all – for the sake of the succession, he would naturally expect the grant of an additional £25,000 a year which had been made to the Duke of York at the time of his marriage to be considered a precedent. He would be content with the same arrangement, and would make no demands 'grounded upon the difference of the value of money in 1792 and at present'. Regarding the payment of his debts, he didn't call them great. The nation would, on the contrary, be greatly his debtor.

Creevey, of course, promptly circulated the story of this 'very curious conversation' among a few favoured friends, including the Duke of Wellington and the Earl of Sefton, who roared with laughter and thought that nothing could be more first-rate than the Royal Edward's ingenuousness. His lordship did not know which to admire more, the delicacy of the Duke's attachment to Madame de St Laurent, or his 'perfect disinterestedness in pecuniary matters'.

But Royal Edward's future was by no means settled yet. Victoire had still not made up her mind, and the atmosphere in the Place Royale was becoming increasingly strained. By the beginning of January 1818, he could stand the suspense no longer, and wrote to Amorbach to insist on an answer one way or the other. The Princess of Leiningen had already been assured that several months of each year could be spent in Germany and now the Prince Regent stepped in, undertaking to persuade the Court of Wards, presided over by the Grand Duke of Baden, to agree that the Leiningen children should remain under their mother's guardianship. All her objections having been met, the Princess capitulated and on 25 January she accepted the Duke of Kent's proposal.

When it came to the point of breaking the news to Madame de St Laurent, the Duke's courage failed him and, with some idea of sparing them both the distress of actually having to say good-bye, he left for England ostensibly on a business trip. Madame accepted the inevitable with dignity, retiring to make her home in Paris, where King Louis XVIII bestowed on her the courtesy title of Comtesse de Montgenet. She and the Duke never met again, although they continued to correspond and he continued to show an anxious solicitude for her welfare.

There's no doubt that he felt a genuine sense of loss, and arrived in London on 23 March to prepare for his wedding with his heart 'half-broke'. 'I hope I shall have the energy to do my duty,' he wrote to a friend. His mood of depression was not lightened by the unsympathetic attitude of the House of Commons, which showed no signs of appreciating the magnitude of his sacrifice. One member remarked that, while it might be desirable for some branches of the royal family to marry, he saw no reason why the country should be called on to enable them all to marry. Another thought that, since the Duke of Clarence was already engaged, 'it was not proper that any other member of the royal family should come to the House and ask for an additional allowance for the same purpose'. They might, he felt, quite well have waited to see if the Clarences could provide the necessary 'increase'.

Parliament was, in fact, becoming increasingly tired of those 'damned millstones' the Royal Dukes, and less and less inclined to subsidize their improvidence. However, as Lord Castlereagh pointed out, it was no more than bare justice to make some provision for the new Duchess of Kent, who would be giving up a comfortable income on her marriage, and in the end the Commons rather grudgingly agreed to settle an extra £6,000 a year on the Duke of Kent, to revert to his widow in the event of his death.

The knowledge that his elder brother had done no better was not much consolation to the Duke, who was about to take on the additional expense and responsibility of a wife with little or no financial compensation. But it was too late now for second thoughts. Mr Brook Taylor, the English minister at Stuttgart, was busy completing the negotiations with the Duke of Baden, with the Princess of Leiningen's trustees and her eldest brother, Duke Ernest of Saxe-Coburg-Saalfeld. The Duke of Kent therefore borrowed another £3,000 from the long-suffering Thomas Coutts, and prepared to set out for Germany.

Victoire, meanwhile, had gone back to Coburg, and her mother, the Dowager Duchess Augusta, noted that the 'dear good child' seemed quite unperturbed at what lay before her, and was looking forward calmly to a new life with a man she had met only once. But Victoire, now approaching her thirty-second birthday, had never been gifted with much imagination and, having made her decision, was untroubled by the last-minute doubts and misgivings which might have afflicted a more introspective character. Cheerful, sociable and affectionate by nature, she was basically a very simple woman and one who, without necessarily being in any way over-sexed, needed male support and companionship.

The Duke of Kent arrived on 26 May, the day before he was expected, and the Dowager, who had confessed to feeling 'rather anxious' about her youngest daughter's marriage to a virtual stranger, was relieved to find him 'a fine man for his age' with 'a pleasant winning manner, and a good-humoured expression'. 'His tall stature helps to give him an air of breeding', she wrote in her diary for that day, 'and he combines a simple soldierly manner with the refinement of a man of the world, which makes intercourse with him easy and pleasant.' On 28 May came the formal betrothal ceremony and exchange of rings between the affianced couple, and on the 29th they were married.

The Coburgs, one of a group of princely families descended from the ancient House of Wettin, had experienced inconvenience, invasion, anxiety and loss of revenue as a result of the Napoleonic Wars, but, more fortunate than some of their neighbours, they had emerged with their sovereign powers intact and were determined to put on a good show for the English.

At half-past eight in the evening Victoire, with her mother and her sister Sophie, drove *en cérémonie* to the Schloss Ehrenburg, the ducal residence, to find Duke Ernest waiting in the State Rooms ready to conduct them into the brilliantly lit Riesensaal, or Hall of Giants, where the bridegroom, resplendent in his Field Marshal's uniform, was already standing under a velvet canopy. Describing him as tall and 'stately', one contemporary at least thought that, in spite of his bald head with its fringe of dyed hair and his tendency to corpulence, 'he might still be considered a handsome man'. The bride, matron though she was, wore white trimmed with white roses and orange blossom and, to her mother's eyes, looked 'charming'. One of her English sisters-in-law was to call her no more than 'very pleasing', but other observers were kinder, and with her glossy dark curls, dark eyes, high colour and generous curves the new Duchess, to judge from her portraits, was good-looking enough in a rather florid style. She was fond of dress, with a penchant for large hats, feathers and bright colours, and might fairly be regarded as an attractive woman.

A salute of guns from the Festung above the town informed the Coburgers that the religious ceremony had been completed, while the family sat down to a state dinner which went on well into the night. The newly-married couple were then escorted to their apartments and the Dowager Duchess, who had prayed that her dear child would find in this second marriage 'all the happiness which she had not quite attained in her last one', went home 'thoroughly tired out'.

Five days later the Kents left for England, Victoire once more followed by her mother's hopes that she would be happy with 'her really very amiable husband, who only in middle age makes acquaintance with family life and will therefore perhaps appreciate it all the more'. The journey, with frequent stops along the way, including one at Brussels with its rather unfortunate associations with Madame de St Laurent, took the best part of a month. But at last, on 30 June, they landed at Dover and Victoire now had to face the prospect of meeting her formidable new in-laws. After a night at Claremont, still full of affecting mementoes of poor Charlotte, she was driven up to London to be presented to the Prince Regent, the Duke and Duchess of York, the Duke of Cambridge complete with his new Duchess, and Princess Mary, Duchess of Gloucester, amid the daunting splendours of Carlton House.

Any gathering of the English royal family was liable to be fraught with dangerous undercurrents, and there was no love lost between the Duke of Kent and his two eldest brothers. The Regent disliked him anyway for being a sanctimonious prig and Whig, and still resented his former friendship with the exiled Princess of Wales; while there was a long-standing, if officially buried, quarrel between York and Kent. Frederick suspected Edward of having had a hand in exposing the Mrs Clarke scandal, and Edward believed that Frederick had been behind his recall from Gibraltar. On this occasion, however, all went well and the Regent who, despite his somewhat grotesque appearance, could still display an astonishing amount of charm, exerted himself to give Edward's wife a gracious welcome.

1818 was a year of weddings. On 7 April the Princess Elizabeth had married the Landgrave of Hesse-Homburg – and promptly earned herself the nickname of Betty Humbug. The Cambridge wedding had followed on 1 June, and on 4 July the Duke of Clarence's betrothed arrived in London. Since the Kents were to go through a second marriage service according to the rites of the

Church of England, it was decided to hold a double ceremony
which took place in the drawing-room at Kew in the intimidating
presence of old Queen Charlotte at four o'clock on the afternoon
of Monday, 13 July, with the Archbishop of Canterbury and the
Bishop of London officiating. The Regent gave both brides away
and Victoire, dressed this time in a robe of gold tissue, lined with
white satin and trimmed with Brussels lace, definitely outshone
the pale, refined Adelaide of Saxe-Meiningen.

The Duke of Kent did not take his bride to Castle Hill. Instead
they stayed at Claremont with Prince Leopold, using Kensington
Palace as a *pied-à-terre*, and the next six weeks or so were spent in a
giddy round of sightseeing and theatre-going. There was a
reception at Carlton House, and on Victoire's birthday, 17
August, a family dinner party was held in her honour. The Duke
was also at pains to introduce his wife to his more serious friends.
They paid a visit to the headquarters of The British and Foreign
School Society and attended a prize giving at the Society's branch
in City Road, where the Duchess was invited to preside over a
newly formed Ladies' Committee – thus making her the first
English royal lady ever to sit on a charitable committee. Much
gratified, the Duke rose to return thanks on her behalf, explaining
that 'she was not yet perfectly conversant with the English
language'.

In fact, Victoire spoke no English at all, and when presented
with a congratulatory address by the Lord Mayor and Aldermen of
the City of London, her reply had to be written out phonetically
and learned parrot-fashion. Inside the family circle this hardly
mattered. Her husband was seldom at a loss for words in either
German or French and there was no shortage of German speakers
among the other royals, but obviously it would be a serious
handicap in public life. So English lessons were arranged and the
Duchess applied herself docilely.

As it turned out, she was to have little opportunity to practise,
for it was already becoming uncomfortably clear that the sooner
the Kents returned to Germany the better. Marriage, far from
solving the Duke's financial problems, was plunging him ever
deeper into debt. The £3,000 borrowed from Mr Coutts had

been swallowed up by wedding presents, by a sum of £500 promised to Madame de St Laurent and £1,500 due to the Duchess under the marriage contract – not to mention bills from milliners and dressmakers for her new finery. By the end of August the holidays were over. The Duke of Cambridge had taken his bride back to Hanover, where he would be resuming his duties as governor of the family's German kingdom. The Clarences had gone with him, also from motives of economy, and early in September the Kents set sail from Dover en route for Amorbach.

First, though, they stopped off at the Duke of Wellington's headquarters, now established at Valenciennes. Three years after Waterloo, there was still an Allied army of occupation in northern France and G.H.Q., with its gay social round of balls, dinners and reviews, had become a great centre of attraction for the travelling English. The Kents witnessed a review of British and Russian troops, and were guests at a ball given by the Russian commander-in chief, the fascinating Count Woronzow. The Duchess daringly 'waltzed a little' and the Duke was seen to 'put his hand upon her cheek to feel if she was not too hot', a display of husbandly solicitude which the ubiquitous Mr Creevey recorded with a certain amount of rather malicious amusement.

From Valenciennes the couple went on to Aix-la-Chapelle to see something of the festivities surrounding a summit conference of European sovereigns at which the four Allied Powers – England, Russia, Austria and Prussia – were to discuss the withdrawal of their occupying armies and consider their future relations with France and with each other. The Kents, of course, were not concerned with international politics (though no doubt the Duke would have been only too pleased to give the treaty-makers the benefit of his advice), but they attended another ball, given by the town of Aix to its distinguished visitors, before leaving for Switzerland. There they paid a visit to another member of Victoire's numerous family, her sister Juliana, and made an adventurous excursion to the Grindelwald glaciers and up the Lauterbourg valley. So that it was the end of October before they were finally settled at Amorbach for the winter.

It had been a strenuous and exciting summer, and despite her abundant vitality Victoire was probably not altogether sorry to get home again and unpack. As for the Duke, he had characteristically found congenial employment by starting an ambitious scheme of improvements to his new home. The territory round the village of Amorbach and its little palace had originally been ecclesiastical property, granted to the Princes of Leiningen in 1801 in compensation for lands taken from them by the French, but picturesque though it might be, the residence scarcely measured up to English princely standards of comfort or convenience. The Duke had therefore imported an architect and a small army of workmen, and set about building new stables, walling in the gardens for extra privacy, and installing a more efficient heating system.

It was all going to be very pleasant and cosy, but when, about the middle of November, the Duchess was able to inform her husband that she was certainly pregnant, he at once addressed himself to the problem of ensuring that the coming child should, as he put it, be BRITON BORN. On 18 November he wrote one of his enormously long letters to the Prince Regent's Private Secretary with the information that the Duchess expected to be confined in the following May, and that consequently they would feel it their duty to set out for England early in April, it being 'incumbent upon us to adopt such measures as will enable the child to be born at home'. However, as the Duke was obliged to confess, the measures he proposed to adopt would depend on the Regent's showing 'the goodness of his heart and his liberality', and he went on to ask for 'pecuniary assistance to perform the journey', the use of the royal yacht for the Channel crossing and the loan of additional accommodation at Kensington Palace for the period of the Duchess's confinement.

The Duke appears to have felt every confidence that these requests would be granted; but unfortunately the self-important tone of his letter was exactly calculated to irritate the Regent, whose own disastrous marriage and now childless condition made him hyper-sensitive on the subject of royal offspring. He had not the slightest intention of showing either goodness of heart or liberality merely to enable his least favourite brother to make a parade of fatherhood under his nose. Instead, he proceeded to administer a sharp snub to Edward's vanity, informing him via the Private Secretary that no assistance, pecuniary or otherwise, would be forthcoming for a journey to England, and reminding him that the Duchesses of Clarence and Cambridge were also in delicate situations. They were both content to have their babies in decent obscurity abroad, and therefore the Regent 'could not resist' recommending that the Kents should do the same.

This came as a grievous disappointment to Amorbach, but in his present state of financial distress, the Duke had little option but to submit. As he told his old friend General Weatherall just before Christmas, he could see no other prospect 'but that of my *necessarily* remaining *here* for the *whole* of the next *five* years'.

This was not a very enlivening prospect, but the Duke of Kent was never cast down for long. He was sustained by a Micawber-like conviction that 'something would turn up' and, whether or not there is any truth in the story that a gipsy fortune-teller had once assured him that he would have a daughter who would be a great Queen, he possessed an unshakeable belief in the future. 'My brothers are not so strong as I am,' he was in the habit of saying to anyone who would listen. 'I have led a regular life, I shall outlive them all; the crown will come to me and my children.' While pronouncements of this kind naturally did nothing to improve his relations with his brothers, anyone gazing upon his large, robust person could scarcely fail to wonder if he might not be right.

Another, more immediate, source of comfort was the fact that his marriage, entered into with so much reluctance and hesitation, had proved a triumphant success. In Victoire, with her warm, outgoing personality, her eagerness to please and be pleased, and her touching reliance on her husband's superior judgement, he had surely found the ideal helpmate and companion, the ideal mother of his children.

On the last day of 1818, although they were under the same roof, he wrote a tender love-letter to his wife:

This evening will put an end, dear well beloved Victoire, to the year 1818, which saw the birth of my happiness by giving you to me as my guardian angel. I hope that you will always recall this year with the same pleasure as I do, and that each time a new anniversary comes round, you will be as contented with your fate, as you make me hope you are today.

. . . I would have wished to be at least able to say all this to you in pretty verses but you know that I am an old soldier who has not this talent, and so you must take the good will for the deed and in accepting this little almanack you will remember that it comes from your very deeply attached husband, for whom you represent all happiness and all consolation. On that I tell you in the language of my country, God bless you, love me as I love you.

Chapter Two
The Little Mayflower

Take care of her for she will be Queen of England.

The Duke of Kent

If 1818 had been a good year for royal weddings, 1819 looked like producing a bumper crop of royal babies, with four Duchesses, Clarence, Kent, Cumberland and Cambridge, all in the family way. Three of the expectant fathers (the Cumberlands were now settled in Berlin) apparently had no particular objection to their infants being born in Germany, and the Prime Minister, Lord Liverpool, felt it would place a severe and unnecessary burden on the royal family to bring the mothers home for their confinements; although he conceded that it might perhaps be 'advisable' to have some British subjects on hand to witness the births.

The Duke of Kent alone remained obstinately determined to do his duty as an Englishman and a patriot by ensuring that *his* child should draw its first breath on British soil. Also, as he repeatedly pointed out, Amorbach was really quite unsuitable for such a momentous event. The house was isolated, fifty English miles from the nearest large town, the accommodation inadequate and the ventilation bad. Opposition to his plans had only stiffened his resolve and if the Regent refused to help, then he must find someone else who would.

He turned, accordingly, to his radical and dissenting 'Methody' friends – earnest, sober and God-fearing men who represented an increasingly influential body of English public opinion, and who could be relied upon to seize any opportunity of embarrassing their arch-enemy, the profligate Prince Regent. Prominent among them were Joseph Hume, M.P. and Alderman Matthew Wood, a former Lord Mayor of London. Both were members of the Duke of Kent's committee of trustees, but it was chiefly thanks to the efforts of Matthew Wood that a sum of money was raised large enough to enable the Duke to satisfy his more impatient foreign creditors and pay for the journey to England.

Although the news was received joyfully in Amorbach, the Duke had been warned not to expect a cordial reception from the family at home, who regarded his insistence on returning as yet another disagreeable example of Edward's putting himself forward. His sister Augusta did not hesitate to declare that he was behaving 'like a fool and a madman', while the Princess Mary feared it was all 'a *deep – very* deep-layed plan'. Certainly the Regent had been out-manoeuvred and was correspondingly annoyed. He now had no choice but to lend the royal yacht – Edward was threatening to bring his wife over on the packet if necessary – and also the apartments at Kensington. But he made his disapproval plain, expressing very deep regret that the Duke should have thought it expedient to subject the Duchess to such an ordeal at this advanced period.

There's no doubt that the Kents were cutting it pretty fine. It was half-way through March by the time the financial arrangements had been sorted out and Victoire was entering the eighth month of her pregnancy – hardly the most propitious moment to embark on a journey of some four hundred miles over shockingly bad roads, with a notoriously stormy sea-crossing at the end of it. Her mother was understandably nervous at the prospect, but when she came on a brief visit to Amorbach to say good-bye, she found dear Victoire looking very well, 'thoroughly happy in her new married life' and looking forward to the journey with 'joyful anticipation'. They both shed tears at parting, but the Dowager was able to comfort herself with the knowledge that her daughter was 'really happy and contented, and that Kent makes an excellent husband'.

The excellent husband admitted that 'the interesting situation of the Duchess' was causing him 'hourly anxiety' and he certainly did his best to ensure her comfort. When the party set out on 28 March 1819, he drove his wife himself in a phaeton – a light open carriage drawn by a pair of horses – which was better sprung and more easily controlled than the more conventional type of conveyance. Behind them came the travelling 'baroutsch' with the Duchess's old friend and lady-in-waiting Baroness Späth, and Madame Siebold the midwife, who could boast the unusual distinction of having qualified 'like a man' at the University of Göttingen. There followed the Duchess's post-chaise, empty, in case it rained, and another post-chaise carrying her daughter Princess Feodore and Feodore's governess. Victoire's son Charles, now rising fifteen, was away at school in Switzerland, but eleven-year-old Feodore was going to England with her mother. Then came the servants and the baggage-train, which included the Duchess's own bed and bedding, plus her precious pet birds and lapdogs, and bringing up the rear was Dr Wilson, the Duke's personal physician, who had 'managed the Duchess to perfection' from the beginning of her pregnancy.

This 'unbelievably odd caravan' – so described by an Englishwoman privileged to see it passing on the road – bowled merrily across Europe. The weather remained the finest under Heaven and there were no accidents of any sort. 'Providence', wrote the Duke triumphantly, 'absolutely prospered our undertaking', and it now looked as if Providence was planning to favour the Kents in more ways than one. On 26 March the Duchess of Cambridge had given birth to a healthy son, but the Clarence baby, born the following day, lived for only seven hours.

The Clarences' disappointment had, of course, greatly increased the dynastic importance of Victoire's child, and the Duke's anxiety to reach England without mishap. But everything continued to go smoothly. The Channel crossing was accomplished in less than four hours and although the Duchess was very sea-sick, her medical attendants were satisfied that no harm had been done. By the end of April she was safely installed at Kensington, and the Duke was able to assure the Dowager in Coburg that 'all has ended well'.

The rooms in the south-east wing of the Palace which the Kents were to occupy had stood stripped and empty for five years and were in a poor state of decoration and repair, but their situation was idyllic. The Duchess's bedroom looked out over the green glades and thickets of the Park, now in all the freshness of its late spring glory, with the still waters of the Basin, or Round Pond, in the foreground. The Duke could congratulate himself that the apartment was 'as quiet as possible' while being conveniently close to town, and with his usual financial insouciance he set to work to make good the deficiencies of the interior décor, spending over £2,000 on furniture from a firm in Bond Street which supplied, among other things, white glazed cambric bed-hangings and curtains, a 'cribb bedstead of mahogany' also hung with white cambric, a child's wardrobe, and a bed-chair and bed-table for the Duchess's convalescence. The fine weather had broken at last and it was discovered that the rotting window sashes behind the elegant new curtains were 'constantly' letting in the rain; but repairs would have to wait, for at ten-thirty on the evening of Sunday, 23 May the Duke sent a hurried note round to his friend General Weatherall telling him that the Duchess's labour had begun.

The distinguished witnesses assembled at Kensington that night included the Duke of Wellington, the Duke of Sussex, the Archbishop of Canterbury, the Bishop of London, the Marquis of Lansdowne, Earl Bathurst, the Chancellor of the Exchequer and Mr George Canning, several of whom still retained uneasy memories of the last occasion when they had been similarly gathered together. But this time their vigil was to be blessedly brief, for at 4.15 a.m. on 24 May, as a damp grey dawn broke over Kensington Gardens, the first lusty cries of a vigorous baby girl could be heard mingling with the birds' chorus.

According to old-established custom, the waiting Privy Councillors were immediately summoned to the lying-in room, where 'the infant was presented to them, and they signed, conjointly with the physicians, a certificate of its birth, together with a report of its perfectly healthful appearance.' Contrary to the legend which grew up in later years, there had been no complications and the official announcement in The London Gazette stated that the Duchess of Kent had been 'happily delivered of a Princess', adding that 'Her Royal Highness is, God be praised, as well as can be expected, and the young Princess is in perfect health.'

The Duke of Kent, who had remained with his wife throughout her labour, positively glowed with relief and parental pride, sending a letter off to Coburg that evening with the news that his daughter was 'truly a model of strength and beauty combined'. 'Thank God', he wrote, 'the dear mother and the child are doing marvellously well.' The Duchess was feeding the baby herself, and while this was considered a rather bourgeois activity in some circles, it met with wide approval among the bourgeoisie itself. However, as the Duke ponderously informed one of his regular correspondents, 'parental feeling and a just sense of duty, and not the applause of the public' had motivated the Duchess's exemplary conduct as a mother. The fond papa, who, as might be expected, was busy supervising every detail of nursery routine, hovered in anxious attendance over the 'process of maternal nutriment' which he found 'most interesting in its nature'.

Although both parents may have been secretly hoping for a son, the Duke was resolute in his denial of any lingering disappointment, being 'decidedly of the opinion that the decrees of Providence are at all times the wisest and best'. There seemed every reason to hope that Victoire would have other children but, in any case, their sex hardly mattered. The Duchess of Cumberland had given birth to a boy on 27 May, but, male or female, the offspring of the Duke of Kent took precedence over his younger brothers'. The little Kent princess therefore occupied fifth place in the succession, with only the lives of three middle-aged uncles – the Prince Regent, and the Dukes of York and Clarence – and her own middle-aged father standing between her and the throne. Unless and until the Duke of Clarence was able to father a legitimate child, or, of course, a brother arrived to supersede her, she would remain the senior member of the latest generation of the royal family. 'Again a Charlotte', wrote Duchess Agusta from Coburg, 'destined perhaps to play a great part one day.' And she added cheerfully, 'the English like Queens.'

The Duke of Kent fully shared his mother-in-law's optimistic outlook, and though in public he was always careful to acknowledge the strong probability of the Clarences' starting a family – the Duchess after all was only twenty-six – among his own friends he could not resist the temptation of showing off his daughter as the future Queen of England.

The baptism of this very important infant now had to be arranged and was to result in another bout of fraternal hostilities. The Regent might not have been able to prevent Edward's child from being born in England, but he could and would prevent its christening being turned into a state occasion. He had accepted an invitation to be godfather (the other sponsors were to be Tsar Alexander of Russia, the baby's eldest aunt, the widowed Queen of Württemberg, and her maternal grandmother, the Dowager Duchess of Saxe-Coburg-Saalfeld) but the ceremony itself was going to be as inconspicuous as His Royal Highness could make it. It would, he decreed, take place at Kensington on 24 June, the parents receiving only two days' notice of the event, and the guest-list being restricted to a handful of close relatives – the Yorks, the Gloucesters, Princess Augusta, Princess Sophia and Prince Leopold. The Duke of York would stand proxy for the Tsar, the Duchess of Gloucester and Princess Augusta for the two godmothers and, since the occasion was a private one, the gentlemen present would wear frock-coats, so no display of uniforms, orders and gold lace.

As far as names were concerned, the Duke of Kent had already submitted his own sonorous choice of Victoire Georgina Alexandrina Charlotte Augusta, but at the last moment he received a message informing him that Georgina was unacceptable. The Regent 'did not chuse to place the name before the Emperor of Russia's, and He could not allow it to follow.' He would, the message added, indicate his pleasure regarding the other names at the ceremony.

The family duly foregathered in the Cupola Room at Kensington Palace, their surroundings having been embellished with crimson velvet draperies hastily borrowed from the Chapel Royal. The seventeenth-century silver-gilt font had been brought over from the Jewel House at the Tower of London and the service, conducted by the Archbishop of Canterbury and the Bishop of London, began promptly at three o'clock. Nothing further had been said about the names, so when the Archbishop, standing poised over the font with the infant in his arms, pronounced the words 'Name this Child', he turned enquiringly to the only sponsor present in the flesh. 'Alexandrina' came the curt reply. An embarrassing pause ensued and, nervously prompted by his brother, the Regent now vetoed both Charlotte and Augusta. When the ruffled parent asked that another name should be given and 'urged' Elizabeth, this too was refused. Finally, having made it insultingly plain that he would not allow his niece to bear any of the traditional royal Christian names, the Regent, with a glare at the unfortunate Duchess of Kent, who had dissolved into tears of mortification, said 'brusquely', 'Give her the mother's name also, then, but it cannot precede that of the Emperor.' So, in an atmosphere heavily charged with rancour and wounded feelings, and to a background of its mother's sobs, the baby was baptized Alexandrina Victoria.

The world in which the four-week-old Princess now took her place as a fully-paid-up member of the Christian congregation was one still precariously balanced between the old and the new, where for many people the process of revolution, both social and technological, had become a desperate exercise in survival. The genteel, pastoral England of Jane Austen, of John Keats and William Wordsworth was also the England of the new industrial age; of dark Satanic mills where small children tended unfenced machinery for up to fourteen hours a day; of coal mines where women and girls, harnessed to heavy trucks, crawled stripped to the waist through dripping, pitch-black tunnels.

In the countryside, the enclosure of the old open fields and commons was undoubtedly making for greater efficiency and higher productivity – as well as vastly enriching the big landowners. But to thousands of smallholders, thus deprived of their immemorial stake in the land they tilled, the new ways all too often meant pauperism; and they and their families, like those other victims of progress, the handloom weavers, were being driven to swell the ranks of the dispossessed, squatting in shanty towns of indescribable squalor which had grown up on the fringes of the industrial areas.

Some parts of London were already illuminated by the new gas lighting, but the alleys and courts behind Oxford Street would have disgraced a mediaeval ghetto. The capital, like the population, was expanding fast, and elegant new streets and squares were appearing almost overnight in Belgravia, Bloomsbury and on the fields of Marylebone; but no law enforcement officer in his senses would have dreamt of venturing into the scabrous rookeries of Seven Dials or Tothill Fields.

Joseph Bramah's water-closet was already on the market, as was Humphry Davy's safety lamp, and Michael Faraday, the blacksmith's son, had constructed his first electric battery. Telford's and McAdam's new metalled highways had increased the speed of the mail coaches to a staggering ten or even twelve miles an hour, while the next decade would see the opening of the first experimental stretch of commercial steam railway. But for the great majority sanitation remained a matter of the communal bucket and open drain, and for most the speed of life was still governed by the pace of a plodding horse, or their own trudging feet. The pioneering work of Edward Jenner had made possible successful vaccination against smallpox, and on 2 August 1819 the Duke and Duchess of Kent took the wise, though still somewhat daring step of subjecting their infant daughter to the process. But in the London slums and the grim factory towns of the north not only smallpox, but typhus, dysentery and cholera remained commonplace facts of life or, more often, of death.

Not surprisingly, few people had yet begun to grasp the full implications of that astonishing tidal surge of energy and inventive genius conveniently known as the Industrial Revolution which, given additional impetus by the necessities of war, had overwhelmed the capacities of a system geared to the needs of an agrarian society. At the same time, a lot of people, alarmed and distressed by the sufferings of the poor in a totally uncontrolled economy, could see the need for reforming the system, and nowhere was that need more glaringly apparent than in the High Court of Parliament itself. The geography of the parliamentary boroughs had scarcely changed since the mid-seventeenth century, with often ludicrous results. Towns or villages which had once been important centres of trade or population were still returning one, or sometimes two members (Old Sarum, most notorious of the so-called rotten boroughs, was not even a village); but great new centres like Birmingham, Manchester, Leeds and Sheffield had no representation at all. Voting qualifications varied from place to place, but were still firmly based on property or status and, in the vast majority of cases, the nomination and election of members were controlled by the influential landowning families.

Obviously this was no longer a reasonable method of governing a modern industrial state, but the reform of the House of Commons was going to mean treading on a great many highly sensitive toes. Unhappily, too, the very word 'reform' had acquired sinister connotations among the property-owning classes. Memories of the excesses of the French Revolution had bred a deep fear and hatred of 'the Mob', while mass demonstrations with their displays of inflammatory banners, tricolour flags and caps of liberty not unnaturally served to strengthen the conviction that any well-meaning tampering with long-cherished institutions would simply be opening the door to bloody revolution.

In good years, when wages were high and bread was cheap, grass-roots agitation for reform tended to die away, but 1819 was a bad year when, it was stated, 'the most perfect stagnation' prevailed in every department of business. The wages of handloom weavers in Glasgow were down to five shillings and there were sporadic outbreaks of violence in Carlisle, where the gingham weavers were out on strike. In July the starving frame-work knitters of Leicester were also out on the streets, and stories of battalions of workers drilling with pikes and bludgeons on remote northern moors struck terror into the hearts of respectable citizens. Some sort of explosion seemed inevitable and it came on a sultry August day, when an apparently endless procession of reformers, carrying banners demanding Universal Suffrage and Annual Parliaments and accompanied by bands of music, marched with well-drilled precision into Manchester to hear an address by Henry 'Orator' Hunt, one of the best known of the radical leaders.

The magistrates, watching nervously from the windows of a nearby house as an estimated crowd of sixty thousand jammed itself into St Peter's Field, ordered the arrest of Hunt and his fellow speakers and, when the Deputy Constable refused to execute the warrant without the assistance of the military, a detachment of yeomanry was sent in to clear a path to the hustings. Afterwards there was to be furious controversy over whether or not the yeomanry had been attacked, but certainly they were quickly swallowed up by the multitude and, in the general confusion, their sabres were certainly drawn. Regular troops had to be called in to restore order and the final casualty list was eleven civilians killed and some four hundred injured.

Although the result of muddle and cold feet rather than deliberate malice on the part of the authorities, the Peterloo Massacre, as it became known, was a horrifying episode which led to a hardening of attitudes on both sides. Lord Grey, the Whig leader, took a thoroughly gloomy view of the situation. 'Every-thing', he wrote, 'is tending . . . to a complete separation between the higher and lower orders of society; a state of things which can only end in the destruction of liberty, or in a convulsion which may too probably produce the same result.' In October Grey told a friend that the leaders of the popular party, or rather of 'the Mob', wanted not Reform but Revolution, and in the same month, at Newcastle, muskets were fired and stones and brickbats hurled in an ugly confrontation between the marines and striking keelmen.

All this seemed a very long way from the family at Kensington, where there was greater interest in a domestic event destined to be of immense significance to the baby kicking in her mahogany 'cribb bedstead'. Madame Siebold, the midwife who had brought Alexandrina Victoria into the world, had gone back to Germany to attend another Coburg accouchement, and on 27 August the Dowager Duchess was able to tell Victoire that her brother Ernest's wife had been safely delivered of a second son, 'as lively as a squirrel', who was to be christened Albert. 'How pretty the little Mayflower will be when I manage to see her in a year!' the Dowager went on. 'Siebold cannot say often enough what a lovely little darling she is.' The little Mayflower had continued to flourish and, at three months, seems to have been an exceptionally sturdy child, but even her doting father felt obliged to admit that 'the little one is rather a pocket Hercules than a pocket Venus'.

The Duchess of Clarence was pregnant again that summer and the Duke, tired of being upstaged by his younger brother, decided to bring her home. But Adelaide proved less resilient than Victoire and she miscarried on the journey. The Kent baby's position thus remained secure, to the imperfectly concealed disgust of her most important uncle. The Prince Regent was making no attempt at all to conceal his impatience for the removal of the entire Kent ménage from his orbit and when Edward and Victoire, plus baby, turned up at a review on Hounslow Heath in August, His Royal Highness was heard to trumpet angrily, 'What business has that infant here?' At a reception given by the Spanish ambassador he cut his brother dead, although deigning to shake hands with his sister-in-law, and generally missed no opportunity of demonstrating that he regarded Edward as a nuisance and a bore.

But Edward, apparently impervious to hints, continued to occupy the apartments at Kensington and to display his daughter to admiring passers-by in the Park. Guests were entertained at dinner-parties and musical evenings, and Victoire took time off from her maternal duties to accompany her husband to the theatre. The family paid a visit to Leopold at Claremont and in September spent two nights, 'bag and baggage', at Windsor, which prompted the Duchess of Gloucester to write maliciously to the Regent of the amusement caused by the fact that the Kents, baby, nurse, Princess Feodore and Baroness Späth all said goodnight at nine o'clock and '*actually went to bed!*'

In spite of the unkind fun being poked at his middle-class habits, the Duke of Kent remained entirely happy in his marriage and was a model husband and father. Little Princess Feodore had grown genuinely devoted to him. 'I loved him dearly', she was to remember years later; 'he always was so kind to me.' With the constant pleasure and pride (not to mention the undoubted dynastic consequence), to be drawn from the plump, thriving baby, and cushioned by the uncritical affection of his own domestic circle, the Duke could have afforded to go on ignoring the hostility of the other royals – if only it had not been for the ever-present anxiety of his chronic insolvency. While committed to spend part of the year in Amorbach, at least until Charles of Leiningen came of age, he had not yet given up hope of being able to base himself in England and bring up his daughter as an English child. But although his trustees were now allowing him an extra £2,000 a year which, with the £6,000 voted by Parliament in 1818, brought his income up to around £14,000, it was once more becoming painfully clear that he could not manage to live in London, however modestly.

In the current political climate any further appeal to Parliament was obviously out of the question (it would, in any case, have been blocked by the Regent), and Castle Hill Lodge, the Duke's only remaining disposable asset, had so far failed to attract a buyer. The Kents would have to embark on another economy campaign – 'We intend wintering in the West', wrote the Duke impressively – and it was decided to look for a house to rent on the Devonshire coast. The climate would be milder, the Duchess could take salt water baths (a fashionable restorative for nursing mothers), and they would all benefit from the sea air. It would also be cheap and out of the way of all but the most adventurous creditors. So, towards the end of October, the Duke, accompanied by his equerry Captain Conroy, set out on a tour of inspection. Torquay, Teignmouth and Dawlish had nothing suitable to offer; but at Sidmouth, Woolbrook Cottage, built in the Gothic style and pleasantly situated in a sheltered valley only about a hundred and fifty yards from the beach, was pronounced to be satisfactory.

Edward got back to town just in time to celebrate his fifty-second birthday with a little family festival. Princess Feodore recited some verses specially composed for the occasion, Prince Charles sent 'filial congratulations' from his school at Geneva, and the infant Princess Victoria, dressed in a white frock trimmed with bows of red and green ribbon, was held up to present her papa with a letter from the Duchess. (Although sometimes called Drina in her baby days, Victoria was always the name preferred by her mother and, later, by herself.)

Preparations for the move to Sidmouth now began, but it was December before the Kents were ready to leave London. The Duke was still trying desperately to raise a capital sum which would break the vicious circle of debt in which he seemed to be permanently trapped; but Thomas Coutts no longer felt able to accommodate him, and while it had been estimated that, broken up, the Castle Hill estate might fetch £20,000, with another £15,000 for the furniture, this was not the moment to sell and the auctioneers all advised waiting till the spring. Plans for a sale by lottery had fallen through, but now some ingenious soul suggested a tontine. Each member of a tontine buys a share and the last survivor becomes the owner of the property. If enough people, four or perhaps five hundred, could be persuaded to put up a hundred guineas, then the problem might be solved. But this would take time to organize, and in the end, leaving his affairs in the hands of 'two or three active members' of his committee, the Duke took his family off to Devonshire about the middle of the month. They spent another night at Windsor on the way and a couple of days at Salisbury, staying with Edward's old tutor, Bishop Fisher, at the Palace, finally reaching their destination on Christmas Day in the middle of a heavy snowstorm.

Woolbrook Cottage, like so many rented houses, was cold, cramped and musty-smelling, a far cry from the splendours of Castle Hill or even the crumbling grandeur of Kensington Palace. Nor was Sidmouth, with its huddle of fishermen's cottages and sprinkling of villas let to summer visitors, particularly enlivening in the dead of an unusually severe winter. But for once Edward seems to have felt no urge to improve his surroundings. It was hardly worth while. In the spring he planned to take his wife and daughter up to Scotland to visit his socialist cotton-spinning friend Robert Owen, and see the model villages he had built for his workers at New Lanark. After that, it looked very much as if he would have to admit defeat and return to. Amorbach for an indefinite period. In the meantime, he was making the best of things, going for long walks with Captain Conroy, writing his interminable letters and playing with the baby. Victoire cannot have found Sidmouth very amusing either, but she conscientiously took tepid sea baths, walked along the shore with Feodore and spent a lot of time in the nursery.

Three days after their arrival there had been a very upsetting incident, when a boy shooting sparrows in the road outside had accidentally shattered one of the windows of the cottage, narrowly missing the little princess and tearing the sleeve of her nightgown. The Duchess, always inclined to be an over-anxious mother, was, not surprisingly, 'most exceedingly' alarmed, but the baby seemed none the worse. She had now been successfully weaned and cut her first two teeth 'without the slightest inconvenience'. At seven months she looked like a child of a year, and was almost indecently strong and healthy, − 'too healthy, I fear', wrote her father in one of his gloomier moments, 'in the opinion of some members of my family, by whom she is regarded as an intruder.'

The New Year came in with a spell of arctic weather. Woolbrook Cottage seemed more cheerless than ever and the whole family was shivering and sneezing. Even the baby developed a sore throat and was fretful. The Duke of Kent had also suffered a nasty gastric attack, the water at Sidmouth having played 'the very deuce' with his bowels, but on 7 January he insisted on going out with Captain Conroy to see to the horses and came back thoroughly chilled. Next day his cold was worse. Dr Wilson prescribed calomel and James's Powder, the universal panacea of the times, but the Duke thought a good night's rest would put him right. By the morning he was running a temperature and the

Duchess kept him in bed. Dr Wilson, who was lodging in the village, called again and looked grave. By 12 January it was clear that Edward was seriously ill, with a high fever, pains in the chest and vomiting. Bleeding, the only known remedy in such cases, brought no relief and Victoire, now very frightened, wrote urgently to London, begging Sir David Dundas, the senior royal physician, to come at once. Unfortunately the old King George III was failing and Sir David could not leave his post. He sent Dr Maton instead and the grim three-cornered battle between Edward's magnificent constitution, pneumonia and medical science went on.

Although sickened by the 'torments' being inflicted on him by the doctors – 'there is hardly a spot on his dear body which has not been touched by cupping, blisters or bleeding' – Victoire nursed her husband devotedly, hardly leaving him for a moment through the long-drawn-out nightmare of his illness. A hundred and twenty ounces, or six pints of blood had now been taken from him. He was often delirious, racked by exhausting spasms of coughing and hiccups, and by an agonizing pain in his side from which he only escaped during merciful spells of unconsciousness.

His friends, Generals Moore and Weatherall, came down to Woolbrook Cottage and Prince Leopold was also summoned, reaching Sidmouth on 22 January together with his secretary and constant companion, the serious young Coburger Dr Christian Stockmar. Stockmar was a qualified and skilful physician who had given up his own career to devote himself to Leopold's interests, but after examining the patient he was obliged to tell Victoire that 'human help could no longer avail'. Later that evening, though, the Duke rallied briefly, spoke quite lucidly and, supported by John Conroy and General Weatherall, managed with an immense effort to sign his will, appointing the Duchess sole guardian of his infant daughter. He died at ten o'clock the following morning, Sunday, 23 January 1820, with his wife, who had not been to bed or changed her dress for five days, kneeling beside him holding his hand.

Once again the efforts of the Coburg family to forge an alliance with the House of Hanover had ended in tragedy; but this time

they did at least have a living child to show for it and Prince
Leopold, a farsighted man of great political shrewdness, made up
his mind from the start that, whatever happened, his sister and the
baby must make their home in England. Although this was undoubtedly the right decision, it was not going to be an easy one to
stick to. The Duke of Kent had left 'nothing in the world but
debts', nor could the Duchess expect anything but 'the *greatest
animosity*' in high places. 'I know not what would have happened
to you and your Mamma if I had not then existed', Leopold was
later to remind his niece.

It was certainly very fortunate for the stunned, grief-stricken
widow, who had not even enough ready money to leave Sidmouth,
that her brother was at hand to take charge. Woolbrook Cottage
was now being invaded by the surgeons, embalmers and under-
takers with all their grisly paraphernalia, and Leopold lost no time
in getting the women and children away; but it was a forlorn little
party which left 'melancholy Sidmouth' under the Prince's
escort. 'That dreary journey, undertaken, I think, on the 26th of
January in bitter cold and damp weather, I shall not easily forget',
he wrote. 'I looked very sharp after the poor little baby, then
about eight months old.'

The Duke's death – 'so strong a man to go in so short a space,
and from, in its origin, so trifling an indisposition' – had come as a
shock to the outside world. Dorothea Lieven was astonished to
hear that 'that Hercules of a man' was no more, and Princess
Augusta, writing to a friend from Windsor Castle on 25 January,
exclaimed:

Think my Dearest Lady Harcourt, that yesterday *five* weeks he was
here on His way to Sidmouth; so happy with His excellent good little
Wife, and his lovely child; and within so short a time was perfectly *well –
ill –* and *no more!* . . . God knows what is for the best, and I hope I bow
with Submission to this very severe trial; but when I think of His poor
Miserable Wife, and His innocent Fatherless Child, it really breaks my
Heart.

To Victoire, her second bereavement came as a crushing blow.
'She quite adored poor Edward', wrote kind Princess Augusta;

'and they were truly blessed in each other.' Poor Edward may
have had his faults – he had been pompous, egocentric, often
foolish and sometimes cruel – but to his wife he had been a kind
and 'chivalrous' husband, who had given her all the consequence
and cherishing she craved, and she mourned him sincerely. Back
at Kensington, alone in a foreign land with a young baby totally
dependent on her, she faced a bleak and uncertain future, not
made any easier by the fact that she was finding it almost
impossible to learn English. Her only consolation, now to become
the centre of her universe, was Edward's child, 'dear sweet little
Vickelchen', completely recovered from her cold and already
beginning to show signs of 'wanting to get her own little way'.

Chapter Three
Le Roi George in Petticoats

Her Royal Highness is remarkably beautiful, and her gay and animated countenence bespeaks perfect health and good temper. Her complexion is excessively fair; her eyes large and expressive, and her cheeks blooming. She bears a very striking resemblance to her late royal father, and indeed to every member of our reigning family.

Anonymous Correspondent

The Duke of Kent was buried on 11 February, but as his immense coffin – seven feet long and weighing more than a ton – was lowered into the family vault at Windsor, his widow, forbidden by etiquette to be present, remained secluded at Kensington Palace, 'sick at heart and very lonely'. She had received visits of condolence from the Dukes of York, Sussex and Clarence, and the Duchess of Clarence was a regular caller. 'Dearest William is so good-hearted', wrote Princess Augusta, 'that He has desired Adelaide to go to Kensington every day, as she is a comfort to the poor Widow; and Her sweet, gentle mind is of great use to the Duchess of Kent. It is a great delight to me to think that they can read the same *Prayers*, and *talk the same Mother Tongue* together; it makes them such real friends and Comforts to each other.'

The family were doing their best to be kind to Edward's widow, but any consolation Victoire may have derived from her sister-in-law's company was inevitably shadowed by the knowledge that Adelaide represented danger, being the only person with the power to oust Edward's daughter from her place in the succession. The threat of a Clarence baby was now all the more to be dreaded by the mother of the Kent baby, especially since recent events had raised 'little Vickelchen' from fifth to third rung on the ladder, her grandfather having followed her father to the grave within a matter of days.

With the death of George III the Prince Regent became George IV, but this long-expected development was quickly followed by another, less predictable. The new King succumbed to an acute inflammation of the lungs and for a few tense days early in February it looked very much as if his reign would end almost before it had begun. 'Heavens, if he should die!' exclaimed Dorothea Lieven. 'Shakespeare's tragedies pale before such a catastrophe. Father and son, in the past, have been buried together. But two Kings!' Catastrophe was, however, averted. The King recovered, though, as Henry Brougham told Mr Creevey, he had been 'as near death as any man but poor Kent ever was before' and only a hundred and fifty ounces of blood let had saved his '*precious* life'. Everyone breathed again and at Kensington Victoire turned once more to face the problem of her future.

If she had followed her own inclinations, she would undoubtedly have returned to Germany, where she would at least have been among friends, and this was the course being most strongly advised by George IV, whose '*great wish*' was to get his brother's widow and intrusive child out of the country without delay. 'It was wonderful', recollected Prince Leopold nearly forty years later, 'how George IV was bent on this idea; and in those days the wish and will of the head of the state was still a very serious concern and the people very subservient to it.' But despite the widow's natural desire to go home and the head of the state's anxiety to be rid of her, Leopold continued to insist that she must stay where she was. He reminded her at every opportunity of Edward's wish that his little girl should be brought up as an English child, and pointed out how vital it would be for her to have an English background were she ever to become Queen. Victoire listened to her brother and, being in the lifelong habit of turning to the nearest male for guidance, she accepted that he knew best. The King's recent brush with eternity had, after all, demonstrated just how close Edward's little girl might be to the throne.

The difficulty, as always, was money. Even returning to Amorbach would have presented serious problems, for the ambitious rebuilding programme started by the Duke of Kent was still unfinished and the house uninhabitable. Several thousands were owing to the architect and workmen, and the Duchess had been troubled by disagreeable business letters even during Edward's last illness. If she stayed in England her only source of income would be the £6,000 jointure voted by Parliament at the time of her marriage, and Leopold himself conceded that no Royal Duchess with children could live on that amount. Although the King would not go as far as actually turning his sister-in-law out of the apartments at Kensington, he made it abundantly plain that he would do nothing to help her stay in them; nor would he recognize his niece's existence by arranging any sort of financial provision for her, and once again it was left to Prince Leopold to come to the rescue. Luckily he was in a position to do so, as he was still drawing the annual pension of fifty thousand pounds settled on him when he married Charlotte, and he now proposed to make his sister and her fatherless infant an allowance of three thousand pounds a year.

Though he was at pains to remind the Prime Minister that he had not grasped at the management of the Princess but was happily undertaking a responsibility delegated to him by the King, Leopold's intervention and the necessity for it did nothing to improve relations between the English royal family and the Coburgs. Even with her brother's help the Duchess of Kent was obliged to borrow quite a substantial sum of money in order to buy herself an 'outfit', since she had been left 'without Furniture, Plate, Linen . . . or, in fact, any one of the Materials of an Establishment'. Leopold summed up her situation rather more brutally when he remarked that 'she had not a spoon or napkin of her own, as everything belonged to the creditors'.

By the spring of 1820 the Duchess had cut her ties with Amorbach, reluctantly resigning the guardianship of her son

Charles, and had settled down to make what she could of life in England. Kensington, which was to be her own and her daughter's home for the next seventeen years, was then a quiet rural suburb of orchards and market gardens, its only excitement being provided by the mail coaches flashing past on the main road to the west. The Palace itself, a rambling red-brick mansion first acquired by the Crown in 1689 from the Earl of Nottingham for the sum of £18,000 and a favoured resort of William and Mary and Queen Anne, had become a backwater with a few old pensioners and royal retainers roosting under the eaves. The enormous, amiably eccentric Duke of Sussex occupied a suite of rooms on the ground floor and the sad Princess Sophia, fourth daughter of George III, still expiating the old scandal of her illegitimate child in self-imposed seclusion, was another resident.

This slumbrous, ghost-ridden retreat was hardly perhaps the most suitable environment for a rumbustious toddler, but Alexandrina Victoria, still blissfully unconscious of the cross-currents, the family feuds and jealousies, the sorrowful memories and avid ambitions surrounding her, seemed able to flourish anywhere. Her own earliest memories were connected with the 'poor old Palace', as she later referred to it, of crawling on a yellow rug spread out for that purpose, and of being told that 'if I cried and was naughty my "Uncle Sussex" would hear me and punish me, for which reason I always screamed when I saw him!' She had an early horror of *Bishops* 'on account of their wigs and *aprons*'. In the case of her father's old tutor, Fisher of Salisbury, this was at least partially overcome by his kneeling down and letting her play with his Garter badge, but with another bishop even the persuasion of showing him her 'pretty shoes' was of no avail. Non-episcopal visitors seem to have had better luck. Solemn William Wilberforce, of abolitionist fame, who was invited to call on the Duchess of Kent in July 1820, told his friend Hannah More that she had received him 'with her fine animated child on the floor by her side, with its playthings, of which I soon became one'.

The Duchess was now beginning to appear occasionally in society and Harriet Granville, who met her at a 'royal morning' during August, found her 'very pleasing indeed and raving of her baby, "C'est mon Bonheur, mes délices, mon existence . . ." Think of the baby,' added Lady Granville. 'They say it is le roi George in petticoats, so fat it can scarcely waddle.'

The baby was not present on this occasion, but two ladies out walking in Kensington Gardens that August were fortunate enough to encounter her taking her daily airing in 'a very elegant child's phaeton', painted bright yellow and bearing her initials and coronet on its panels. The fifteen-month-old Princess, dressed in a white cambric pelisse and large straw bonnet, was tied into this interesting conveyance with a broad black ribbon round her waist and was being pulled along by her sister Feodore, with her nurse and Baroness Späth in attendance. The two passers-by reported that they had walked alongside the carriage for a considerable distance, 'which appeared to please her Royal Highness greatly, as she never once turned her face from us, but continued talking the whole time very distinctly, and with great intelligence for her age. She noticed with vivacity every thing that passed, and continually addressed us as "lady", looking after us whenever we fell a little behind her chaise, as though unwilling to part company.'

The Princess's new friends, regretting they had not had 'some trifling toy' with which they might have amused and pleased her, were anxious to make good the omission, and on their next excursion took with them 'a little spun glass lancer on horseback' which they found an opportunity of presenting at the palace door. This charming, if not very suitable offering for a young child was courteously accepted by Baroness Späth, and the little Princess, who seemed 'highly pleased', was reaching out for it when the voice of nanny, wise in her generation, could be heard saying, 'If you give it to the Princess, it will be broken in a minute.' History does not reveal the immediate consequences of this damping remark, but the interview appears to have terminated somewhat abruptly. A few days later, however, having been once again overtaken by the royal entourage passing through the courtyard of the palace, the two ladies were agreeably surprised to be immediately recognized by their 'little darling', who turned

quickly to her nurse and said 'in a loud and authoritative tone,
"lady" '.

This time the baby's admirers were invited to walk in 'to have
the honour of kissing the Princess's hand' and Baroness Späth told
them she had known they were to be asked in and had pointed
them out the moment she saw them – 'a most extraordinary
instance of acuteness in so very young an infant.' 'She seemed
perfectly to understand', continues the anonymous authoress of
this sworn-to-be-'authentic' anecdote,

> that it was we who gave her the man and horse, for which she was
> frequently desired to thank us, but apparently a little too wilful to obey
> the mandate, she merely smiled and looked very arch. She held out her
> pretty, fair, fat little hand to be kissed with the utmost grace and
> dignity; and on our taking leave some minutes after the subject had been
> mentioned, said of her own accord, 'thank you', most plainly and
> distinctly.

This seems to have marked the end of their acquaintance, but
the strangers carried away a highly favourable impression of the
Princess Victoria, who

> was at this period a beautiful child, bearing a very strong resemblance
> to her father, and indeed to the royal family generally. Though small and
> delicately formed, she was very fat, and might be called a remarkably
> fine child for her age; her eyes were large and blue; her complexion
> extremely fair, with a rosy colour expressive of high health, and her
> curled lips continually parted, shewed her four pretty white teeth. She
> was forward in her speech; very lively, and appeared of a gentle, happy
> temper; occasionally a sweet and merry smile animated her intelligent
> countenance.

After allowing for a due measure of baby and royalty worship,
there seems no reason to doubt the accuracy of this portrait of a
healthy, handsome, intelligent child, with a happy outgoing
disposition who took a vigorous interest in the world about her. It
was still a very small world, of course, and peopled exclusively by
friends. After Mamma came Feodore, and despite the twelve-year
gap in their ages a deep and lasting bond of affection was to unite
the two half-sisters. Equally important at this stage was the nurse

Mrs Brock, or Boppy as she was called by her small charge, and kind sentimental Späth, who frankly doted on the little Princess. Two other figures, not yet fully in focus but destined in their different ways to exercise an incalculable influence on her development, were Fräulein Louise Lehzen and Captain John Conroy.

Louise Lehzen, the daughter of a Lutheran pastor from Hanover, had been engaged by the Duke of Kent to be Feodore's governess on the understanding that she would in due course instruct the Princess Victoria as well, and she had joined the household in December 1819, just in time for the fatal visit to Sidmouth. Lehzen, as she was always known, was then in her mid-thirties, slim, dark-haired and not unattractive. Charles Greville, a discerning observer, was to describe her as 'a clever agreeable woman', and certainly she possessed considerable shrewdness and strength of character, together with an almost limitless capacity for single-minded devotion.

John Conroy was an Irishman from Connaught, tall, good-looking, plausible and unscrupulous. Less perceptive than Lehzen, he too possessed an immense capacity for devotion – to the advancement of John Conroy, although his progress had so far been disappointing. The Duke of Kent had held a high opinion of his 'intelligent factotum' but, even with royal recommendation, the military establishment continued to display an obstinate reluctance to make further use of this promising young officer's capabilities, and when his patron died, Conroy, at thirty-three, was still no more than the Duke's equerry. With a family of six children to support on a small private income, he naturally did not relish the prospect of being out of a job and chose instead to remain with the Duchess as her Comptroller, private secretary and confidant. He was, in fact, taking a deliberate gamble on the future, or rather on the Princess Victoria's future, but the Duchess, never one to look beneath the surface, had accepted his services and protestations of loyalty thankfully and without question.

In contrast to Prince Leopold, who was inclined to be both pompous and gloomy, Conroy had plenty of gay Irish charm and an invincibly optimistic outlook on life which the harassed widow found very comforting in those first dismal months. He was always at her elbow, always sympathetic and cheerful, happy to take all the tiresome financial and practical details off her shoulders and generally make himself useful. Not surprisingly Victoire found him invaluable and was soon heavily dependent on his support and companionship, while his second daughter, another Victoire, made an ideal playmate for the Princess, who was almost exactly the same age.

Throughout the summer and autumn of 1820 the country was convulsed by the reverberating scandal of the Queen's trial. George IV's marriage to Caroline of Brunswick had been a disaster from the beginning. The bridegroom is said to have called urgently for brandy when he first set eyes on his uncouth slummocky bride, while the bride was to swear that the groom spent their wedding night lying on the floor in a drunken stupor. The couple had separated within a year, and two months after the birth of her child the Princess of Wales set up house at Blackheath, where her convivial goings-on provided the gossip-mongers with an inexhaustible source of supply. In 1814 she had gone abroad and proceeded to cut a swathe through Europe – a stout, middle-aged playgirl parading about the streets of Genoa in a mother-of-pearl phaeton shaped like a seashell and driven by a child wearing spangles and flesh-coloured tights; turning up at parties in an advanced state of nudity and accompanied everywhere by a handsome Italian gigolo, Bartolomeo Bergami. So, when she landed in Dover in June 1820 bent on claiming her rights as Queen Consort, Lord Liverpool's government was thrown into an agony of embarrassment.

Caroline had always been eccentric and difficult, but there was no question that she had been disgracefully treated by her husband and his family, and the government was only too well aware that the opposition and the opposition press would extract every ounce of political capital from her present predicament. Alderman Wood – the same who had organized the Duke and Duchess of Kent's return from Amorbach the previous year – was at the port to greet her and she received a rapturous welcome from large crowds of well-wishers, who saw her as the persecuted victim of an intensely unpopular administration.

An 'immense multitude' surrounded her carriage as she approached the capital and Charles Greville, who had ridden out as far as Greenwich to see the fun, reported that 'she was everywhere received with the greatest enthusiasm'. Caroline was staying with Alderman Wood in South Audley Street and for several days London was in an uproar, with disorderly crowds roaming the West End forcing passers-by to shout 'God Save the Queen!', demanding illuminations in her honour, smashing windows and 'pelting those who would not take off their hats as they passed Wood's door'. Pro-Caroline demonstrations spread to the provinces and the slogan 'No Queen, no King!' became the battle-cry of her supporters. The mob screamed 'Nero!' under the windows of Carlton House, until the King, very gouty and in a furious temper, retreated to Windsor, no doubt to brood on the enviable freedom enjoyed by some of his predecessors when it came to disposing of superfluous wives. An especially alarming feature of the crisis was the fact that the army, the only effective force of law and order, was showing every sign of becoming infected with the prevailing Queen-fever, and a battalion of the Guards mutinied. 'The extinguisher is taking fire,' remarked one wit, a circumstance which led the Duke of Wellington to reflect seriously on the imperative need for the provision of some form of civilian police.

Caroline, greatly heartened by the strength of public sympathy for her cause, refused to accept a compromise settlement, while the King, who had long been agitating for a divorce, equally flatly refused to recognize her as his consort and was threatening to abdicate rather than allow her name to be included in the liturgy. The government, whose emissaries had been stoned on their visits to South Audley Street and who saw red revolution staring it in the face, was therefore forced to bring in a Bill of Pains and Penalties, designed to prove Caroline's adultery with Bergami, to dissolve her marriage and deprive her of her title.

The 'trial', which took place in the House of Lords against a background of intense popular excitement, did nothing to improve the royal family's image. Few people, including her own counsel, who listened to the all-too-explicit evidence or watched the Queen, with her outlandish black wig and coarse red face, lolling in her chair and occasionally shrieking reproaches at one of the Italian witnesses, had any real doubt of her guilt; but the Bill secured only a slender majority on its third reading and the government, terrified of the counter-disclosures which might result if it was debated in the Commons, decided to drop the whole measure. Its political opponents, and all those who chose to regard the establishment's tactical retreat as a victory for innocence and liberty, celebrated with a three-day debauch, but thereafter the general hysteria began to subside. The following February Parliament made no difficulty about voting to exclude the Queen both from the Prayer Book and the Coronation, and when the King ventured to appear again at the theatre there were only isolated shouts of 'Where's your wife, Georgy?'

The chief interest which these stirring events had roused at Kensington was centred on speculation as to whether the King would marry again if he got his freedom. Of far greater immediate significance was the fact that on 10 December the Duchess of Clarence had given birth to a living daughter, born six weeks prematurely but said to be doing well. This was a dreadful blow to the Duchess of Kent and to John Conroy, who observed with his usual clumsy flippancy that 'our little woman's nose had been put out of joint'. The King marked his relief and pleasure by conferring the royal names of Elizabeth Georgina on his latest niece, but the second Clarence baby survived for no more than three months, dying suddenly of 'an entanglement of the bowels' on 4 March 1821. The Princess Victoria was thus reinstated and her second birthday received respectful notice in 'the public journals', whose editors thought it expedient to inform their readers that Her Royal Highness was a very beautiful and interesting child, and had entered upon her third year with every promise of health, strength and spirits.

George IV's Coronation took place in July, a ceremony almost oriental in its magnificence but chiefly remembered for the ludicrous spectacle of the unhappy Queen trying frantically but unsucessfully to gain admittance to the Abbey. Napoleon Bonaparte died that summer and so did the poet John Keats, while the Duchess of Kent and her daughters went on holiday to Bognor, spending two months at 'this secluded watering place', walking and riding on the seashore and 'gathering a store of health for the ensuing winter'. The little Princess was also strengthened by 'a regular course of sea-bathing' which she appeared to enjoy very much.

Back at Kensington she resumed her daily outings, which had been greatly enlivened by the addition of Dickey the donkey, a present from the Duke of York. Dickey was such a success that it was only with considerable difficulty that she could be persuaded to part with him at the end of their various expeditions. The fair-haired Princess, either riding on patient Dickey's back or in the little carriage he pulled, or else scampering 'with astonishing rapidity' hand in hand with Feodore along the gravel walk, had by now become one of the sights of Kensington Gardens. Her likeness to the rest of the royal family was already noticeable and with her blooming cheeks and large, expressive, rather prominent blue eyes she reminded some sentimental souls of the 'late beloved Princess Charlotte'.

She continued to be the friendliest child, seldom passing anyone without a brisk 'How do you do' or 'Good morning, Sir' or 'Lady', and was always ready to enter into conversation with anybody who would talk to her, 'returning their compliments or answering their questions in the most distinct and good-humoured manner'. She was fascinated by other children, especially babies, rarely allowing one to pass her without demanding 'to see it close'. On those occasions when she could be seen playing on the lawn outside the Palace, an audience usually gathered at the railings but this never disconcerted her Royal Highness in the least. She would curtsy and kiss her hand to the spectators, prancing up to talk to them at the first opportunity. When led away by a disapproving Mrs Brock, she would often wriggle free, returning 'again and again . . . to renew the mutual greetings between herself and her future subjects'.

As well as widening her circle of acquaintance among her future subjects, the young Victoria was beginning to get to know her father's family. One of her earliest memories was of going to Carlton House Terrace to see the artist Thomas Lawrence painting her Aunt Mary, the Duchess of Gloucester, and she grew very fond of her uncle the Duke of York, remembering him as 'tall, rather large, very kind but extremely shy'. He always gave her beautiful presents and, on one never-to-be-forgotten day, arranged a Punch and Judy show for her in a friend's garden. There was also kind Aunt Adelaide, who wrote to her touchingly in May 1821, only two months after the death of her own baby: 'My dear little Heart, I hope you are well and don't forget Aunt Adelaide who loves you so fondly.' A year later came another little note: 'Uncle William and Aunt Adelaide send their love to *dear little Victoria* with their best wishes on her birthday, and hope that she will now become a *very good Girl*, being now *three years old.*'

In May 1823 the Princess made her debut at Court. George IV had not forgiven the Duchess of Kent, either for her bad taste in marrying Edward or for her obstinate insistence on staying where she was not wanted, but having failed to get rid of her he was now grudgingly prepared to be civil and to take some interest in the child who, it now seemed, was all too likely eventually to succeed to the throne. So, on Victoria's fourth birthday, she received 'a superb token of remembrance' from her Uncle King: a miniature portrait of himself set in diamonds, and shortly afterwards His Majesty issued invitations for a state dinner party, informing the Duchess of Kent that he wished the Princess Victoria to accompany her and be presented to the assembled guests. Mother and daughter accordingly arrived at Carlton House at half-past six on the appointed evening to be 'received with all the honours due to royalty, and conducted immediately to the drawing-room'. The Princess, dressed in a plain white frock with her birthday gift pinned on her sleeve, seems to have done her Mamma credit, for during the half-hour she was with the King 'her engaging and

interesting manners, the result of a lively, affectionate
disposition, were displayed to great advantage' and His Majesty
'expressed himself greatly delighted with his little niece'. The
company present were also 'much gratified with the opportunity
thus afforded of seeing the royal child, whom they could not but
look upon with the deepest interest as their probable future
sovereign'.

But outings like these were extremely rare, and daily life at
Kensington normally followed a very simple pattern. Breakfast
was at eight and on fine summer days would often be served out of
doors, the Princess sitting beside her Mamma at her own little table
and chair eating her bread and milk and fruit. After breakfast
Feodore and Lehzen retired to the schoolroom, while Victoria set
out for an hour's ride with Dickey. If the weather was bad 'a
carriage airing' would be substituted at about twelve o'clock, but
normally the rest of the morning was spent indoors with the
Duchess, who was now trying, not very successfully, to give her
little daughter her first lessons, and playing with her toys or
galloping up and down the galleries and corridors of the Palace.
Lunch was at half-past one, always 'the plainest and most
wholesome fare', and in the afternoon there were either more
lessons, a drive with Mamma and Feodore or a visit to some
favoured member of the Duchess's circle. The Princess would
then ride or walk again in the Park and sometimes in the summer
the whole afternoon might be spent out in the garden. Grown-up
dinner was at seven, and unless there was 'a regular dinner party'
the baby of the family would be present, with Mrs Brock in
attendance, to have her supper of bread and milk out of a silver
basin. Tea she remembered only as a great treat in later years.
When she had finished, she was allowed to get down and play until
dessert was on the table, and at nine o'clock she would be taken
off to bed, sleeping always in her mother's room.

Queen Victoria was later in the habit of complaining about her
sad, dull childhood but this sounds quite a sensible regime for a
young child – a quiet, regular life with plenty of fresh air and
exercise – and these earliest years seem to have been happy ones, if
a little lonely. There was to be another invitation to Carlton

House to meet her Cambridge cousins – George, two months older than herself, and Augusta, born in 1822 – who were over on a visit from Hanover, and occasionally some carefully selected child or children would be introduced to play at Kensington; but the Princess had no real friends of her own age and knew nothing of the rough-and-tumble of ordinary nursery life. As a result she was becoming more than a little spoilt and, being 'naturally very passionate', tantrums and storms were not infrequent.

The Duchess of Kent continued to take her family on a summer holiday in August and September. Tunbridge Wells was the choice one year, but gradually Ramsgate became their favourite resort and the Princess Victoria could often be seen digging industriously on the sands, or running up to her ankles into the sea, wearing thick shoes over her boots! It is recorded that 'Her Royal Highness was occasionally permitted to play with the children of the gentry, whom she met upon the beach; but if she attempted to take unfair advantage of her exalted rank, the ladies in attendance always interfered to set her right.' She was described by someone who knew her at Ramsgate as being 'a charming child, very high-spirited, and being much indulged, but little disposed to abide by any will but her own'. Certainly she was an energetic and naturally cheerful child. Once, having tripped and fallen while running very fast along the sands, she was picked up by a convenient passer-by who enquired solicitously whether she had hurt herself. 'Oh, no!' answered Victoria gaily. 'I am not hurt, but mamma will say the Princess of England should not be so giddy.'

Prince Leopold, who sometimes joined the family party at the seaside, continued to be a familiar figure during these early years and his two nieces came to regard visits to Claremont as the high spots of their young lives. Feodore 'always left Claremont with tears for Kensington Palace' and Victoria especially remembered the joy 'of being under the roof of that beloved Uncle' and of going to see dear old Mrs Louis, once Princess Charlotte's faithful dresser and friend, 'who doted on the little Princess who was too much an idol in the House'.

When she was five years old it was decided that Princess

Victoria had outgrown her nurse, and 'Boppy' departed, to be replaced by Louise Lehzen, who had for some time been watching with disapproval the way in which the little Princess was being handled. Everyone, of course, worshipped 'the poor little fatherless child' but although – as time was to prove – she yielded to no one in devotion to her charge, Lehzen had enough common sense to see the destructive effects which too much uncritical adoration were beginning to have on a strong-willed, assertive temperament.

The young Victoria resembled her father's family in more than looks, possessing a full share of the Hanoverian temper and over-flowing animal spirits which, uncontrolled and unchannelled, were all too apt to manifest themselves in screaming fits and violent explosions of rage. The Duchess of Kent unfortunately lacked the strength of mind necessary for dealing with the 'storms' so enthusiastically created by the nursery tyrant, complaining rather ineffectually that 'the ladies of the household *would* spoil her little girl, an evil which she did not exactly know how to remedy.' Lehzen, now undertaking the over-due task of instilling some notions of discipline, had no patience with this defeatist attitude and Feodore was to remember with amusement how fiercely she scolded the two worst culprits, poor Späth and Mrs Louis.

Victoria herself took a certain simple pride in the tempests she created. On one occasion, when a visitor enquired if she had been good, the Duchess replied that she had been good that morning, 'but yesterday there was a little storm'. 'Two storms, Mamma,' came the complacent reminder, 'one at dressing and one at washing.' Devastatingly honest, she remained immune to the age-old sophistry of maternal logic: 'When you are naughty you make me and yourself very unhappy.' 'No, Mamma, not *me*, not myself, but *you*!' But although accustomed by this time to setting 'pretty well *all* at defiance', she could recognize authority when she saw it and, like many children of her type, responded gratefully to Lehzen's policy of kindness but firmness.

According to one of the anecdotes painstakingly related by a Lady whose Sources for Collecting the Same were 'of the Highest

Character', the Princess could generally be seen out on the grass during the haymaking season with her little rake, fork and cart, busily employed in collecting the hay. But

> she had one day completely fatigued herself with filling and re-filling her cart; and at length threw down her rake when it was but half-loaded. Her governess immediately desired her to resume it, and to finish filling her cart; she replied she was too tired. 'But Princess, you should have thought of that before you began the last load, for you know we never leave any thing unfinished'; and her Royal Highness was thus most judiciously persuaded to complete the work she had begun.

Under Lehzen's calming influence storms were gradually becoming a thing of the past and the attachment between governess and pupil grew stronger. It was affection always tinged with respect on the Princess's side, for Lehzen never relaxed her high standards, although she came to live entirely for the child in her care. While she was undoubtedly something of a handful, Victoria must have been an easy child to love, with her warm demonstrative vitality and engaging gift for mimicry and repartee, which was also 'in the Family'. Never one to sulk, she was always 'very contrite' after an outburst of screaming and foot-stamping, and remembered being taught from the first to beg her maid's pardon for any naughtiness or rudeness.

Education had already made its appearance in the shape of the Reverend George Davys, a gentle young evangelical clergyman who had been recommmended to the Duchess of Kent as an English tutor by the vicar of Kensington. The Duchess was so pleased with her progress that she invited Mr Davys to take on the still more challenging assignment of teaching her daughter to read. Victoria, who was 'not fond of learning as a little child' had so far successfully baffled all her Mamma's attempts to teach her her letters, but Davys had the brilliant idea of turning this boring process into a game – writing letters and words down on bits of cardboard and hiding them round the room. Lehzen read little stories aloud to her while she was being dressed to get her out of the habit of talking in front of the servants and sometimes the Princess would invent her own plots, saying 'Let me tell a story.'

Now the reading material was becoming more educational in its nature, but not even Lehzen could yet persuade her charge to sit still for long enough to absorb formal lessons.

Wisely, no attempt was made to force her but, all the same, babyhood was drawing to an end, and the chatty, roly-poly infant who had held court in Kensington Gardens or flirtatiously blown kisses to her admirers through the Palace railings was growing up. Soon she would be an altogether different child, slimmer and more serious and beginning at times to wear an oddly strained and anxious look.

Chapter Four
The Kensington System

In the family it is noticed that you are cutting yourself off more and more
from them with your child.

Duchess of Clarence to the Duchess of Kent

In May 1825, 'without any application or representation on her
part', the Duchess of Kent received the first public recognition of
her services to her adopted country, when the government asked
the House of Commons to approve a grant of £6,000 a year 'for the
purpose of making an adequate provision for the honourable
support and education of Her Royal Highness the Princess
Alexandrina Victoria'.

In the debate on the motion not a single dissentient voice was
raised. 'All parties agreed in the propriety of the grant,' declared
Mr Secretary Canning, 'and if the government had anything to
answer for on this point, it was for having so long delayed in
bringing it before the House.' Mr Canning did not wish to
mention the Duchess of Kent on this occasion, 'because he was
sure that to be the subject of a discussion would be as painful to her
feelings as it would be repugnant to that unobtrusive delicacy
which characterised her conduct, and which rendered her an
ornament to her exalted station.' Nevertheless, Henry Brougham
took the opportunity of complimenting her on the assiduous
manner in which she was devoting herself to the education of the
young Princess, whom he described, gratifyingly if inaccurately,

as the heiress presumptive. The Chancellor of the Exchequer also had some kind remarks to make about the general excellence of the Princess's upbringing, and in the Lords the Prime Minister praised the Duchess's exemplary conduct 'for propriety, domestic affection and moral purity'. The Earl of Darnley, who was an old friend of the Kents, added that 'knowing perhaps more of her Royal Highness than most of their Lordships, he could safely say that she showed herself unexampled in prudence, discretion, and every amiable quality that could exalt and dignify the female character.'

There was no question that the extra money would be welcome at Kensington, for despite the simplicity of her life-style, the Duchess was by now quite heavily in debt; but the tributes lavished on her by both Houses of Parliament came as balm to her soul, going a long way towards making up for the humiliations and deprivations of her early widowhood. They were balm to Prince Leopold, too, vindicating his prescience in persuading Victoire to stay in England and boding well for the future fortunes of the Coburg family. He told his sister that he would continue her allowance, at least for the time being, and advised her to enlarge her household now that Victoria's importance had been officially recognized.

There was quite a gathering of Coburgs down at Claremont that summer when the Dowager Duchess Augusta came over on a visit, escorted by Prince Charles of Leiningen, now nearly twenty-one. At the age of sixty-seven the Dowager was still a lively, vigorous old lady, and her granddaughter was to remember her as 'a most remarkable woman, with a most powerful, energetic, almost masculine mind, accompanied with great tenderness of heart and extreme love of nature'. Certainly she took a keenly observant interest in her surroundings. From the moment of her arrival she was fascinated by the English stage coaches which 'with their elegant red-uniformed postillions, look like carriages of the nobility' and, like most foreigners landing at Dover, was much impressed by the cleanliness of the inns, the good roads and the lush prosperity of the Kentish countryside.

'The country houses,' she wrote to her eldest daughter,

Countess Mensdorff-Pouilly, 'the uniquely delightful villages, cannot be described; everywhere is not only neat but subtly elegant; an abundance of flowers! In one village, the pastor's residence was like something out of a novel. Sittingbourne, where we stayed overnight, was a so-called village; only two rows of houses, but how pretty they were!' Approaching Chatham there was the busy port and dockyard to be admired – 'this sight of the broad rough river alive with innumerable ships is unique!' – and at the top of Shooters Hill a first intoxicating glimpse of 'the most beautiful view in the world'.

Stretching out at our feet lay unending London, with its parks covered by a thin veil. The whole neighbourhood seems like a big park with gardens, and big and small country houses scattered around. Camberwell seems to be a part of London, since the rows of buildings are continuous, like the mail and stage coaches. We changed horses again here and rode from country house to country house. One cannot think of anything more diversified or prettier; some are quite new and have been built on speculation. The older ones either have fine gardens full of flowers . . . or large parks, in whose shade they stand. So many-sided, so delightful, all drawings of English country houses, lodges and cottages scarcely give one the right impression.

Arrived at Claremont, Duchess Augusta thought that Victoire, whom she had not seen for more than seven years, looked ill, and had lost so much weight 'that I had to force myself not to burst into tears'. Feodore she found growing 'rather pretty, clever, amiable', while Victoria, 'the flower of May', was 'ein schönes Kind' – a fine child. The Dowager, in fact, was soon in raptures over her little granddaughter – 'big and strong as good health itself . . . agile, poised, graceful in all her movements . . . a lovable child, so vivacious and so friendly.' 'The Little One' was soon on the best of terms with grandmamma, painstakingly correcting her English – 'such natural politeness and attentiveness as that child shows has never come my way before'. At the same time, grandmamma held strong views on naughty children. 'I shall never forget her coming into the room when I had been crying and naughty at my lessons', wrote Queen Victoria nearly fifty years

later, 'and scolding me severely, which had a very salutary effect.'
The Queen also remembered being sent on long carriage drives
with her grandmother and not enjoying them 'as, like most
children of that age, I preferred running about'.

But the Dowager was an indefatigable sightseer and was out
nearly every afternoon exploring the Surrey lanes. There was a
trip to Hampton Court and another to Box Hill, visits to Oatlands
and Bushey Park, drives through Walton and Weybridge and
farther afield to Kingston and Richmond, where the scenery by the
river was 'indescribably pretty'. 'The country people are nice and
friendly,' she commented, 'their villages are darling little towns
. . . On Sundays the inhabitants sit quite relaxed in front of their
pretty houses, or in their gardens. Only the workmen wear
peasant clothing.'

After about a fortnight at Claremont, Duchess Augusta went
up to stay at Kensington. She found the old Palace 'a tiny bit
sad' and rather dark, but 'the garden or, more precisely park,
since there are avenues and little woods of the most heavenly
trees, is very lovely'. On 17 August Victoire celebrated her
thirty-ninth birthday. 'To be here, with my children, on her
dear birthday, is something that at my age I had no longer
counted on', wrote the Dowager. Feodore woke her mother
with a serenade and the Little One had dressed all her dolls in
their Robes of State.

The rest of the month was spent in more sightseeing – the
Tower, of course, and Westminster Abbey and St Paul's, a trip
on the river down to the West India Docks, and a delightful
carriage drive to Hampstead 'from which one can see the whole
town as well as a wide stretch of countryside'. There was another
memorable drive over Battersea Bridge, beyond which were
'meadows, hedges, lovely trees and nice little country houses',
and back via Vauxhall Bridge – 'hundreds of boats carrying
holidaymakers were sailing on the river.' There were visits to the
Opera, where she was half-blinded by the glaring gaslight, and to
the Haymarket Theatre. The actors were excellent and, even with
her inadequate English, the Dowager could follow enough of the
performance to be amused. Regent Street, 'the newest and most

beautiful part of the town', reminded her of St Petersburg, but everything in the shops was horribly expensive.

Duchess Augusta was enjoying herself very much, but she was glad to get back to the fresh clean air of 'charming, homely Claremont' and more of the company of her little granddaughter. 'The Little One is nothing less than a beauty, yet a darling clown', she wrote on 12 September. 'She is incredibly precocious for her age and very comical, I have never seen a more alert and forthcoming child. She talks to everyone and thinks a lot about what has been said. When she speaks German she is adorable. She will not do it with me, "Grandmamma speaks English", but she does with the young ladies.' This rather seems to dispose of Queen Victoria's own later contention that she never spoke German as a child, and was 'not allowed to'. Probably she did not in public – her image as an 'English' child was always carefully cultivated and she once refused to say something in German to an inquisitive lady in Kensington Gardens. But accustomed to hearing it constantly spoken around her by the predominantly German household from her earliest infancy, it is a little hard to believe that she was not bilingual as a small child.

At Claremont her comical little ways continued to delight her grandmother.

Since one is six years old with impunity, there is often bargaining whilst going to bed . . . In the morning, she sometimes does not want to get out of bed, preferring to tell all sorts of tales. Lehzen takes her gently from her bed, and sits her down on the thick carpet, where she has to put on her stockings. One has to contain oneself not to burst out laughing, when she says in a tragic tone of voice, 'Poor Vicky! She is an unhappy child! She just doesn't know which is the right stocking and which is the left!'

The hopes of the entire Coburg clan, centred as they were on the merry, sturdy little girl, received a sharp warning against over-confidence during that month. There was an outbreak of dysentery at Esher and several children died, including the daughter of a local doctor. Princess Victoria caught the infection and for a few anxious days she was seriously ill. Mr Blagden, a specialist from London, was summoned and the Princess made a good recovery, though she remembered 'being very cross and screaming dreadfully at having to wear, for a time, a flannel next to my skin'.

By the end of September the Duchess Augusta's holiday was drawing to an end. The parting with Victoire and the Little One was inevitably tearful, and the old lady felt the sad 'for the last time' deep in her heart. It was, in fact, to be the last time. She died six years later without seeing her daughter and grand-daughter again.

On 24 May 1826 the Princess Victoria's seventh birthday was marked by a grand fête given in her honour by Uncle Leopold at Claremont, and among the 'costly tokens of respect and affection which awaited Her Royal Highness on this occasion' was one present calculated to delight the heart of any small girl – a matched pair of tiny Shetland ponies, the gift of the Marchioness of Huntley. 'These pretty little animals were speedily provided with a handsome harness . . . a low, light phaeton was also immediately built, just large enough to hold the young Princess and her governess; a lilliputian postillion, in a neat livery of green and gold, with a black velvet cap, was mounted on one of the ponies, and an outrider on horseback preceded the little equipage.' Not surprisingly, the Princess 'was quite in love with her new acquisition; and every morning during the summer months, and generally again in the afternoon, she rode round the park or into the country in her favourite vehicle.'

Another excitement that summer was her first visit to Windsor. The Duchess of Kent and her daughters had been honoured with an invitation to spend a few days at Cumberland Lodge and the Princess always remembered the King taking her by the hand, saying, 'Give me your little paw.' The preposterous sight of the monarch, heavily rouged, bewigged and, despite his restraining corsets, enormously fat, might have terrified a less robust child. But Victoria, although repelled by the greasepaint, kept her self-possession. She was, after all, accustomed to the almost equally bizarre figure of Uncle Sussex, and Uncle King was just another large, gouty old gentleman, though one with 'wonderful dignity and charm of manner'. Even now, when George IV set out to please, he could be irresistible, and his seven-year-old niece proved an easy conquest.

Lady Maria Conyngham, daughter of the King's current mistress, was deputed to entertain the Princess, and she was taken driving in Windsor Great Park and to Sandpit Gate to see the royal menagerie, 'with wapitis, gazelles, chamois, etc., etc.' The next day, she remembered long afterwards,

> . . . we went to Virginia Water, and met the King in his phaeton in which he was driving the Duchess of Gloucester, – and he said, 'Pop her in', and I was lifted in and placed between him and Aunt Gloucester, who held me round the waist. (Mamma was much frightened.) I was greatly pleased, and remember that I looked with great respect at the scarlet liveries, etc . . . . We drove round the nicest part of Virginia Water and stopped at the Fishing Temple. Here there was a large barge and everyone went on board and fished, while a band played in another!

The Princess came after dinner to hear the band playing in the Conservatory 'which was lit up by coloured lights'. 'Now, Victoria,' said His Majesty on one of these occasions, 'the band is in the next room, and shall play any tune you please; what shall it be?' 'Oh, Uncle King,' came the tactful reply, 'I should like God save the King better than any other tune.' She was quick to repeat her success when asked which of the various treats provided for her she had enjoyed most. 'The ride I took with you, Uncle King.' Uncle King, much gratified, was moved to bestow a pair of diamond bracelets upon this eminently satisfactory niece and 'absolutely forbad any contradiction of her inclinations during her visits to him'.

The Duchess of Kent and John Conroy viewed these developments with some alarm. The hothouse atmosphere of George IV's Court, with all its extravagant sensuality, was admittedly unsuitable for an impressionable little girl, and no conscientious mother could be blamed for reluctance to expose her daughter to its pernicious attractions; but John Conroy, who had his own reasons for wanting to prevent the Princess from becoming too much of a favourite with the royal family, was already frightening the Duchess with dark hints of worse dangers than moral corruption which Victoria might encounter at the hands of her wicked uncles. What, for instance, of the sinister Duke of Cumberland, widely suspected of having murdered his valet and of fathering his sister's bastard? After the elderly and childless Dukes of York and Clarence, only Victoria's 'delicate life' stood between Cumberland and the throne. How easy for such a blackguard to arrange some convenient 'accident' for the little Princess or, alternatively, to have her kidnapped and removed to the King's care. Once at Court, how easy to spread rumours that she was ailing, and either by means of slow poison, drugs or neglect, bring about an apparently 'natural' death.

The credulous Duchess, always inclined to be an over-protective mother, redoubled her precautions. Victoria was never left alone for a moment, day or night, or permitted to see any outsider unless Lehzen or some other trusted member of the household was present. It is said that even her bread-and-milk was tasted, and she was not allowed to walk downstairs without someone holding her hand.

In later years Queen Victoria indignantly and categorically repudiated all insinuations against her Uncle Ernest and no shred of evidence was ever produced to support Conroy's allegations; but, in fairness to the Duchess of Kent, it has to be remembered that at the time many people shared her dread of the Duke of Cumberland, believing him capable of almost any crime. Certainly his was an intimidating and abrasive personality, and his bitter tongue, arrogant disregard of public opinion and ferocious Toryism all combined to make him intensely unpopular. Even his appearance was against him, his luxuriant whiskers and heavily scarred face (the result of a wound honourably received in battle) giving him the air of a stage villain.

But he was not a villain. In fact, he possessed a good deal of courage and his principles, or prejudices, were sincerely held. He had not murdered his valet, nor was he the father of Princess Sophia's child. He did, however, dislike and distrust the Duchess of Kent for her tendency to 'Whiggishness', and he undoubtedly exercised a malign influence over the King.

It is also true that George IV, who 'was as great a despot as ever lived', was at one time contemplating removing the Princess Victoria from her mother's guardianship. This, at least according to Charles Greville, he would inevitably have done but for the Duke of Wellington, who, 'wishing to prevent quarrels, did all in his power to deter the King, not by opposing him when he talked of it, which he often did, but by putting the thing off as well as he could.' In 1828 Wellington strongly advised the Duchess of Kent to make a civil gesture towards the Duchess of Cumberland, who was still being cut by the rest of the family. 'She did as he suggested', reported Greville, with the result that the Duke of Cumberland 'ceased to blow the coals.'

Another anxiety afflicting the Duchess of Kent at this period concerned her elder daughter. Feodore at eighteen was beginning to resent her mother's discipline (there was never any risk of Feodore becoming spoilt), and to show signs of rebellion against the restrictions of life at Kensington. An exceptionally pretty girl, she was also beginning to attract unwelcome interest in high places. During the visit to Windsor the sharp-eyed Victoria had not failed to notice that 'the King paid great attention to my Sister, and some people fancied he might marry her! She was very lovely then . . . and had charming manners, about which the King was extremely particular.' That George IV at sixty-four really cherished any serious intentions towards the Princess Feodore seems highly improbable, but he might easily have taken it into his head to interest himself in her marriage and, in any case, the Duchess and Jonn Conroy were taking no chances – there was no room for a leading role for Feodore in the scenario they were planning. It was obviously time to get her safely off the stage, and towards the end of 1827 her betrothal was announced to Prince Ernest of Hohenlohe-Langenburg. The wedding took place privately at Kensington Palace the following February with Princess Victoria as bridesmaid: 'dearest little girl as you were, dressed in white . . . going round with the basket presenting the favours'.

As it turned out, Feodore found more happiness with her Ernest than she had 'ever thought of possessing', but the Hohenlohe-Langenburgs were as poor as church mice and a girl with her beauty and connexions might have expected to make a more brilliant match. She had, however, married neither for love nor position, but simply to escape from Kensington which was falling increasingly under the rule of John Conroy, or Sir John as he had now become, George IV having created him a Knight Commander of the Hanoverian Order.

Conroy, who could see the odds on that long-term bet he had made with the future back in 1820 beginning to shorten, was growing steadily more confident. He was, in fact, now staking everything on another regency – a contingency which seemed more probable with every month that passed. The King, despite all the rumours, had not married again and his health was precarious. Apart from gout and obesity, he suffered from an agonizingly painful bladder complaint, for which he regularly dosed himself with astonishing quantities of laudanum washed down with brandy or claret. The Duke of York had died in January 1827, and there had been no more Clarence babies. This danger could not yet be entirely discounted but it was growing more and more remote. William, Duke of Clarence was now himself over sixty and also suffered from gout, or arthritis, and severe bronchial asthma. Royal personages, it was true, came of age at eighteen, but there were still a good ten years to go before Princess Victoria's eighteenth birthday and the likelihood that she would accede to the throne while still a minor was a very strong one. Equally strong was the likelihood that the Duchess of Kent, that ornament to her sex and her exalted station, would be appointed Regent. The Duchess might hold the title, but the power, if Conroy knew anything of the matter, would be his.

The glittering prospects thus opened up were enough to dazzle a less ambitious man than John Conroy, and John Conroy was nothing if not ambitious. He was neither a subtle man nor a particularly clever one, but he wanted power and riches with quiet, steady desperation and was prepared to do most things to achieve them. The first step, of course, was to make certain of his domination over mother and daughter by cutting them off as much as possible from all outside influences, and here circumstances combined to smooth Conroy's path. The Duchess of Kent had never been given any great cause to like or trust the English royal family and still harboured a smouldering resentment over the snubs and slights she and the Duke had been subjected to during their short married life. She needed very little encouragement to go on harbouring it.

Years later, Prince Albert was to blame Uncle Leopold for his failure to guide Mamma and keep her out of Conroy's clutches, but unfortunately Leopold was seeing a good deal less of Kensington these days. For one thing he was in the middle of a peculiar affair with a young German actress who bore a startling resemblance to the dead Charlotte, and for another he was increasingly preoccupied with the question of his own future. Still a comparatively young man and, in his way, as ambitious as Conroy, he was not anxious to remain a pensioner of the English government for the rest of his life (the English government was even less anxious that he should), and was busy considering offers of the tenancies of certain vacant European thrones. Conroy, as plausible as adventurers of his type generally are, was careful to keep on friendly terms with Leopold – at the same time warning the Duchess that her brother was planning to compete with her for the regency – and Leopold seems to have been genuinely unaware how strongly Sir John was entrenching himself, or how completely Victoire had fallen under the spell of his specious charm.

Conroy had been afraid that Feodore, so devoted to her little sister, might have offered a threat to his regime – especially if married to a man of influence – and had played an important part in getting her banished to her obscure German principality, but he and the Duchess of Kent both seem to have regarded Lehzen as harmless. Ironically enough, in view of later events, Lehzen owed her appointment as Princess Victoria's governess and constant companion very largely to Conroy's belief in her negligibility. An Englishwoman in that position would have possessed independent social status and possibly undesirable political connexions but Lehzen, a humble foreigner entirely dependent on the Duchess's patronage, could surely be trusted to do as she was told without question. Indeed, it was apparently to forestall objections that Lehzen was *too* humble for her position that Conroy, using Princess Sophia as his intermediary, persuaded George IV to make her a Hanoverian baroness when he received his own knighthood.

The King seems to have rather liked Conroy – he always had a weakness for scamps – and Conroy, of course, took pains to ingratiate himself with the right people at Court. Princess Sophia had become his devoted slave and the Duke of Sussex was also considered friendly 'in part'. But while studiously cultivating the acquaintance of anyone in the outside world who looked like being useful to him, Sir John, with the insensitivity of the totally self-absorbed, never bothered to ingratiate himself with the one person who really mattered.

To the outside world, the Princess Victoria still seemed the very picture of a happy, healthy, unaffected child, being brought up in a refreshingly simple and natural manner by a thoroughly sensible mother – a picture which Conroy, with his undoubted flair for public relations, was careful to promote at every opportunity.

In the summer of 1826, George Keppel, then in waiting on the Duke of Sussex at Kensington Palace, remembered mornings when he stood watching the movements of 'a bright, pretty little girl' dressed in a plain white cotton frock and large straw hat, who was in the habit of watering the plants immediately under the window, and being amused to see 'how impartially she divided the contents of the watering-pot between the flowers and her own little feet'. Leigh Hunt, the journalist, remembered 'the peculiar kind of personal pleasure' it gave him to see the Princess Victoria out walking in Kensington Gardens, holding another little girl by the hand and followed by a magnificent footman, who looked 'somehow like a gigantic fairy'. In the summer of 1827, Charles Knight, another journalist, used to walk to work through the Park 'when the sun was scarcely high enough to have dried up the dews

of Kensington's green alleys', and would sometimes catch a
glimpse of the Duchess of Kent and her daughter having breakfast
on the lawn before the Palace. Knight thought this 'a vision of
exquisite loveliness . . . the matron looking on with eyes of love,
whilst the ''fair soft English face'' is bright with smiles'. It
seemed to him a beautiful characteristic of the training of this
royal girl 'that she should not have been taught to shrink from the
public eye . . . that she should enjoy the freedom and simplicity of
a child's nature – that she should not be restrained when she starts
up from the breakfast-table and runs to gather a flower in the
adjoining parterre – that her merry laugh should be as fearless as
the notes of the thrush in the groves around her.' 'I passed on and
blessed her', he wrote, thanking God that he had lived to see the
golden fuits of such training.

These favourable impressions of the 'Kensington System' as it
became known, were not confined to casual passers-by alone. At
the beginning of May 1828, Harriet Arbuthnot, the Duke of
Wellington's friend and a sensible, highly intelligent woman,
visited the Palace and was introduced to the Princess Victoria,
whom she found 'the most charming child I ever saw. She is a fine,
beautifully made, handsome creature, quite playful and childish,
playing with her dolls and in high spirits, but civil and well bred
and Princess-like to the greatest degree.' The Duchess of Kent,
concluded Mrs Arbuthnot, 'is a very sensible person and educates
her remarkably well.'

All this, conflicting as it does with Feodore's vivid
recollections of 'that dismal existence of ours' and her
commiserations over the 'years of imprisonment' which her poor
darling sister had to endure, together with Victoria's own
memories of her 'melancholy' childhood, presents something of a
puzzle. Probably the truth is that until she was seven or eight she
was a reasonably happy child, if an over-watched, over-protected
one. But from then on the constant, domineering presence of John
Conroy grew steadily more oppressive, until virtually every
youthful memory became coloured with her detestation of him.
She soon began to recognize and to resent his attempts to separate
her from her Uncle King, and to smart under his heavy-handed

teasing. This seems to have been partly his natural manner and partly his notion of helping to keep the Princess in her place – which he intended should remain very definitely subordinate to her mother and himself. But Victoria already had a strong sense of family pride and she naturally hated to be told that she looked like her semi-imbecile cousin Silly Billy, the Duke of Gloucester, or being chaffed for 'closeness' over her pocket-money like old Queen Charlotte. Lehzen came in for much the same sort of treatment – her comical German habit of scattering caraway seeds over her food being the cause of much Irish hilarity – and Victoria resented this even more fiercely on her beloved governess's behalf.

As the Duchess of Kent became identified ever more closely with John Conroy, so Victoria turned more and more to Lehzen. Her education was now proceeding in earnest, still under the general supervision of George Davys, who had come to live in the Palace. Visiting masters taught arithmetic, calligraphy, music, dancing and drawing. A good deal of time was devoted to languages, and there were tutors for French, German and Italian. The Duchess of Kent claimed that she herself was 'almost always' present for at least some part of every lesson – a claim which her daughter later refuted – but faithful Lehzen was always there chaperoning the Princess. When the household went on its usual summer holiday round of Tunbridge Wells, Ramsgate or Broadstairs, Victoria did her lessons in Lehzen's bedroom. She still slept in her mother's room, but it was Lehzen who sat on guard until the Duchess came upstairs. It was Lehzen who went walking and driving with her in the pony carriage, Lehzen who read aloud to the Princess while her hair was being brushed, Lehzen whose clever fingers helped to dress her growing collection of little wooden dolls in their elaborate historical or theatrical costumes. It was Lehzen who, with a mixture of patience, firmness and tact, had tamed the little Hanoverian termagant and to whom the credit for her civil, well-bred and Princess-like demeanour properly belonged. It was Lehzen who, by her unfailing comforting presence, provided the security which Victoria craved, and in return the Princess lavished on her governess all the intensity of love with which her emotional nature overflowed.

The Duchess of Kent does not appear to have noticed the situation developing under her nose, and Lehzen, so quiet, so outwardly deferential to her employer, was far too intelligent to obtrude the closeness of her relationship with the Princess – or to allow Victoria to do so. The Duchess only saw that Lehzen was devoted, that she seemed to have the knack of managing Victoria and took all the tedious chores of sitting in at lessons, supervising piano practice, reading aloud and driving endlessly round the Park off her own shoulders, leaving her free at last to enjoy some of the social life due to her position.

Conroy had not, of course, been able to isolate the Princess entirely from the Court. There was at least one other visit to Windsor after 1826, and in 1829 Victoria attended a children's ball given at St James's Palace in honour of Maria da Gloria, the young Queen of Portugal. Charles Greville, getting his first sight of 'our little Victoria', was not impressed: 'a short, plain-looking child, and not near so good-looking as the Portuguese.' The good-looking Portuguese, however, unfortunately fell down and hurt herself and left the party in tears, while Victoria, happily unaware of Mr Greville's strictures on her appearance, made the most of this rare treat, entering into 'the merry dance with great spirit and animation'.

Her birthday that year happened to fall on a Sunday and, at morning service, the Reverend Mr Davys did not miss the opportunity of

solemnly impressing on the mind of the Princess, who had now completed her tenth year, and was, therefore, old enough to understand the precepts of Christianity and to act upon reason and principle, the duties imposed upon her, in common with all her fellow-creatures, as a being responsible to her Creator and placed in this world for the purpose of trial . . . and also the duties imposed upon *her* individually by her exalted station.

But at the age of ten, Victoria was old enough to understand more than the precepts of Christianity, and that autumn she received and understood a frightening object lesson on the extent to which her mother had now fallen under John Conroy's influence – and the lengths to which he was prepared to go in order to consolidate his tyranny over the household at Kensington.

The occasion was the Duchess of Kent's dismissal of her middle-aged lady-in-waiting, Baroness Späth – a familiar and much-loved figure of Victoria's little world ever since she could remember. Späth had been with the Duchess for twenty-five years and had shared all the vicissitudes of her adult life. She had been her companion and friend during the dull, lonely years of her first marriage; had supported her through her first widowhood and the days of the Duke of Kent's courtship; had been with her on that memorable journey to England in the spring of 1819 and had watched with her beside the dying Edward in the cold misery of Sidmouth. In the first anxious, poverty-stricken months at Kensington Späth had stayed loyally at her post, ready to share her mistress's exile in an unfriendly foreign land as uncomplainingly as she had shared all the rest. But now, all of a sudden, it seemed she was too German, her manners were unsuitable, she talked too much, saw too many visitors and spoiled the Princess Victoria. More to the point, she allowed her jealousy of Conroy and his family to show and had been foolish enough to criticize the Kensington system.

Some people attributed Späth's downfall to a passage of arms between her and Conroy's daughter, Victoire. Others had no difficulty in thinking of a more scandalous reason. The Duke of Wellington was later to tell Charles Greville that Victoria had 'witnessed some familiarities' between Conroy and her mother. 'What She had seen She repeated to the Baroness Spaeth, and Spaeth not only did not hold her tongue, but (the Duke thought) remonstrated with the Duchess herself on the subject. The consequence was that they got rid of Spaeth, and they would have got rid of Lehzen too if they had been able.' Greville remarked that he concluded Conroy was the Duchess of Kent's lover, and the Duke said 'he supposed so'.

Whispers of an improper relationship could be heard in certain quarters as early as 1829 and Späth's dismissal naturally added to the gossip. The kind Duchess of Clarence was shocked. She warned Princess Sophia that poor Späth's going would 'make a great noise in the world', for it would surely kill her. Mr Paget, one of the gentlemen-in-waiting, had burst into tears when he heard the news, and exclaimed: 'Going! Impossible! Oh, who has done this? It is not the Duchess of Kent, she is so good, so kind. How cruel after so many years of faithful service to send her away!' Lehzen would go next, and it would be impossible to find another Lehzen. Another was not wanted, retorted Princess Sophia sharply. The Court had always grumbled that there were too many foreigners at Kensington, that there ought to be more 'nice English Ladies'. Well, now they would get them.

There was no reprieve for Späth, who found sanctuary with Princess Feodore. But Lehzen stayed. Wiser than Späth, she had been 'prudent enought not to commit herself', to steer clear of the petty feuds, the jealousies and intrigues seething beneath the bland surface of Kensington Palace. By the time Conroy and the Duchess of Kent woke up to the fact that Lehzen was not quite so docile as they had believed, that intelligent woman had dug herself in too securely to be dislodged. 'She was beside powerfully protected by George 4th and William 4th,' commented Mr Greville, 'so that they did not dare to attempt to expel her.' But Lehzen and Späth had been close friends and from 1829 onwards there was war to the knife between the governess and John Conroy.

In January 1830 the Duchess of Clarence wrote bluntly to her sister-in-law, warning her of 'the general wish' that she should keep Conroy in his place, for it was being noticed in the family that she was cutting herself off more and more from them with her child. 'This', continued Adelaide,

they attributed to Conroy, whether rightly or wrongly I cannot judge; they believe he tries to remove everything that might obstruct his influence, so that he may exercise his power *alone*, and alone, too, one day reap the fruits of his influence. He cannot be blamed for cherishing dreams of future greatness and wanting to achieve a brilliant position for his family . . . but everyone recognises these aspirations, towards which his every action is directed . . . It is well known who Sir J.C. is; he cannot make himself higher or lower than he is, nor does he need to, as a man of merit; only he must not be allowed to forbid access to you to all but his family, who in any case are not of so high a rank that they *alone* should be the entourage and the companions of the future Queen of England.

Both the Duchess of Kent and Conroy angrily resented this well-meant piece of advice and from now on the Clarences were regarded as being openly hostile to Kensington.

Whether or not there was any truth in the rumour that Victoire and her 'confidential servant' were lovers remains a matter of speculation. To worldlings like Charles Greville and the Duke of Wellington it offered an obvious explanation for the young Queen Victoria's unconcealed and implacable detestation of her mother's friend and, on the face of it, it looks quite plausible. Conroy and the Duchess were the same age, both were handsome, vigorous and warm-blooded, constantly in each other's company and, in their own ways, fond of each other. Victoire was lonely, and Conroy's wife, usually present somewhere in the background, was a delicate, invalidish creature, described by her own grandson as 'a perfect cipher'. On the other hand, the Duchess of Kent was an intensely conventional, sincerely pious woman, and Conroy had more important things on his mind than sex.

There may very well have been 'familiarities' – Sir John had a boisterous, bouncing way with him towards all women – but in the goldfish bowl atmosphere of Kensington it would have been virtually impossible to conceal the existence of a serious affair, and any real evidence of misbehaviour would have been seized on joyfully by the Duke of Cumberland and others as an excuse to remove the Princess Victoria from her mother's charge. It would also have put paid to the Duchess's chances of being nominated as Regent. Most probably there was never anything more than a little flirtation, some hand-squeezing and languishing glances, possibly a few kisses, which may or may not have been witnessed by the

Princess. All the indications, however, are that her dislike of Conroy was entirely on her own account. She must certainly have known about his attempt to separate her from Lehzen, and by the time she was into her teens she had plenty of purely personal reasons both to fear and to loathe him.

Chapter Five
I Will be Good

We have everything to hope from this child.

The Duchess of Kent

The beginning of the 1830s effectively marked the end of Victoria's private childhood and the beginning of her long career as a political figure and public monument. This process was accelerated by an astute campaign, master-minded by Conroy and carried out by the Duchess of Kent, intended both to draw attention to the Princess and to emphasize the exemplary nature of her upbringing. Its timing was influenced in part by the need to silence nasty-minded gossip and in part by the fact that George IV was dying at last. He was now nearly blind and suffered from acute attacks of breathlessness, so that he could only sleep sitting up with his arms resting on a table; nor were ever-increasing doses of laudanum any longer having much effect on the pains in his bladder. It was clear that the end could not be long delayed, and the Duchess of Kent might be glad of support from some unimpeachably respectable quarter against the time, in the next reign, when a Regency Bill would be discussed.

On 1 March, therefore, she addressed a long letter to the Bishops of London and Lincoln on the subject of her daughter's education, reminding them pathetically that 'by the death of her revered father when she was but eight months old, her sole care and charge devolved to me. Stranger as I then was,' she went on, 'I became deeply impressed with the absolute necessity of bringing her up entirely in this country, that every feeling should be that of Her native land, and proving thereby my devotion to duty by rejecting all those feelings of home and kindred that divided my heart.'

The Princess's education had begun 'in a moderate way' when she was four years old and the Duchess naturally hoped she had 'pursued that course most beneficial to all the great interests at stake'. But she felt the time had now come when this should be put to some test, so that 'if anything has been done in error of judgement it may be corrected, and that the plan for the future should be open to consideration and revision.' She did not presume to be over-confident. 'On the contrary, as a female, as a stranger (but only in birth, as I feel that this is my country by the duties I fulfil, and the support I receive), I naturally desire to have a candid opinion from authorities competent to give one.' With that end in view, she was sending their lordships a paper setting out the general plan of the Princess's studies, together with reports of her progress, and asked that they should personally conduct an examination before advising her further. Mr Davys, added the Duchess, would explain the nature of the Princess's religious instruction 'which I have confided to him, that she should be brought up in the Church of England as by Law established.'

The bishops' examination duly took place at Kensington during the first week of March and resulted in a triumph for the System. Their lordships reported that

> in answering a great variety of questions proposed to her, the Princess displayed an accurate knowledge of the most important features of Scripture History, and of the leading truths and precepts of the Christian Religion as taught by the Church of England, as well as an acquaintance with the Chronology and principal facts of English History remarkable in so young a person. To questions in Geography, the use of the Globes, Arithmetic and Latin Grammar, the answers which the Princess returned were equally satisfactory.

Due attention appeared to have been paid to modern languages, nor could their lordships help admiring the Princess's pencil sketches, which had been executed 'with the freedom and correctness of an older child'.

The bishops, in short, had no fault to find and did not hesitate to recommend that 'the Princess should continue, for some time to come, to pursue her studies upon the same plan which has been hitherto followed, and under the same superintendence.' Thus encouraged, the Duchess of Kent went on to approach even higher authority, the Archbishop of Canterbury, spiritual head of the Church of England and surely the most unimpeachably respectable supporter that could be desired. Victoria underwent another examination in the presence of His Grace and once more emerged triumphant from the ordeal, Dr Howley pronouncing himself 'perfectly satisfied that Her Highness's education in regard to cultivation of intellect, improvement of talent, and religious and moral principle, is conducted with so much care and success as to render any alteration of the system undesirable.'

Victoria's education has often since been a target of ridicule among biographers and, admittedly, it was neither inspired nor inspiring. But what is not so often remembered is that her schooldays coincided with a period of low educational standards generally, and especially for girls. It was a time when young ladies were either taught at home by governesses, whose gentility was regarded as their most important qualification; at pretentious and expensive 'seminaries', such as the one attended by Amelia Sedley and execrated by Becky Sharp; or at honest, old-fashioned boarding-schools, 'where a reasonable quantity of accomplishments were sold at a reasonable price, and where girls might be sent to be out of the way, and scramble themselves into a little education, without any danger of coming back prodigies.'

Certainly few parents wanted a prodigy or a blue-stocking. The era of the New Woman, of Miss Buss and Miss Beale and of Girton College was still nearly a generation away, and independent minds like Mary Wollstonecraft, Hester Thrale and Elizabeth Montagu had found little sympathy among their contemporaries. Music, dancing, needlework, water-colour sketching, a little French or

Italian formed the basis of a young lady's preparation for life and marriage. Enough arithmetic for the casting up of household accounts was felt to be desirable and more down-to-earth mothers initiated their daughters into the mysteries of household management; but anything other than a smattering of history and geography, together with a passing and heavily censored acquaintance with English literature, was widely considered unnecessary, if not actively harmful to a girl's prospects.

Against this background, the syllabus offered by the Kensington Palace schoolroom was definitely above the average, and the Duchess of Kent, in no sense a liberated or a well-educated woman, deserves credit for at least taking the matter seriously. Not that Victoria herself was in any way intellectually inclined. Always painfully aware of her limitations in this direction, she tended to be ill-at-ease in intellectual company, but while she probably would not have benefited from the kind of intensive academic training available to her Tudor predecessors, she was very far from being stupid. A conscientious child, she worked hard at her lessons which, although frequently dull, did have the advantage of inculcating useful habits of concentration and application. She had an ear for languages and for music, which she enjoyed and appreciated — Italian opera became a passion. She possessed undoubted artistic talent which was encouraged and fostered, and by her teens she was reading far more widely, both in English and French, than most girls of her age.

Buttressed by the weight of so much ecclesiastical approval, her mother and John Conroy faced the future with increased confidence, and the future was now beginning to press in on Kensington. The Duchess had informed the Bishops of London and Lincoln that, as yet, the Princess was not aware of the station she was likely to fill. She was, however, 'aware of its duties, and that a Sovereign should live for others; so that when Her innocent mind receives the impression of Her future fate she receives it with a mind formed to be sensible of what is to be expected from Her, and it is to be hoped, she will be too well grounded in Her principles to be dazzled with the station she is to look to.'

The Bishop of London had sought further clarification on this point. How soon was the Princess to be told of her probable destiny, and would her education now be planned with the declared aim of preparing her to be Queen? In an interview on 10 March, the Duchess told Dr Blomfield that she had not made up her mind as to the best way of breaking the news. She rather hoped that her daughter would 'come to the knowledge by accident, in pursuing her education'.

According to Lehzen's memory of the occasion, this 'accident' was arranged to take place on the following day, and at her suggestion. With the agreement of the Duchess of Kent, a genealogical table was slipped into the Princess's history book and when she came on it, she is supposed to have exclaimed in surprise, 'I see I am nearer to the Throne than I thought.' Again according to Lehzen, she then took her governess by the hand, declaring solemnly, 'I will be good.'

Lehzen wrote her account of that momentous March day nearly forty years later and embellished it with a good deal of dramatic licence, but although the Queen, who claimed to recollect the circumstances perfectly, corrected its most obvious inaccuracies, she did not actually deny having spoken the famous words which have become her signature tune. She may well have said them, or something very like them – it would have been entirely in character – but at the time she probably meant no more than that she would be a good, obedient child and try harder at her lessons. Whether the news itself came as a complete surprise is doubtful. Walter Scott, who met her when she was celebrating her ninth birthday, had wondered if 'a little bird' had already carried the truth into her heart, and it seems likely that she must at least have guessed the truth by then. Certainly she must have known her father's place in the family pecking order, and would also have known enough about the laws of inheritance and of precedence, which loomed so large in royal circles, to have worked out the implications for herself. But it is one thing, at ten years old, to think vaguely about a distant future, quite another to have one's guesses ceremoniously confirmed by so respected an authority as the beloved Lehzen. If, as the Queen remembered, the Princess 'cried much' on learning of her destiny, it would have been a natural emotional reaction to a real sense of shock.

Just over three months later, destiny took a step closer. George IV died on 26 June 1830 and was succeeded by his brother William. There was little pretence at public mourning. 'King George had not been dead three days', observed Charles Greville, 'before everybody discovered that he was no loss.' 'There never was an individual less regretted by his fellow-creatures than this deceased King,' added *The Times*, which did not even wait until the deceased King was in his grave before attacking his 'reckless, unceasing and unbounded prodigality', his 'indifference to the feelings of others' and his course of life, 'the character of which rose little higher than that of animal indulgence'. A few people, remembering past glories and past kindnesses received from that 'most extraordinary compound of talent, wit, buffoonery, obstinacy and good feeling', genuinely grieved for 'poor Prinny'. But the country in general was unmoved, except by relief. The usual decencies were perfunctorily observed, though on the day of the funeral *The Times* noticed 'no solemn expression of feeling nor much decorum of behaviour' and all Windsor was said to have been drunk that night.

George IV's death marked the end of an era. As that intelligent Frenchman Prince Talleyrand put it: 'King George IV was *un roi grand seigneur*. There are no others left.' Perhaps it was just as well. Certainly no one could accuse the new King of overdoing the grandeur. William IV, at sixty-five, was a bluff, red-faced, good-natured old gentleman with a curiously pineapple-shaped head who, according to Mr Greville, looked like a respectable old admiral. He at once set about promoting the image of a simple sailor with no interest in luxury and magnificence and no patience with French cooking, fal-lals or 'knick-knackery' of any kind.

The late King had spent the last years of his life in almost total seclusion, taking elaborate precautions against being seen or stared at by his subjects. The new King was embarrassingly ready to be friends and nearly caused a riot by going off on a ramble by himself round the West End. He was recognized in St James's Street and 'was soon followed by a mob making an uproar'. He had been kissed on the cheek by a street-walker before the outraged members of White's Club issued forth in a body and escorted their wandering sovereign back to St James's Palace, 'amid shouting and bawling and applause'. The King seemed quite unconcerned by the results of his excursion. 'Oh, never mind all this,' he told his rescuers cheerfully; 'when I have walked about a few times they will get used to it, and will take no notice.' But Queen Adelaide quite saw it would not do, and said that in future William must take his walks early in the morning or in some less public place, so Greville thought there were hopes 'that his activity may be tamed.' William might be unconventional to the point of eccentricity, but the Duke of Wellington, now Prime Minister, found him refreshingly tractable and told Greville that he was able to get through more business in ten minutes with his new master 'than with, the other in as many days'. 'Altogether,' wrote Greville, 'he seems a kind-hearted, well-meaning, not stupid, burlesque, bustling old fellow, and if he doesn't go mad may make a very decent king.'

The new reign had triggered off a burst of self-assertive activity at Kensington, and the day after George IV's death the Duchess of Kent addressed a long letter to the Duke of Wellington to be submitted to the new King. The Princess Victoria, she declared, should now be regarded as Heir Apparent, while the offices of Regent and Guardian should be 'vested fully, and without any interference whatsoever, in Her Mother'. If she consulted her own inclinations, went on the Duchess unblushingly, she would choose not to be Regent, but her conscience and her judgement told her it would be contrary to the Princess's interests if she hesitated to bear that heavy burden should the Princess succeed before she came of age. As the Princess's position was now totally different, the Duchess wanted some lady of rank to be appointed as her State Governess, and suggested the Duchess of Northumberland. She herself now wished to be treated as Dowager Princess of Wales and to be given an appropriate income. No additional grant should, however, be made to the Princess. Until she was of age it would be in her best interests for her mother to remain in sole charge of their joint finances.

Inured as he had become to the antics of royalty during the two years of his Premiership, the Duke of Wellington was appalled by this preposterous communication, and wasted no time in informing the Duchess that her proposition was 'altogether inadmissible'. He did not intend to show her letter to the King, or even to his colleagues, and earnestly advised her to consider it as 'a Private and Confidential Communication, or rather as never having been written'. Her affairs and those of her 'August Daughter' would shortly be coming before Parliament, and it would be better for them both if the question of a settlement was considered in the regular way by the King and his Ministers, than as the result of claims put forward by her. In any case, he could assure Her Royal Highness that 'no Party, nor no Individual of an influence in the Country' had any idea of injuring her daughter's interests, and no measure affecting either of them would be adopted without 'being imparted to her and the fullest information given her'.

Whether or not the Duchess and Conroy had really expected to win an engagement of this kind with the Iron Duke, the Duchess was foolish enough to take offence and, according to Greville, refused to speak to Wellington 'for a long time after'. In September, when the Regency Bill was being framed, the Duke, true to his promise, offered to call on her to show her the draft and explain it to her, but Victoire, with the unattractive small-mindedness which was to characterize her behaviour all too often during the next few years, sent a message that she was out of town (the family was at Claremont) and asked to have the Bill sent to her in the country.

The Duchess's only serious rival for the regency was the Duke of Cumberland who, as the next heir in blood, would, in normal circumstances, have had a strong claim at least to share the office with her. The Duke had his supporters among those who regretted that on the accession of a Queen regnant, England would be separated from Hanover, where the Salic Law limited the succession to men only. There were also some people, not entirely happy at the prospect of a female sovereign in the present violently unsettled state of the country, who felt that a Salic Law might usefully be introduced into England. But Cumberland's party commanded little influence – his evil reputation, his extreme unpopularity and the still widely held belief that he was plotting against the Princess Victoria's life told too heavily against him – and when Parliament reassembled in November 1830, the Lord Chancellor, Lord Lyndhurst, rose to announce that it was impossible to recommend any other individual for the high office of Regent than the Princess Victoria's mother.

The manner in which Her Royal Highness the Duchess of Kent has hitherto discharged her duty in the education of her illustrious offspring [declared his lordship] – and I speak upon the subject, not from vague report, but from accurate information – gives us the best ground to hope most favourably of Her Royal Highness's future conduct. Looking at the past, it is evident that we cannot find a better guardian for the time to come

The Duchess did not get the honorary title of Dowager Princess of Wales – to which, of course, she had no shadow of right – and the financial settlement was disappointing, an extra £10,000 a year instead of the £20,000 she had been hoping for, but she had been named sole Regent in the event of a minority and that was the main thing. It was, she exclaimed, with a burst of tears, her first happy day since the death of the Duke of Kent, and when she appeared with the other royal ladies at the House of Lords, the mother of the heir, buxom, blooming and triumphant, positively eclipsed poor, pale, childless Queen Adelaide.

It might have been supposed that, having won the coveted assurance of the regency and routed the Cumberland clique, Kensington's relations with the Court would have improved. Unhappily for all concerned, they grew rapidly worse and the fault, it must be said, rested with Kensington. Any appearance of an open breach had been avoided as long as George IV was alive – the Duchess of Kent had been more than a little frightened of that unpredictable monarch – but no one could be frightened of genial, clownish old Sailor William or gentle, pious Adelaide, and thus freed from restraint the Duchess proceeded to exhibit all the symptoms of a classic case of swollen-headedness. Victoire had

been a success as a wife – at least as the Duke of Kent's wife –
and had shone as a forlorn widow, but she possessed neither the
inner confidence, the experience nor the mental equipment
necessary to cope gracefully with the demands of public life.
Encouraged of course by Conroy, she developed an absurd
touchiness about her rights, and her idea of keeping up her
position was to put on queenly airs, noticeably incompatible
with that 'certain German homeliness' which her rustling silks,
elaborate curls and the large feathered hats she loved could
never quite conceal.

In the circumstances, the King and Queen showed considerable
forbearance. William was fully prepared to acknowledge his niece
as the heir presumptive (though neither he nor Adelaide had yet
entirely given up hope of having a child of their own) and the
Queen remained genuinely fond of the little Princess. 'My
children are dead', she had once written pathetically to her sister-
in-law, 'but yours lives and She is mine too.' The King and Queen
were both anxious to see more of Victoria and wanted her to take
her place at Court as often as possible, but John Conroy and the
Duchess of Kent were equally determined to keep her away. They
had no intention of loosening their grip on their priceless asset by
allowing her the opportunity of leading any sort of independent
existence, or of making friends on her own account. The Princess
appeared, dressed in deep mourning, at a chapter of the Order of
the Garter held at St James's Palace in July 1830, and was present
at her first Drawing Room in February 1831, but the King, who
had been watching her closely, complained that she looked at him
stonily.

The eleven-year-old Victoria, increasingly aware of her
uncomfortable position as bone of contention between the
opposing factions, was increasingly taking refuge behind a barrier
of 'stoniness', foreign to her nature and correspondingly
damaging. She was now very much alone – Uncle Leopold having
departed to become King of the Belgians – and she, once so
energetic a creator of 'storms', was beginning to dread the scenes
created by her mother. Her only defence at this stage was silent
withdrawal and the patience counselled by Lehzen, but the depth

and bitterness of the resentment building up beneath that impassive exterior was to come as an unpleasant shock of surprise when the dam finally burst.

The King was naturally hurt and irritated by the rejection of his friendly overtures, but he had more serious matters on his mind during the first two years of his reign – a period when it seemed to many thinking people that the most important question affecting the monarchy was not when the little girl at Kensington would succeed to the throne, but whether there would be a throne for her to succeed to.

During the summer and autumn of 1830 renewed economic distress, especially in the south, was bringing renewed pressure for Parliamentary reform and this time the pressure was not to be denied. Reports were coming in almost daily of alarming disturbances in Kent and Hampshire, where desperate agricultural workers were burning ricks and barns and destroying farm machinery under the supposed leadership of the legendary but dreaded 'Captain Swing', while in the great conurbations of Manchester, Birmingham and London the Radical Societies were organizing themselves for a last great push.

At the beginning of November the Duke of Wellington unwisely delivered himself of the pronouncement that 'the Legislature and the system of representation possess the full and entire confidence of the country.' The result was a panic in the City, violent demonstrations in the streets and the threat of a general insurrection. The Duke was obliged to advise the King not to attend the Lord Mayor's banquet and to warn him that the authorities could not guarantee his safety if he did. In the crisis of confidence which followed, Wellington's government fell, to be replaced by a Whig administration headed by Lord Grey and committed to a policy of Reform.

'London', wrote Charles Greville gloomily on 1 December, 'is like the capital of a country desolated by cruel war or foreign invasion, and we are always looking for reports of battles, burnings and other disorders.' Several members of Greville's acquaintance were convinced that revolution was now not merely inevitable but imminent, and while poor Queen Adelaide feared she would not make a very attractive Marie Antoinette, she was heard to murmur that 'please God she would prove a courageous one'.

The elegant, patrician Charles Earl Grey of Fallodon, with his self-confessed 'predilection for old institutions', did not exactly look the part of a revolutionary leader and the King was, on the whole, agreeably surprised by his new Prime Minister. But he still dreaded the whole 'perilous question' of Parliamentary Reform, which seemed all too likely to end in an eyeball-to-eyeball confrontation between the Lords and Commons 'upon a matter affecting a main feature of the Constitution of the country'.

The Great Reform Bill was introduced into the House of Commons on 1 March 1831. It swept away sixty boroughs of less than 2,000 inhabitants and cut down the representation of nearly fifty others, distributed ninety-seven new seats among new centres of population and enfranchised the £10 householders, not in themselves a noticeably revolutionary body. There was as yet no question of manhood suffrage – the principle of 'one man one vote' being just as repugnant to Lord Grey as to the King and the Duke of Wellington – but the Bill was, nevertheless, regarded as unexpectedly far-reaching. That sturdy old Whig Thomas Creevey was delighted and astonished at its boldness, while it was greeted with cries of anguished incredulity by the Tory opposition. It passed its second reading in the Commons at 3.00 a.m. on 23 March by a majority of one. 'They say the excitement was beyond anything,' noted Charles Greville. In April the government was defeated in committee and the King at last agreed to Grey's demand for an appeal to the country, hurrying down to Westminster with the crown jammed crookedly on his head before the Lords could pass an address protesting against dissolution. Both Lords and Commons had worked themselves into a state of near hysteria and 'the whole scene', according to Greville, 'was as much like the preparatory days of a revolution as can well be imagined.'

The general election which followed had, of course, to be fought on the old system, but it still resulted in a landslide victory for the reformers and on 8 July the Bill once more passed its second reading in the Commons, this time by a majority of 136. All that summer the country seethed and boiled with Reform fever, which subsided only briefly early in September for the King's Coronation. William would have preferred to do without a Coronation altogether, on the grounds that it was a 'useless and ill-timed expense', as well as offering a quite unnecessary excuse for more 'popular effervescence'. He was advised that some ceremony was essential but stuck to his determination to make it as short and simple as possible. When some of the Tory peers threatened to boycott the occasion, he remarked cheerfully that he anticipated 'greater convenience of room and less heat', and the peers capitulated.

There was, however, to be another more serious boycott which did nothing to improve relations between the King and his sister-in-law which were already being exacerbated by the ostentatiously Whig atmosphere of Kensington. When it came to the Coronation, trouble blew up over a matter of precedence. It appeared that the Princess Victoria's place in the procession was to be after the King's brothers. The Duchess of Kent insisted that Victoria, as heir presumptive, should precede the Royal Dukes. Neither side would give way and the Duchess therefore announced that neither she nor her daughter would attend. In a not very convincing attempt to keep up appearances, it was given out that the fatigue would be too much of a strain on the Princess's health, but Charles Greville heard from his friends at Court that the Duchess was seizing 'every possible occasion of showing her impertinence and hostility to the King and Queen', and *The Times* declared that her absence from the Coronation was 'in pursuance of a systematic opposition on the part of Her Royal Highness to all the feelings of the present King'. 'The presence or absence of the Duchess herself', continued the Thunderer at its most thunderous, 'is a matter of comparative indifference, it is merely disrespectful; but that of the Princess Victoria, which must, as to its immediate cause, be imputed to her mother, cannot fail of being considered by the public as indecent and offensive.'

The person who suffered most, of course, was the Princess

Victoria herself. 'Nothing could console me,' she remembered afterwards, 'not even my dolls', and she wept copious tears of bitter disappointment on Lehzen's sympathetic bosom. The newspapers had dropped hints about the Duchess of Kent's 'advisers', but Victoria was in no doubt whom to blame for her exclusion from Westminster Abbey and it knocked yet another nail in John Conroy's coffin.

The Coronation passed off without further incident, but then it was back to Reform and in October came the collision which the King had dreaded all along, when the House of Lords threw out the Bill by a majority of forty-one votes. The immediate consequence was an explosion of violence. The Duke of Wellington had his windows broken for the second time in a year and several other anti-Reform peers suffered attack on their property or their persons, while in Regent Street and Bond Street prudent shopkeepers hastily put up their shutters. In London the New Police maintained a precarious control over the situation, but in Bristol towards the end of the month there was a very nasty riot which destroyed half the centre of the city and resulted in several hundred deaths, and there were other sporadic disturbances in Derby, Nottingham and Blandford.

Parliament was prorogued for a cooling-off period while behind-the-scenes efforts were made to lobby the more moderate peers, but in January 1832 Grey was obliged to report the failure of these negotiations. The dangers of a second rejection by the Lords scarcely needed spelling out, and the Prime Minister asked the King to make an addition to the Upper House. William agreed reluctantly, though he stipulated that the new creations should be heirs to existing peerages. When this became known, it was enough to persuade the 'waverers' and in April the Bill passed its second reading in the Lords by nine votes, but after the Easter recess the government was again defeated in committee. Grey demanded a mass creation of at least fifty peers. The King refused and Grey and his ministers resigned.

There were no disturbances like those of the previous autumn; on the contrary, everything was 'fearfully quiet', but no one doubted that this was the lull before the storm or that England was as close to civil war as it had ever been during those May days while the Duke of Wellington tried dutifully but hopelessly to form a government. The temper of the House of Commons made it quite plain just how hopeless his task was, and the radical press intensified its campaign of vilification against the Duke, the Lords and the monarchy. 'The King, the Queen, and Royal Family are libelled, caricatured, lampooned and balladed, by itinerant singers hired for the purpose, to a degree not credible,' wrote the Tory John Wilson Croker. 'They are constantly compared to Charles and Henrietta, and to Louis and Antoinette, and menaced with their fate . . . Depend upon it, our Revolution is in a sure, and not slow progress.'

Revolution was indeed in progress, but there was no civil war, no Day of the Barricades. The Reform Bill had to be passed. Charles Greville had known that as long ago as March 1831. 'The country *will* have it, there is a determination on the subject, and a unanimity perfectly marvellous.' By the middle of May 1832 everyone else knew it too. Grey came back into office and William came to heel. On 4 June the Bill got its third reading – Wellington and the diehards abstaining – and the crisis was over.

The passing of the Great Reform Bill did not result in a 'rabbleocracy', nor did it usher in a new millennium of social justice. In fact, in typical English fashion, it made very little immediately obvious difference at all, the new electors, like the old, continuing to send solid men of substance to represent them in the House of Commons. But the disappearance of the rotten boroughs had broken the stranglehold of patronage and from now on real power would pass gradually but inevitably away from the great landed families to the towns and cities of the new England.

On Wednesday, 1 August 1832, 'at 6 minutes past 7', the young Victoria set out from Kensington Palace to see something of the new reformed England she was to inherit. This was not, of course, her first formal contact with the public. She had been used from babyhood to acknowledge the loyal greetings of Ramsgate and Broadstairs and Tunbridge Wells, whose inhabitants had once presented her with a magnificent specimen of Tunbridge ware, 'a table of kingwood elegantly inlaid, containing a complete work box and bag, reading desk, writing desk and painting-box, all elaborately furnished'. In the summer of 1830 the family had made a more ambitious tour, 'attended with much more publicity and state than had hitherto been observed', going as far north as Leamington Spa and Birmingham, where they visited the Soho Foundry and the Society of Arts, before spending a holiday at Malvern. They had returned by way of Gloucester, where they watched the whole process of pin-making at the manufactory of Messrs Durnford, Clifton, where they received a visit from the mayor and corporation of Bristol, Bath, where a new park was christened in honour of the Princess, Devizes, Salisbury, Southampton, Portsmouth and then home via Claremont.

The 1832 excursion was therefore really the second of those semi-official journeys, or 'royal progresses' as they were to be dubbed by an irritated King William, which were intended by the Kensington camp to introduce the Princess to the people and to build up a popular following for her mother and herself. But this time the Duchess had presented her daughter with a small leather-backed notebook in which, on 31 July, the thirteen-year-old Victoria inscribed a careful heading: 'This book Mamma gave me, that I might write the journal of my journey to Wales in it.'

The journey took them by way of St Albans – 'the situation is very pretty and there is a beautiful old abbey there' – Dunstable – 'there was a fair there; the booths filled with fruits, ribbons, etc. looked very pretty' – Stony Stratford – 'the country is very pretty' – Towcester – where the party stopped for lunch – Daventry – 'the road continues to be very dusty' – Braunston – 'where there is a curious spire' – Dunchurch – it was raining by this time – Coventry – 'a large town where there is a very old church' and where they changed horses for the eighth time – and at last to Meriden 'at ½ past 5' where they were to spend the night. The fatigues of the day had been too much for Mamma, who was 'not well' and had to lie down on the sofa before dinner, but Victoria seems to have survived unscathed and 'was asleep in a minute in my own little bed which travels always with me'.

Next day it was still raining and the scenery no longer pretty.

We just passed through a town where all coal mines are . . . The men, women, children, country and houses are all black. But I can not by any description give an idea of its strange and extraordinary appearance. The country is very desolate every where; there are coals about, and the grass is quite blasted and black. I just now see an extraordinary building flaming with fire. The country continues black, engines flaming, coals, in abundance, every where, smoking and burning coal heaps, intermingled with wretched huts and carts and little ragged children.

But by the time they reached Shrewsbury the desolation had vanished and the journey turned into something very like a triumphal progress. At Welshpool the royal party was met by a troop of yeomanry 'who escorted us for a long time', and the town was decorated with 'arches, flowers, branches, flags, ribbons, etc., etc.' As they drove up through the park to Powys Castle, cannon fired a salute, a band played and the Earl of Powys was waiting to greet them. At Caernarvon, a week later, they were met 'not only by an immense crowd, who were extremely kind and pleased, but by the Corporation also, who walked before the carriage, while a salute was firing.' On Anglesey, where they were to spend the next two months staying at Plas Newydd, there were more bands and salutes and loyal addresses. But when these formalities were over, the Princess was able to enjoy herself riding Rosa, her pony, 'who went at an enormous rate she literally *flew*', or sailing in the *Emerald*, tender of the Royal Yacht, and was sorry when the time came to leave '*dear* Plas Newydd' on 15 October.

The way home took them to Eaton Hall, where they were entertained by the Grosvenor family, Chester – where the Princess opened the Victoria Bridge over the Dee – and then to Chatsworth for three strenuous days as guests of the Duke of Devonshire. The magnificences of Chatsworth proved rather too much for the diarist's powers – 'it would take me days were I to describe minutely the whole' – but she did her best over several pages of painstaking architectural and horticultural detail. On 24 October the royal party lunched in splendour off gold plate with Lord Shrewsbury at Alton Towers and on 8 November paid a state visit to Oxford. Here they were welcomed 'most WARMLY and ENTHUSIASTICALLY' by the undergraduates, 'all in their caps and gowns'. Mamma received an address presented by the Vice-Chancellor and John Conroy was made a Doctor of Civil Law. Mamma received another address from the Corporation of Oxford and John Conroy the freedom of the City. They made a tour of the colleges and saw the Bodleian Library. 'Amongst other curiosities', noted the Princess, 'there is Queen Elizabeth's Latin exercise book when she was of my age (13).' Next day 'at about $\frac{1}{2}$ past 5', they were back in their old rooms at Kensington after an absence of more than three months. The journey was over but the Journal continued and was to become a lifelong habit.

The year ended with a family Christmas at Kensington, celebrated in German style on Christmas Eve. In the morning the Princess distributed Christmas boxes to her old nurse, Mrs Brock, 'and all our people'. Dinner was at 'a $\frac{1}{4}$ to 7' with the whole Conroy family, and then everyone trooped upstairs to the room where the presents had been arranged on tables round a Christmas tree decorated with lights and sugar ornaments. 'Mamma gave me a little lovely pink bag which she had worked herself', recorded Victoria, 'with a little sachet likewise done by her; a beautiful little opal brooch and earrings, books, some lovely prints, a pink satin dress and a cloak lined with fur.' Lehzen got a writing table from the Duchess and gave her 'a little white and gold pincushion and a pin with two little gold hearts hanging on it'. The Princess gave Mamma 'a white bag which I had worked', a collar and steel chain for her dog and an Annual, and received 'a *very* pretty white bag worked by herself' from Victoire Conroy and a silver brush from Sir John. As a sign of her new teenage status 'Mamma then took me up into my bedroom with all the Ladies. There was my new toilet table with a white muslin cover over pink, and all my silver things standing on it with a fine new looking-glass.'

Certainly she was growing up. In his birthday letter that year Uncle Leopold had felt he could hardly venture to call her any longer ' a little Princess', though she was still short for her age with a tendency to plumpness. It was clear by this time that she would never be a beauty but the Tory Lady Wharncliffe, who had dined at Kensington during the Reform Bill uproar, had been 'delighted with our little future Queen', finding her very much grown, with 'a nice countenance' and her manner 'the most perfect mixture of childishness and civility I ever saw . . . When she went to bed we all stood up and after kissing *Aunt* Sophia, she curtsied, first to one side, and then the other, to all the Ladies, and then walked off with her governess.' Lady Wharncliffe, in short, looked to the Princess 'to save us from Democracy, for it is impossible she should not be popular when she is older and more seen.'

Chapter Six

I Was Very Much Amused

I dare not wish thee joy, unmixed with sadness –
'Twere vain to wish thee bliss unknown to pain;
But oh! may all thy sorrows end in gladness,
And all thy pleasures pure and bright remain.

Lines addressed to H.R.H. the Princess Alexandrina Victoria
on the Anniversary of her birthday, 24 May 1835

The spring and summer of 1833 were filled with quite a whirl of
social activity. On 31 January the Kensington Palace party (which
invariably included some or all the members of the Conroy family)
were at Drury Lane to see a performance of *The Barber of Seville*. 'I
was very much *amused*,' recorded the Princess. On 9 February
they went to the ballet, which was *Kenilworth*, the part of Amy
Robsart being taken by Mlle Pauline Leroux, who danced and
acted *beautifully* and looked quite *lovely*. On 13 April they were at
the opera again, but very much *disappointed* not to see Taglioni
dance. On the 27th they saw Rossini's *La Cenerentola*, and this time
Taglioni appeared in the ballet. 'She is grown very thin, but danced
beautifully, so lightly and *gracefully*, and each step so finished! . . .
She looked *lovely*, for she is all-ways smiling.' On 3 May came a visit
to the Exhibition at Somerset House to see some 'very fine pictures',
and on the 11th the Princess was once more being delighted by Mlle
Taglioni, 'who danced and acted QUITE BEAUTIFULLY' in a ballet
called *Nathalie*, and was '*very much* amused'.

As well as all this theatre-going, the Duchess of Kent was entertaining lavishly at home. On 24 April there had been a very grand dinner party at Kensington for the King and Queen. The Queen, unfortunately, was not well and had to cry off at the last moment, but the King and an impressive array of Dukes and Duchesses and other exalted personages were present. Princess Victoria did not appear at dinner, but 'at 20 minutes past 9', went into the saloon with Lehzen to meet the company. On 8 May there was another big party for the Duke of Orleans, with the band of the Coldstream Guards playing during dinner, and again, punctually 'at 20 minutes after 9', Victoria, attended by Lehzen, came downstairs to mingle with her mother's guests.

On 24 May it was the Princess's birthday. 'I am to-day fourteen years old! How *very old*!!' There was a constant stream of callers at the Palace and all day the presents piled up – from Mamma, 'a lovely bag of her own work, a beautiful bracelet, two lovely féronières [*sic*], one of pink topaz, the other turquoises; two dresses, some prints, some books, some handkerchiefs, and an apron'; from Lehzen, a pretty little china figure, a china basket and another print. (It was then fashionable for young ladies to make a collection of prints, which were housed in large cardboard folders covered with marbled paper and brought out to be looked at in the drawing-room after dinner.) Sir John Conroy offered a life-size portrait of 'dear sweet little Dash', the King Charles spaniel who had become Victoria's favourite pet; and George Davys, now elevated to the status of Dr Davys and Dean of Chester, brought his pupil a parcel of books. From the King and Queen came a pair of diamond earrings, and from the Queen alone a gold and turquoise brooch in the form of a bow. The other members of the royal family also gave jewellery – a férronière of pearls from Aunt Gloucester, Aunt Sophia and Uncle Sussex, a turquoise bracelet from the Cumberlands, a turquoise pin from Prince George of Cumberland and 'a brooch in the shape of a lily of the valley' from Prince George of Cambridge. And so the list continued – trinkets and prints and albums, needlecases and sandalwood boxes, pincushions, 'a blue topaz watch-hook', handkerchief sachets and china trays and baskets – quantities of the sort of elegant and useless bric-à-brac accumulated by every fashionable young lady, and which nowadays command high prices in fashionable sale-rooms.

Uncle Leopold in Belgium had a mind above such trifles. He sent his niece a set of views of the former Kingdom of the Netherlands and a long letter, in which his sincere good wishes were accompanied by a few reflections 'which the serious aspect of our times calls forth'. He urged the need for regular *self-examination* and warned Victoria that 'persons in high situations must particularly guard themselves against selfishness and vanity'. 'The position of what is generally called great people', continued the new King of the Belgians sombrely,

has of late become extremely difficult. They are more attacked and calumniated, and judged with less indulgence than private individuals. . . . They are much less secure than they used to be, and the transition from sovereign power to *absolute want* has been as frequent as sudden. It becomes, therefore, necessary that the character should be so formed as not to be intoxicated by greatness and success, nor cast down by misfortune.

Victoria doubtless took her uncle's 'sermon' to heart, for she was still devoted to him and regarded him as a fount of wisdom, but on her birthday itself she had other things to think about. That evening the King and Queen gave a Juvenile Ball in her honour at St James's Palace, taking the precaution of inviting Madame Bourdin, the Princess's dancing teacher, to help keep the large party of teenage guests from getting out of hand. Victoria opened the ball by dancing with her cousin George Cambridge, but there were '*many* other children whom I knew' and her partners included Prince George Lieven, Lord Brook, the Earl of Warwick's heir, the young Earl of March, the Earl of Athlone and Lord Fitzroy Lennox. At supper, when her health was drunk, she sat between the King and Queen, and then danced one more quadrille with Lord Paget. 'I danced in all 8 quadrilles', she reported and the entry in the Journal for that great day ended triumphantly: 'We came home at ½ past 12. I was VERY much amused.'

There was more excitement in store when, on 16 June two grown-up cousins, 'Princes Alexander and Ernst Württemberg, sons of Mamma's sister, my Aunt Antoinette', came to stay at Kensington. Victoria, whose experience of young men had hitherto been strictly limited, was entranced by the proximity of these godlike beings. 'They are both *extremely tall*,' she confided to her journal. 'Alexander is *very handsome* and Ernst has a *very kind expression*. They are both EXTREMELY *amiable*.' There were drives with the cousins, visits to exhibitions and, on 27 June, the opera again, with another ecstatic glimpse of the ethereal Taglioni and her Austrian rival, Fanny Elssler, who 'danced also *very well*'. The Princess stayed up till half-past one and was 'VERY MUCH AMUSED'.

Unhappily, though, there were some less amusing moments during that summer. Queen Adelaide had given another ball in June, and invited the whole Kensington contingent with the kindly intention of pleasing her sister-in-law by showing a special welcome to the Württemberg princes. But something – possibly the sight of Victoria sitting on the royal dais and getting on altogether too well with the Queen – caused the Duchess of Kent to take umbrage and, behaving with extraordinary rudeness, she swept her party away long before the evening was over on the excuse that her stalwart nephews, '6 feet high and very stout for their age', had been at a review and were 'fatigued'.

On 1 July a procession of carriages containing the Duchess and her daughter, her son Charles Leiningen, Lehzen, the Conroys and the Württembergs set out from Kensington *en route* for Portsmouth and the Isle of Wight on the first stage of another 'royal progress', and immediately there was more trouble. The King, already annoyed by the blatant manner in which his heir was being paraded through the kingdom, had taken particular exception to the 'continual popping' of royal salutes whenever the Kents appeared on the horizon. 'He did not choose that this latter practice should continue,' reported Charles Greville, and had signified his pleasure accordingly. In an effort to keep things friendly, the Service Chiefs, in consultation with the Prime Minister, had opened negotiations with the Duchess 'to induce her of her own accord to waive the salutes', suggesting hopefully that when she went to the Isle of Wight she might send word that, 'as she was sailing about for her amusement, she had rather they did not salute her'. Needless to say, these negotiations failed, the Duchess insisting on her right to be popped at on every available opportunity, and Greville heard that Conroy was, as usual, behind her intransigence, having said 'that as Her Royal Highness's *confidential adviser* he could not recommend her to give way on this point.' In the circumstances, the only recourse was to an Order in Council laying down that in future the Royal Standard was to be saluted only when the King or Queen was present.

It was, as Greville remarked, 'a foolish business', but the squabbling and jostling going on at Kensington did not surprise that well-known sophisticate Dorothea Lieven. 'The cause', she told Lord Grey, 'is that German *morgue* and little-mindedness which are rampant in that quarter. Those people are wrong-headed to the utmost possible degree, all of which, however, is a great pity, for, after all, the future of England is placed in their hands.'

Meanwhile, the holiday-makers on the Isle of Wight were established at Norris Castle, with the Conroys staying at nearby Osborne Lodge, and, even though the 'popping' had now ceased, were receiving a most gratifying reception wherever they went. When they visited Southampton on 8 July 'the crowd was enormous', despite the fact that it was pouring with rain. Four days later the Württembergs left for home and Victoria was 'VERY UNHAPPY' to see them go. They were '*always satisfied, always good humoured*' and talked about such interesting things. 'We shall miss them at *breakfast*,' she wrote mournfully, 'at *luncheon*, at *dinner, riding, sailing, driving, walking*, in fact *everywhere.*'

The Princess continued to miss the cheerful companionship of her cousins. On 18 July the royal party crossed over to Portsmouth and went on board the *Victory*. They saw the spot where Nelson fell, explored the ship and even tasted some of the men's beef and potatoes, 'which were excellent, and likewise some grog', but Victoria still wished that '*dear* Alexander and *dear* Ernst' had been there.

At the beginning of August the Princess and her entourage set off down the coast in the *Emerald*. The Duchess and Lehzen were seasick, and as the *Emerald* was being towed into Plymouth harbour there was very nearly a nasty accident. 'As we entered the harbour, our dear little Emerald ran foul of a hulk, her mast broke and we were in the *greatest danger*. Thank God! the mast did not fall and no one was hurt. But I was *dreadfully* frightened for *Mamma* and for all. The poor dear Emerald is very much hurt I fear.'

The following day, Saturday, 3 August, was taken up with a full round of public engagements. Mamma received the inevitable address from the Mayor and Corporation of Plymouth and the royal party then attended a review, where the Princess presented new colours to the 89th regiment, punctiliously noting the names of the ensigns who received them. This was followed by lunch with the Admiral and a tour of the dockyard. After a sail round the Eddystone lighthouse on Monday, the return journey was made by way of Torquay, Exeter and Weymouth, which was illuminated in honour of the visit. Everywhere enthusiastic crowds were waiting to cheer the Princess, and from Weymouth mother and daughter drove in an open carriage, escorted by the local yeomanry, to stay at Melbury with Lord Ilchester. By the middle of the month they were back on the Isle of Wight and on the 22nd the Duchess of Kent entertained the local gentry at a large 'rout' and evening party, while Victoria occupied herself by collecting specimens of seaweed, embroidering a watch case for Uncle Leopold and completing her third Journal book.

Home again in the autumn, she resumed her daily round of lessons with Dr Davys, and walks and drives with Lehzen, while over her head the feud between Kensington and the Court rumbled on like distant thunder. One of the numerous causes of dissension was the uncompromising attitude adopted by the Duchess of Kent towards the royal bastards. 'She has always chosen to be peculiarly uncivil to his [the King's] children', wrote Greville, 'and will not be personally acquainted with any of them, and this she perseveres in, even at Windsor Castle in the King's own house, where she is a guest.' The Duchess, of course, maintained that she was simply keeping up the high moral tone she owed to her innocent daughter, but it's difficult to disregard the suspicion that, by ostentatiously cutting the FitzClarences, Victoire had found yet another means of paying off old scores against the royal family.

In the polite world it was considered both bourgeois and ill-bred to make an issue over such a matter. If the Queen was prepared to receive the *bâtards*, as they were generally known (these things always sounded much better in French), then so could the Duchess of Kent. In any case, as Greville pointed out, she forgot 'that the women, who are all married, have their husbands' rank, in which the stain of their own birth is merged, and that Lord Munster [the eldest FitzClarence] being a peer of the realm, has a constitutional position of his own.'

It was not easy to ignore the *bâtards*, who were all thoroughly at home at Windsor, and poor Queen Adelaide found herself in the embarrassing position of having to try, often unsuccessfully, to keep them out of sight during the Kents' visits. Like most peacemakers, she got little thanks for her efforts and, in the autumn of 1833, confided to a friend that the Duchess, with whom she had always been on sisterly terms, now seemed to be avoiding her. As Duchess of Clarence, Adelaide had been in the habit of dropping in at Kensington whenever she was passing and wandering cosily through the Palace till she found Victoire, and Victoire had done the same to her; but when the Queen called on the Duchess, she was made to wait 'in some particular Room' until her hostess, who apparently wished 'to be on great form', chose to appear. King William, who was devoted to his wife, strongly resented this sort of snubbing behaviour on her behalf, and relations were growing increasingly strained. The Duchess of Kent was making herself unpopular in other quarters, too, and Lord Duncannon at the Board of Works was having 'the devil's own trouble' with her and her perpetual demands 'for alterations, additions, furniture, etc., etc., on her Royal Residence'.

Although John Conroy no doubt deserves the lion's share of the blame for encouraging the Duchess's general tiresomeness, he was not the only culprit. Prominent among the little clique of troublemakers who, in the circumstances, had gravitated naturally towards Kensington was John Lambton, Earl of Durham, otherwise known as 'Radical Jack'. Now that Reform Bill fever had burnt itself out, Lord Grey's government was beginning to look distinctly shaky and according to Thomas Creevey, Durham was deliberately doing all he could to drive the Prime Minister to resign and to succeed him. 'As he has quarrelled openly with most of the present Government,' wrote Creevey, 'he can expect no support from them, nor can one have a conception how a man so generally odious as he is, can find support from any quarter, *except one*, and that one is demonstrably his game. I mean the Duchess of Kent and her Daughter.'

Durham evidently saw the Duchess as a potentially useful tool in his campaign to embarrass Grey, and the Duchess, who unfortunately lacked even the grain of political sense necessary to see when she was being made use of, was pathetically easy game.

She is the most restless, persevering, troublesome devil possible [Creevey went on], neither the King nor Lord Grey will answer her applications any more, and every thing is referred to Duncannon. In return, thro' Conroy to Duncannon, she expresses the most violent indignation both against the King and Grey, considers and states that as Mother of the Princess Victoria she is entitled as *matter of right* to every thing she asks, that she will receive nothing as matter of favour etc., and Conroy upon more than one occasion has had the folly to add that her Royal Highness having consulted the Earl of Durham had the entire sanction of his opinion in her favour. Was there ever . . . ?

No hint of these unseemly goings-on ruffled the placid pages of Princess Victoria's Journal — which was, of course, read by Mamma as well as by Lehzen. On 9 December she went, with the usual party of Conroys, to Drury Lane to see William Macready in Shakespeare's *King John*, followed by a 'very horrible but *extremely interesting*' melodrama called *The Innkeeper's Daughter*. They stayed to the very end and the Princess was 'VERY MUCH AMUSED'. On 27 December there was a new experience, when a Mr T. Griffiths came to the Palace to lecture on Physics before an audience which included Sir John and Lady Conroy, Victoire

Conroy, Lehzen and Dr Davys. According to the Princess's notes, Mr Griffiths covered the

Objects of Alchymy, viz. Transmutation of Metals, the Elixir of Life, and the Universal Solvent; – Objects of Chemistry, viz. the investigation of every substance in nature – Chemistry a science of experiment – Results of chemical action – Arts and Manufactures dependent on chemistry – Importance of Heat as a chemical agent – Its action on various substances – Conductors and Non-conductors of Heat – Nature of Flame.

These subjects were illustrated by some 'very curious and interesting experiments' and Victoria, solemnly drinking it all in, was '*very much amused*'. Two days later a Mr Walker arrived to complete Kensington's scientific enlightenment with a lecture on 'Properties of Matter – Particles infinitely small, divisible and hard – Cohesion – Capillary attraction, Magnetic attraction, etc., etc.,' By way of contrast, the day ended with a visit to the pantomime, *Old Mother Hubbard and her Dog*, at Covent Garden, which was pronounced to be 'very pretty' but did not receive the usual accolade.

In March 1834, Victoria was laid up for several weeks with an 'indisposition'. Her health had been noticeably less robust over the past few months and she was to continue to feel 'poorly' off and on with headaches, backache, sore throats, colds and 'biliousness' for nearly another two years. Much of this was undoubtedly due to the emotional strain she was living under. The constant friction between her mother and the King caused her both private distress and public embarrassment, while at home the atmosphere was growing more and more fraught with tension. There was no escaping the constant, detested presence of John Conroy, with his coarse, bullying familiarity, and the fact that the Duchess of Kent refused to listen to a word against him was erecting an impenetrable barrier between mother and daughter. Lehzen remained the Princess's only refuge, and the two clung together in a desperate but vulnerable alliance against the common enemy.

One of the few outsiders who realized something of the true nature of the power struggle raging behind the bland façade of

Kensington Palace was the Duchess of Northumberland who had
been appointed State Governess to the Princess Victoria in 1832.
But the Duchess, though sympathetic, was given no opportunity
to see Victoria alone or to receive confidences, and it's scarcely
surprising that the Princess's increasing sense of isolation and
helplessness should sometimes have overwhelmed her.

On the surface life went on as usual. In April there were two
more evenings at the opera to see *Anna Bolena* and *Otello*, and
Victoria acquired another idol in the person of the Italian soprano
Giulietta Grisi, who was young, pretty and acted and sang '*most
sweetly and beautifully*'. The Princess, who could always forget her
troubles in the joys of her beloved opera, was 'VERY MUCH
AMUSED INDEED!!!'; but the high spot of the year was the visit,
in June, of Feodore, her husband and two eldest children. The
sisters had not met for six years and their reunion was a happy
occasion for them both. Victoria thought Feo looked very well
but grown much stouter and was enchanted with the children,
'the DEAREST little loves I ever saw'. On 11 June the whole
party went to stay at Windsor and attended the Ascot races, where
the Princess enjoyed herself enormously in spite of the rain and
made a bet with the King, winning, much to her delight, a
beautiful little chestnut mare called Taglioni after the ballerina.
Back at Kensington, she and Feodore went out driving with
Lehzen, quite like old times, and were able to spend some hours
alone together, which no doubt gave Victoria a chance to
unburden herself to her '*dearest* sister'. But at the end of July the
visit had to end. The parting was 'indeed *dreadful*' and the Princess
sobbed and cried inconsolably for a whole morning.

Baron Stockmar, King Leopold's invaluable factotum and
trusted confidant of the whole Coburg clan, was also in London
during the summer and the Duchess of Kent, who had at last begun
to grasp that all was not well in her household, asked him to act as
peacemaker between the opposing factions. In a long letter, dated
4 July 1834, Stockmar told her bluntly that the task was
impossible. 'How can my words help when nobody wishes to
change and nobody wants to give in?'

The Duchess, of course, blamed Lehzen's influence for

Victoria's antipathy towards her 'confidential adviser', but Stockmar disagreed. In his opinion the main difficulty lay in the Princess herself and Sir John Conroy. 'The latter seems to me to be an excellent business man', he wrote, 'and absolutely devoted to your Royal Highness. But how can I overlook that he is vain, ambitious, most sensitive and most hot tempered?' The Baron's letter makes it clear that Conroy was already planning to install himself as Private Secretary when Victoria came to the throne, and he did his best to make the Duchess (and Conroy) see how impractical and short-sighted their schemes were. Apart from the fact that it was more than doubtful whether it would be in Victoria's power to nominate a secretary, even if she wanted to, if her constitutional advisers opposed it, would Conroy have the necessary qualities, 'the self-control, modesty and flexibility', to fill such a delicate position? And what about the future? Supposing he got his way and Victoria had confidence in him, how long did he think his influence would last? Certainly no longer than until she married. 'Would a dignified, able, determined Prince suffer such an exclusive influence? Not for an hour! And could one allow the Princess to marry an incompetent husband? Would she accept one?'

The Princess might differ in her views, sentiments and opinions from Sir John Conroy (she might even sometimes differ from her mother), but she had a mind of her own and it would be wrong to look for the explanation solely in the influence of Baroness Lehzen.

I rather think [Stockmar went on judicially] that the real reasons for those differences are to be found in the innate personality of the Princess, in the inner circumstances at Kensington and in the behaviour of Sir John towards the Princess. . . . Wherever she looked in the house, she encountered Sir John as the sole regulator of the whole machine. As soon as she felt something unpleasant in the house . . . she recognised the main cause of it in the person of Sir John. Such impressions go deepest at a youthful age.

The Princess was, after all, well aware of her royal rank and, as she grew up, would naturally come to resent 'what must have looked to her as an exercise of undue control over herself' by a mere employee. And Stockmar reminded the Duchess, 'Your Royal Highness yourself has agreed with me that Sir John's personal behaviour towards the Princess has been apt only too often to worsen this state of affairs.' The Baron wisely refused to become involved in the Battle of Kensington, but he ended his letter with a definite warning. 'May Your Royal Highness not do anything that could *produce coldness and distance between you and the Princess,* neither *now nor in the future.'*

There is no indication that the Duchess paid any attention to her old friend's advice. Nor did she listen when he urged her to stop treating her fifteen-year-old daughter like a child and give her the chance to start choosing her own friends. So far, the only young companionship provided for her had been the two Conroy girls. Jane, eight years the elder, was delicate and languid like her mother, but Victoire, named after the Duchess and her god-daughter, was the same age as Victoria, a lively, intelligent girl intended by her father to be the Princess's constant companion and bosom friend. In their nursery days they had played together and shared walks, dancing lessons and seaside holidays, but the friendship never developed and although Victoire's name appears frequently in the Journal, no hint of warmth is ever attached to it. She is merely recorded as being among those present, and soon even the Christian name disappears and she becomes 'Miss V. Conroy'.

Stockmar thought it was high time the Princess had her own ladies, nominating them herself. If she suggested someone whom her mother had 'real, considerable reasons' for thinking unsuitable, then the matter should be discussed quietly and settled in a 'cordial manner'. But when, in June 1834, the Duchess decided to widen her circle by appointing Lady Flora Hastings as lady-in-waiting, Victoria was neither consulted nor given any opportunity of putting forward an alternative choice.

No 'journey' was planned for that year, but the Duchess transferred her little Court, including, of course, all the Conroys, to Tunbridge Wells for the autumn, and on 4 November they went on to St Leonards. Here they received a royal welcome from cheering, waving crowds, and passed through streets decorated with flowers and flags and triumphal arches. 'An immense concourse of people' accompanied the carriages, which were escorted by the mayor and aldermen of Hastings and a band of music. 'It was indeed a splendid reception,' commented the Princess. 'One sight was extremely pretty. Six fishermen in rough blue jackets, red caps and coarse white aprons, preceded by a band, bore a basket ornamented with flowers, full of fish as a present for us.'

Not long after their arrival, the Princess and her mother were involved in quite an adventure. They were out driving in a landau with Lehzen, Lady Flora and the much-loved spaniel Dash, when one of the horses kicked up, became entangled in the traces and fell down, pulling the other with it. With both horses on the ground, 'kicking and struggling most violently', there was a danger that the carriage would be overturned, but fortunately two passing gentlemen came to the rescue, holding the first horse's head down while the occupants of the landau 'got out as fast as possible'. The Princess's first thought was for 'poor dear little Dashy' who was in the rumble, and she ran on with him in her arms, calling Mamma to follow. Meanwhile, the traces were cut and the second horse, which had managed to get back on its feet, bolted off down the road, so that the ladies had to take refuge behind a wall. It had been a frightening experience and Victoria very properly felt that 'we ought to be *most grateful* to Almighty God for His merciful providence in thus preserving us, for it was a *very narrow escape*.' She made a careful note of the two gentlemen who had come to their assistance and four years later one of them, who rejoiced in the name of Mr Peckham Micklethwaite, was rewarded with a baronetcy 'for a personal service rendered to Her Majesty and the Duchess of Kent'.

The rest of the winter passed uneventfully. The Duchess and her family became familiar figures in both Hastings and St Leonards, shopping, walking on the Parade or along the beach towards Bexhill and attending the parish church. The Duchess contributed generously to local charities, giving £30 towards a new school and '£10 in aid of a subscription to establish a Life-boat off Hastings', while the Princess announced her intention of 'taking the Society of St Leonards Archers under her special patronage, and of presenting them with two annual prizes, in addition to a banner.' Victoria liked St Leonards for its nice walks and absence of fog. Their house was comfortable and she enjoyed looking out of her window and seeing the people walking by on the esplanade, also 'seeing the sun rise and set, which was quite beautiful.' But she was still feeling rather ill most of the time and sleeping badly. Her lessons, of course, continued. She was now corresponding regularly with Uncle Leopold and they discussed her studies. She was reading Russell's *Modern Europe* and Clarendon's *History of the Great Rebellion* with Dr Davys, and French history (in French, naturally) with Lehzen, as well as Racine's tragedies and the letters of Madame de Sévigné. Leopold recommended history as being 'the most important study for you' and promised to send her a copy of Sully's *Memoirs*, adding a caveat that, 'as they have not been written exclusively for young ladies', it would be as well to read them with Lehzen, who could judge what ought to be left for some future time.

Leopold was also now beginning in his letters to prepare Victoria seriously for the future and on 19 November 1834 she wrote: 'I am much obliged to you, dear Uncle, for the extract about Queen Anne, but must beg you, as you have sent me to show what a Queen *ought not* to be, that you will send me what a Queen *ought to be*.' 'A very clever, sharp little letter', he responded and promised that he would certainly tell her what a Queen should be, a task 'I will very conscientiously take upon myself on the very first occasion which may offer itself for a confidential communication.'

Christmas was spent at St Leonards. The new year came in and on 27 January the Princess, with a sudden access of energy, wrote in her Journal: 'I *love* to be *employed*; I *hate* to be *idle*.' The household was just then 'all in the bustle of packing' for the return to Kensington in two days' time, and Victoria arrived home on the evening of the 29th to find her sitting-room 'very prettily newly papered, newly furnished, and has a new carpet, and looks very pretty indeed.' The bedroom she still shared with the Duchess had also been redecorated and looked very nice and clean.

But new paint and wallpaper did nothing to lighten the atmosphere at the Palace. If anything, matters had become rather worse since the advent of Lady Flora Hastings, for Lady Flora, a sharp-tongued, sharp-witted young woman in her late twenties, had quickly formed an alliance with John Conroy and joined with him in baiting the unfortunate Lehzen. The spring of 1835 seems to have marked the opening of a new campaign to drive Lehzen out, and she was being treated with such contempt and harshness that, on 6 March, the Duchess of Northumberland took it on herself to write to Princess Feodore, suggesting that King Leopold should be asked to intervene.

Her letter made Feodore tremble.

Dear Duchess, We must do everything to preserve Baroness L. The King [William] is the person to uphold her and say she *must* and *shall* remain with the princess . . . for what sort of person may be put near her, to further the plans of that man. As the Queen knows of it I am sure she will do all in her power to protect poor L, but I think it is only the King, as head of the family, that can speak a decisive word in this business. . . . How very good it would be if your Grace could communicate with B. L[ehzen] and advise her what to do at such a moment, but I know, but too well, how difficult, almost impossible that is at the Palace.

In fact, provided she could continue to put up with the undisguised hostility of the Conroy clique, Lehzen's position was probably secure enough by this time. The King and Queen would certainly have moved to protect her if need be, and so would Leopold. It has to be said that John Conroy was not the only person hoping to profit by his close relationship with the future Queen of England. Leopold had invested a good deal of emotional and financial capital in his little niece and counted his influence over her as a priceless potential asset. He regarded Lehzen as his ally, relying on her for confidential on-the-spot reports on the situation as it developed at Kensington, and would never have stood aside while she was ousted by Conroy. Unfortunately, though, Victoria was so closely supervised, so effectively cut off from any uncensored communication with the outside world, that it was almost impossible for her well-wishers to reassure her without causing the sort of scenes and scandals everyone was most anxious to avoid, and as a result she suffered much unnecessary mental stress.

Early in May there was another short visit to Windsor Castle and a note of defiance creeps into the Journal. 'I was very much pleased there, as both my Uncle and Aunt are *so very kind* to me.' Her sixteenth birthday was now approaching and on 19 May the Duchess of Kent arranged a private concert to be held at Kensington Palace as a special treat. The performers included Luigi Lablache, the finest bass singer of his day, and Victoria's current heroine, Giulia Grisi, who proved to be '*quite beautiful* off the stage' and 'very quiet, ladylike and unaffected in her manners'. The programme consisted of a selection of arias from the Princess's favourite operas, the artists being accompanied on the piano by Michael Costa, conductor of the orchestra at Covent Garden, and for young Victoria it was an evening of sheer enchantment. She stayed up till twenty minutes past one and was 'MOST EXCEEDINGLY delighted'.

On Sunday, 24 May, the entry in the Journal begins on a note of slightly self-conscious solemnity. 'Today is my 16TH birthday! How very old that sounds; but I feel that the two years to come till I attain my 18th are the most important of any almost. I now only begin to appreciate my lessons, and hope from this time on, to make great progress.' There was the usual stream of callers and the usual shower of gifts which ranged from an ivory basket of barley-sugar and chocolate from Dashy, the spaniel, to a pair of sapphire and diamond earrings from the King. There was a leather pencil-case and a very pretty print of Marie Taglioni from Lehzen, a handkerchief sachet embroidered in silver from faithful old Späth in Germany and an enamel bracelet with hers and the children's hair from *dearest* Feodore. Mamma's main present, which had shown a rare touch of imagination, had been that *delicious* concert, but she also gave her daughter a bracelet, a pair of fine china vases, a lovely shawl and some English and Italian books. There was a gold and turquoise bracelet from Uncle Sussex and more jewellery from the other uncles and aunts, a prayer book and a very kind letter from the Queen, and another prayer book presented by 'a bookseller of the name of Hatchard'.

Victoria took her religious faith with great seriousness, though she remained admirably free from bigotry and was very much shocked by a rabidly anti-Catholic sermon preached before her at Ramsgate later that year. Her thoughts were running on religious matters during the summer of 1835, for she was to be confirmed at the end of July; but, unhappily, even this pious occasion was to be marred by more family squabbles.

Trouble began when the Duchess of Kent, receiving a message from the King connected with the Princess's confirmation, via the Duchess of Northumberland, sent a reply over Her Grace's head to be conveyed to William by the Archbishop of Canterbury. This was a deliberate piece of provocation and a blatant breach of etiquette. The Duchess and Conroy had begun to distrust the Duchess of Northumberland and were planning to use Victoria's advancing years as a pretext for dispensing with her services as well as Lehzen's. But they had made a serious mistake in tactics. The King was roused to real fury by the discovery that Kensington had been rude to the Duchess of Northumberland, who was not only an esteemed friend of both their Majesties but also one of the greatest ladies in the land. It was therefore made plain to the Duchess of Kent that she must send her reply through the proper channels. The Duchess of Kent refused and William's exasperation drove him to the extreme step of writing in his own hand to the Bishop of London, forbidding him, as Dean of the Chapels Royal, to allow the Princess Victoria to be confirmed in any of them. The Duchess was forced to give in, but this preliminary skirmish did not bode very well in terms of proper Christian spirit.

Victoria herself approached her confirmation, 'one of the most solemn and important events . . . in my life', with the firm determination 'to become a true Christian, to try and comfort my dear Mamma in all her griefs, trials and anxieties, and to become a dutiful and affectionate daughter to her. Also to be obedient to *dear* Lehzen who has done so much for me.' The ceremony, conducted by the Archbishop of Canterbury and the Bishop of London, was to take place in the Chapel Royal, St James's and the

Princess wore a white lace dress and white crape bonnet, trimmed with a wreath of white roses. Mother and daughter, attended by Lehzen and Lady Flora Hastings, were received in the King's Closet, before making their way to the Royal Pew to join the Queen, Aunt Sophia, the Cumberlands and the Cambridges. The Duke and Duchess of Northumberland and various other personages connected with the Court were also present, but as soon as the King caught sight of John Conroy among the congregation, he declared that the Duchess of Kent's retinue was too large and Sir John had to leave.

The thunderous atmosphere in the Chapel must have been strongly reminiscent of Victoria's christening (ironically enough, there had recently been some discussion about the advisability of changing her name to something more English, such as Elizabeth), and acute embarrassment, the natural emotionalism of the occasion, intense July heat and the awesome nature of the Archbishop of Canterbury's sermon all combined to overwhelm the Princess, who was 'frightened to death and drowned in tears'. The Duchess also wept – tears of rage.

Matters were not improved when, later that day, Victoria was handed a letter from her mother informing her that she had now reached a period of her life 'that brings changes with it' and, in consequence, her manner to Lehzen must change. In future that devoted attendant was to be set at a distance and treated with dignity. Dignity and friendly manners were 'quite compatible', but Victoria must always confide first in her mother, whose sacrifices on her behalf had been so great and under whose guidance she would remain until she was at 'the age of either eighteen or twenty-one years'. This was quite a new idea. Royal persons came of age at eighteen. Was Victoria for some reason to be treated differently and her present bondage extended? In the circumstances it's no wonder that she should once more have become 'very much affected indeed'.

Chapter Seven
Albert Is Much Handsomer

The German Princes still continue to pour into this country, and the little Princess is regularly besieged. There is a regular communication kept up amongst the whole race; and when it is found this one has no chance of success, another is sent for.

Press report, 19 June 1836

At the beginning of August 1835 the Kensington family was on the move again. They stayed two nights at Buxted Park with Lord Liverpool, half-brother of the former Prime Minister, whose daughter, Lady Catherine Jenkinson, was Woman of the Bedchamber to the Duchess of Kent, and then went on to Tunbridge Wells. By the beginning of September they were back in London, getting ready to set out on an ambitious 'progress' through the north-east.

Victoria did not want to go. She was feeling so poorly and wretched with constant headaches and backache that she dreaded the prospect of another journey, with all its attendant publicity. Besides this, she knew of and could understand the King's dislike of seeing his heir touring the provinces under the management of John Conroy. At his birthday dinner in August, William had publicly expressed a hope that his successor would be of age when she came to the throne (a hope which his successor devoutly shared), and had gone on to speak of his 'great distrust' of the persons who surrounded the Duchess of Kent, another sentiment fully shared by his niece.

But when the Princess tried to put her point of view to Mamma, she got no sympathy. Instead she got another letter, for matters were now reaching the stage when the Duchess found this an easier method of communicating with her daughter on sensitive subjects. 'You may imagine', she wrote on this occasion, 'that I feel very much disappointed and grieved, that the journey we are to commence tomorrow is not only disagreeable to you, but that it makes you even unhappy; that the fatigue of it will make you ill, that you dislike it. . . . You will not see, that it is of the greatest consequence that you should be seen, that you should know your country, and be acquainted with, and be known by all classes.' The King's objections were brushed aside as mere senile jealousy: '. . . if he really loved you he would, instead of wishing to stop our Journey . . . even press me to them.' Victoria must pull herself together and reflect on her future station, its duties and responsibilities. 'I must tell you, dearest Love, if your conversation with me could be known, that you had not the energy to undertake the journey, or that your views were not enlarged enough to grasp the benefits arising from it, then you would fall in the estimation of the people of this country.'

The Duchess, of course, was right in that it *was* of great importance that the Princess should see something of the country, get to know the people and be seen by them. If only the Journeys could have been freed from the taint of Conroyism and a nagging suspicion that the heir to the throne and her mother were being exploited for private ends, no one could reasonably have objected to them.

From the point of view of what it was intended to achieve, this particular Journey was a triumphant success. After two and a half days of strenuous travelling, the royal party reached York (which was a good deal further north than royalty usually penetrated), on Saturday, 5 September. They were to stay with the Archbishop at his official residence just outside the city and on the Monday, after a civic reception at the Mansion House, the Duchess and her daughter toured the Museum of the Yorkshire Philosophical Society and visited nearby Castle Howard. The rest of the week was taken up by attending a music festival held in York Minster. A performance of the *Messiah* was the main item on the programme, but although Grisi sang the 'Rejoice greatly' *most beautifully*, the Princess found it very 'heavy and tiresome'. 'I am not at all fond of Handel's music,' she wrote. 'I like the present Italian school such as Rossini, Bellini, Donizetti etc., *much better.*' Everywhere they went, the royal visitors were mobbed by enthusiastic crowds and before leaving York Victoria was presented with a length of claret coloured cashmere from the mills of Messrs Hargreaves and Co. of Kirkstall, a fabric so exquisititely beautiful as to rival the finest French merino and which was greatly admired as a superb specimen of the perfection of British manufacture.

From York the party went on to spend a quiet weekend with the Lascelles family at Harewood House, and from there to Wentworth to stay with Earl Fitzwilliam and attend the Doncaster Races. The towns they passed through – Leeds, Wakefield and Barnsley – were all *en fête* with flags and flowers, triumphal arches and pealing bells, and everywhere the crowds of cheering, jostling, inquisitive onlookers were immense; so much so that it was often impossible to change horses at the regular staging posts, and it was noticed that the Princess looked pale and seemed nervous.

After Wentworth, where they were received with 'princely hospitality', the travellers continued their tour of the stately homes of the North Midlands, going from Belvoir Castle to Burghley House near Stamford. At Stamford an address was read to the Duchess by the Marquess of Exeter, and Charles Greville, who was present, did not fail to notice that 'Conroy handed the answer, just as the Prime Minister does to the King.' A grand dinner at Burghley House was 'very handsome' and went off well, except that 'a pail of ice was landed in the Duchess's lap, which made a great bustle.' The ball for three hundred guests of rank and fashion which followed was opened by the Princess and Lord Exeter, but Victoria had 'a dreadful headache' and went to bed after the first dance.

The route now took them eastward, by way of Peterborough, Wisbech and King's Lynn, where the inhabitants insisted on taking the horses out of the royal carriage and drawing it round the

Edward Duke of Kent in
1818

The Duchess of Kent in
1829

The 'Royal Pregnancies' cartoon

Woolbrook Cottage, Sidmouth, where the Duke of Kent died

The widowed Duchess of Kent and Princess Victoria in 1821

Left: Uncle Leopold

Below far left: Prince Charles of Leiningen

Below left: Princess Feodore in 1828

Above right: Baroness Lehzen sketched by Princess Victoria

Below right: Sir John Conroy

Above: Princess
Victoria as a baby

Above right: Aged four

Right: From a painting
by her drawing master,
Richard Westall

Left: The Duchess of Kent and Princess Victoria in 1834

Below left: Queen Adelaide

Below right: King William IV

'Susanna and the Elders'. Queen Victoria out riding with Lord Melbourne and the Home Secretary, Lord John Russell

Lady Flora Hastings

Queen Victoria in 1839

town – a demonstration which upset the schedule and made the visitors very late arriving at Holkham Hall, seat of the famous agriculturist Coke of Norfolk. 'A magnificent dinner was almost immediately served to the Illustrious Guests, and a select party invited to meet them', but the Princess Victoria again went early to bed, 'having been considerably fatigued by the many ceremonies which the warm-hearted loyalty of her future Subjects had imposed upon her throughout the day.'

Victoria's ordeal was now nearly over. A brief stay with the Duke and Duchess of Grafton at Euston Hall brought the tour or 'triumphal procession' to an end, and on 25 September she was back at Kensington. 'Though I liked some of the places very well,' she recorded in the Journal, 'I was much tired by the long journeys and the great crowds we had to encounter. We cannot travel like other people, quietly and pleasantly, but we go through towns and crowds and when one arrives at any nobleman's seat, one must instantly dress for dinner and consequently I could never rest properly.' There was still to be little opportunity for rest, for almost immediately they were off again to Ramsgate, but this time Victoria had the joyous prospect of seeing Uncle Leopold again.

King Leopold, having now succeeded in establishing himself reasonably comfortably on the Belgian throne, had decided the moment was ripe for a family reunion and was coming on a short private visit to Ramsgate, bringing his new young wife with him. The royal couple were to stay at the Albion Hotel and the Princess and the Duchess with Lehzen, Lady Conroy and Lady Flora Hastings watched anxiously from a window as the steamer from Ostend entered the harbour amidst loud cheering and a salute of guns from the pier. A quarter of an hour later, a waiter came up to tell them that 'their Majesties were coming' and they hurried downstairs to greet the visitors. 'What a happiness it was for me', wrote Victoria ecstatically, 'to throw myself in the arms of that *dearest* of Uncles who has always been to me like a father, and whom I love so *very dearly*! I had not seen him for 4 years and 2 months!'

For the Princess her uncle's visit, brief though it was, brought an incalculable sense of relief and reassurance. They were able to have two private conversations, talking over 'many important and serious matters', and Uncle Leopold gave her some '*very good and valuable advice*'. Uncle Leopold was later to take the credit on himself for having had the courage 'to tear apart the whole web of intrigue' by which the Princess was surrounded, and he appears to have taken the opportunity of doing some straight talking both to his sister and John Conroy. Still more important, Victoria now had the personal promise of his support. She and Lehzen were no longer quite alone, and her frightening sense of isolation began to recede.

As well as the benefit of Uncle's good advice – 'he is the best and kindest adviser I have' – she also had the pleasure of getting to know her new aunt. Louise of Orleans, Queen of the Belgians, was only seven years older than Victoria and seemed more like an elder sister. The two young women discussed clothes and hairstyles – Louise was well known for her excellent taste – and quickly became firm friends. But even during this happy week the Princess was far from well, feeling sick and headachy and off her food. Although 'very poorly', she managed to keep going until Uncle Leopold and Aunt Louise left for home on 7 October and then collapsed, lying on her bed feeling '*so ill*'.

The Duchess and John Conroy had always been inclined to disregard her symptoms. It was part of Conroy's policy deliberately to create the impression in certain quarters that the Princess Victoria was backward for her age and of below average intelligence, a silly little girl who would continue to need guidance and supervision even after she was technically of age. Her irrational dislike of himself, so devoted to her interests, her reluctance to undertake Journeys, her headaches, fatigue and sickness were merely 'whims' and vapourings in which she was encouraged by Lehzen, and which only went to prove her incapacity to fill a great position unaided by those who knew and understood her shortcomings.

But in October 1835 there was no denying that Victoria was seriously ill, though even then, according to Lehzen, the Duchess and Sir John tried at first to make light of her condition and a full week went by before Dr Clark, later Sir James Clark, was called in. However, when he did finally see and examine the Princess, Dr Clark at once realized the gravity of the situation. The exact nature of the illness which was to keep her confined to her room for over a month remains in some doubt. Dr Clark himself diagnosed 'bilious fever' and other sources describe it as an attack of typhoid, but Cecil Woodham-Smith, Victoria's latest biographer, believes the trouble may have been due to septic tonsils which had been systematically poisoning her, and causing the aches and pains, nausea, sore throats, colds and general debility of the past two years – aggravated, of course, by the emotional strain of her position.

Whatever its true cause, her naturally strong constitution enabled her to throw off the infection, which was fortunate, as she had to fight illness and John Conroy together. Conroy was no longer quite so sanguine about the future. With Victoria now half-way through her seventeenth year and King William, although over seventy, still disappointingly hale and hearty, the odds on a regency were lengthening and Sir John, alarmed perhaps by Leopold's visit, decided the time had come to hedge his bets. The barely convalescent Princess was therefore confronted with a none too gentle demand that she should promise to place herself unreservedly in Conroy's hands when she came to the throne by appointing him as her Private Secretary, and a written pledge to this effect was thrust before her to sign. She refused. With Lehzen at her side to give her courage and the memory of Uncle Leopold's valuable advice fresh in her mind, she said No and went on saying it. 'I resisted in spite of my illness', she was to remark later and for the first time Conroy found himself brought up against the 'vein of iron' which lay beneath that deceptively demure exterior.

No direct reference to this alarming episode appeared in the Journal when it was resumed at the beginning of November, but there was a significant tribute to *dear good* Lehzen, who 'takes such care of me, and is so unceasing in her attentions to me that . . . I never can sufficiently repay her for all she has *borne* and done for me. She is the *most affectionate, devoted, attached* and *disinterested* friend I have, and I love her most *dearly*.'

On 3 November Victoria was able to tell Uncle Leopold that

she was much better and getting stronger, but had grown *very* thin. Her hair, too, had been coming out in handfuls, so that she was 'literally now getting *bald*'. As a last desperate resort they had had to cut it nearly all off, and it was once so thick that Lehzen could hardly take it in her hand. However, she was now definitely on the mend and soon the loyal inhabitants of Ramsgate were being rejoiced by the sight of the Princess and her Mamma promenading briskly to and fro on the eastern and western piers for upwards of an hour at a time. These rather chilly outings, enlivened only by looking at the foreign fishing boats in the harbour, were part of a new regime of fresh air and exercise which Dr Clark had prescribed for his patient. She was not to study for too long at a time and to change her position frequently, a standing desk would be better than too much sitting still. She was to take a warm bath twice a week, use Indian clubs to improve her circulation and sleep in a well ventilated room.

On 13 January, 'a bitterly cold day, though bright and clear', the royal party left Ramsgate for Kensington and when they arrived home, after an absence of three and a half months, immediately went up *two* staircases to their handsome new sleeping and sitting apartments. The Duchess of Kent had been agitating for more and better accommodation for the past three years, and in 1832 had commissioned the fashionable architect Jeffry Wyatville to draw up plans creating a spacious new suite on the second floor of the Palace for the Princess and herself. The Duchess had a point. The modest rooms on the ground and first floors to which the Duke of Kent had brought his bride after that epic journey across Europe in 1819 were cramped and gloomy, and had certainly become quite inadequate for their present purpose. If only she had presented her case with a modicum of tact, William would probably have listened sympathetically. But as it was, he had become so irritated by his sister-in-law's graceless insistence on her 'rights' that he had flatly refused to consider Wyatville's scheme. The Duchess had therefore proceeded to help herself. All the alterations vetoed by the King had been carried out (with the obvious exception of improvements to the exterior of the building) and now, relying on the general inefficiency and lack of supervision over the royal establishments, she was moving in without his knowledge.

Victoria, blissfully unaware that they had been illicitly acquired, spent a happy afternoon exploring her new quarters.

Our bedroom is very large and lofty, and is very nicely furnished, then comes a little room for the maid, and a dressing-room for Mamma; then comes the old gallery which is partitioned into 3 large, lofty, fine and cheerful rooms. One only of these (the one near Mamma's dressing-room) is ready furnished; it is my sitting-room and is *very* prettily furnished indeed . . . .. The next is my study and the last is an anteroom.

The Princess paid a nostalgic visit to her old bedroom (where Lehzen was now sleeping), and her 'poor former sitting-room' which she could not help looking at with affection and pleasant recollections, 'but our new rooms are much more airy and roomy.'

She enjoyed herself over the next few days running up and down stairs, arranging her books and china, getting rid of 'two ugly oil pictures of my Father and Mother' and hanging 'Hayter's drawing of Mamma and I' in their place. The workmen were still busy in her study and making a great noise, but by the end of the month life had settled back into its old routine. Dr Davys came every morning and they were now ploughing through Blackstone's *Commentaries on English Law* and Milton's *Paradise Lost*. The Princess read the English newspapers every day with Lehzen in order to keep up with current affairs (though there's not much evidence that these interested her greatly) and kept up her habit of reading aloud while her hair was 'doing'. She was still working her way through Madame de Sévigné and Sully's *Memoirs*, and had begun writing a weekly letter in French to Aunt Louise. In obedience to Dr Clark's instructions, she was also being taken three or four times a week to the bracing heights of Finchley or Hampstead Heath for health-giving walks. Her health was, in fact, much better and continued to improve, though, as she wistfully remarked in one of her letters to Uncle Leopold, '*pleasure* does more good than a hundred walks and drives.'

There was, however, pleasure in prospect. The opera season

was once more in full swing and in March came the thrill of a visit from more Coburg relations, the Duchess of Kent's brother Ferdinand, who had married the Hungarian heiress Antoinette Kohary, with his two sons Ferdinand and Augustus. Ferdinand junior was on his way to Portugal and marriage to the young Queen Maria da Gloria, who had once shared a children's party with Princess Victoria, and the family were planning to give him a brilliant send-off.

The Kohary Coburgs were to be received at Windsor, and on 17 March there was a grand dinner followed by dancing in the Waterloo Gallery. The Princess danced three quadrilles and was 'much amused and pleased'. As usual, she was in raptures over her cousins. Ferdinand was tall and very good-looking, with beautiful dark eyes and a very sweet mouth. He talked 'so dearly and sensibly' that it was impossible not to love him, in spite of his habit of speaking through his nose in 'a slow funny way'. Dear Augustus was also tall and very handsome and 'a dear good young man'. He was very quiet and shy, but Victoria felt certain that there was a great deal in him.

The party stayed two nights at Windsor before returning to Kensington, where the Duchess was giving a ball in honour of her nephews. The King and Queen were present, but were not shown upstairs. Two days later there was another ball, in fancy dress this time, and Victoria danced seven quadrilles before supper. The stimulus of congenial young company acted powerfully on her spirits and Ferdinand, when not on show, proved that he could be 'most funny and childishly merry', which delighted his cousin, merriment being an all too scarce commodity at Kensington. Unhappily he had to leave for Portugal on 27 March. 'Oh! when I think how *very soon* I shall not see that *dear dear* Ferdinand any more I feel quite *wretched* . . . I love him *so* much, he is *so* excellent.'

Augustus stayed on for another week and, although inferior to his brother, was some consolation. 'He is a dear boy, and is so extremely good, kind and gentle; he has such a sweet expression and kind smile.' He would come and sit quietly in the Princess's sitting-room, reading the newspaper and never getting in the way.

On one occasion he helped her to seal her letters. 'We both made a mess, and he burnt a cover in sealing it, dear boy, for me, which made us both laugh.' When the visit came to an end early in April there were tears— 'it seems like a dream that all our joy, happiness and gaiety should thus suddenly be over.'

On 19 April Victoria started singing lessons with Luigi Lablache. She was so nervous at first that no sound would come, but Lablache, a big, genial man, half Neapolitan, half Irish and said to have been the finest Leporello in musical history, soon persuaded her to relax— 'personne a jamais eu peur de moi.' 'I am sure nobody ever can be who knows him', wrote the Princess and the lessons became a continuing delight. 'I wish I had one every *day* instead of every *week*.'

Meanwhile, another family visit was looming. With Victoria about to enter her all-important eighteenth year, Uncle Leopold felt the time had come to introduce her to her cousins Ernest and Albert, sons of his own and the Duchess of Kent's eldest brother, the reigning Duke of Saxe-Coburg and Gotha — a piece of avuncular solicitude which was to prove fraught with diplomatic awkwardness. It had long been an open secret that the Coburgs were planning a match between Albert and Victoria; but King William, in common with a number of fellow monarchs, regarded the encroaching spread of Coburg influence (master-minded by busy Uncle Leopold) with disfavour, and had already let it be known that he had other plans for his niece.

Victoria, the greatest heiress in Europe, was now of an age when her betrothal would normally have already been a settled thing. Unfortunately, owing to the quarrels rending the royal family, the matter had never been sensibly discussed among the interested parties. In fact, it had scarcely been discussed at all and was predictably to become the cause of more bad feeling and damaging displays of petulance and ill-temper.

The English royals wanted to keep their Princess in the family. A marriage between Prince George of Cumberland and Princess Victoria of Kent would, for example, have had the obvious advantage of preserving the union between England and Hanover, and rumours that it was under serious consideration had first

appeared in the press as early as 1828. There's a long-standing
tradition that the Princess had a fondness for her Cumberland
cousin, a gentle, attractive boy who tragically went blind by the
age of fourteen; but although the idea of a match had certainly
been talked of – the Duke of Wellington is said to have favoured it
at one time – it was never a serious possibility. William's and
Adelaide's preference was for George Cambridge, whom they had
helped to bring up and who was a great pet of the Queen's. He and
Victoria met frequently at Windsor, at parties and Court
functions, but while the Cambridges would undoubtedly have
welcomed their future Queen as a daughter-in-law with open
arms, the young people themselves showed no particular liking for
each other.

Now, in the spring of 1836, King William made a move to
forestall King Leopold (whom he detested) and widen the
Princess's field of choice, by inviting the Prince of Orange to
bring his two sons to England, at the same time doing his best to
stop a further incursion of Coburgs.

These rather clumsy manoeuvres provoked an outburst of
wrath from Leopold. 'My dearest Child,' he wrote to Victoria on
13 May,

. . . I am really astonished at the conduct of your old Uncle the King;
this invitation of the Prince of Orange and his sons, this forcing him
upon others, is very extraordinary. . . . Not later than yesterday I got a
half official communication from England, insinuating that it would be
highly desirable that the visit of *your* relatives *should not take place this year*
– *qu'en dites-vous?* The relations of the Queen and the King, therefore, to
the God-knows-what-degree, are to come in shoals and rule the land,
when *your relations* are to be *forbidden* the country. . . . Really and truly I
never heard or saw anything like it, and I hope it will a *little rouse your
spirit*; now that slavery is even abolished in the British Colonies, I do not
comprehend *why your lot alone should be to be kept, a white little slavey in
England*, for the pleasure of the Court, who never bought you, as I am
not aware of their having gone to any expense on that head, or the King's
even having *spent a sixpence for your existence*. I expect that my visits
in England will also be prohibited by an Order in Council. Oh
consistency and political or *other honesty*, where must one look for you! I
have not the least doubt that the King, in his passion for the Oranges,

will be *excessively rude to* your relations; this, however, will not signify much; they are *your guests* and not *his*, and will therefore *not* mind it.

As it turned out, Leopold need not have worried. The King had been unsuccessful in his attempt to prevent the visit of the rival suitors – the Duchess of Kent informing him triumphantly that the Coburg party was already on its way – and Victoria had been too well schooled by Uncle to find anything attractive about the Oranges. She had, in fact, already made their acquaintance by the time his letter reached her. The Prince of Orange, she informed him, seemed embarrassed and the boys were both very plain and had a mixture of Kalmuck and Dutch in their faces. 'They look heavy, dull and frightened and are not at all prepossessing.'

So much, then, for the Oranges (it was ironical to remember that the Prince of Orange had once been rejected by Princess Charlotte in favour of a Coburg), and Victoria could now look forward happily to meeting her own relations. Princess Feodore had already prepared her for the treat in store. 'I am very fond of them both', she had written. 'Ernest is my favourite, although Albert is much handsomer, and cleverer too, but Ernest is so honest and good-natured. I shall be very curious to hear your opinion upon them.'

The visitors arrived at Kensington on Wednesday, 18 May and the Journal records that:

At a ¼ to 2 we went down into the Hall, to receive my Uncle Ernest, Duke of Saxe-Coburg-Gotha [Saalfeld had been exchanged for Gotha in 1825] and my Cousins, Ernest and Albert, his sons . . . Ernest is as tall as Ferdinand and Augustus; he has dark hair, and fine dark eyes and eyebrows, but the nose and mouth are not good . . . Albert, who is just as tall as Ernest but stouter, is extremely handsome; his hair is about the same colour as mine; his eyes are large and blue, and he has a beautiful nose and a very sweet mouth with fine teeth; but the charm of his countenance is his expression, which is most delightful; *c'est à la fois* full of goodness and sweetness, and very clever and intelligent. . . . Both my Cousins are so kind and good; they are much more *formés* and men of the world than Augustus; they speak English very well, and I speak it with them. Ernest will be 18 years old on the 21st of June and Albert 17 on the 26th of August.

Three days later the Princess was getting into her usual enthusiastic stride. Both cousins drew very well, particularly Albert, and were exceedingly fond of music. 'The more I see them the more I am delighted with them, and the more I love them. They are so natural, so kind, so *very* good and so well instructed and informed; they are so well bred, so truly merry and quite like children and yet very grown up in their manners and conversation.'

Contrary to Uncle Leopold's gloomy prognostications, the King was being perfectly civil, inviting the Duke and his sons to dinner at St James's Palace and welcoming them at the state ball for Victoria's seventeenth birthday. The Duchess of Kent had planned a strenuous programme for her nephews. There was a large dinner party at Kensington on 23 May and another grand ball on the 30th, at which the Orange princes were also present. Victoria kept it up till half-past three and felt 'all the better for it next day'; but the unaccustomed bright lights, late hours and rich food were too much for sixteen-year-old Albert, who suffered agonies of sleepiness after half-past nine at night and was obliged to retire precipitately from several of the entertainments so lavishly provided for him. On 26 May the Princess had to report that Albert had succumbed to 'a smart bilious attack . . . by dint of starvation, he is again restored to society, but looks pale and delicate.'

Fortunately for Albert the last week of the visit was rather less demanding. He and Victoria played the piano and sang duets together, twice sharing a singing lesson from Lablache. On 8 June there was a final visit to the opera and on the 9th the royal party attended the annual service for the London charity children at St Paul's Cathedral and lunched afterwards with the Lord Mayor. Then, on Friday the 10th came

our last HAPPY HAPPY breakfast, with this dear Uncle and those *dearest*, beloved Cousins, whom I *do* love so VERY VERY dearly; *much more dearly* than any other Cousins in the *world*. Dearly as I love Ferdinand, and also good Augustus, I love Ernest and Albert *more* than them, oh yes, MUCH *more*. . . . Dearest Ernest and dearest Albert are so grown-up in their manners, so gentle, so kind, so amiable, so agreeable, so very sensible and reasonable, and so *really* and truly good and kind-hearted. They have both learnt a good deal, and are very clever, naturally clever, particularly Albert, who is the most reflecting of the two, and they like very much talking about serious and instructive things and yet are so *very very* merry and gay and happy, like young people ought to be.

Albert especially was full of fun, at breakfast and everywhere, and had played so nicely with dear little Dashy. The parting brought bitter tears, but Victoria decided that her nerves must be getting stronger, for she could bear things more calmly now.

Both young people were aware of the plans being made for them but, as Albert later testified, 'not a word in allusion to the future' had passed between them, despite confident reports in the foreign press that their engagement was about to be announced. Prudent Uncle Leopold had, however, taken the precaution of writing confidentially to Lehzen on the subject. There could, of course, be no question of marriage or even a public betrothal at this stage. The Princess must wait for her eighteenth birthday, perhaps longer; much would have to depend on the general state of her health and physical development. Albert, too, was still very young, still being groomed and trained for the consort's career mapped out for him by Leopold and Baron Stockmar. He needed time to grow up, acquire more social poise and overcome his distressing tendency to fall asleep at the dinner-table. All the same, for the sake of her own peace of mind, Leopold felt that Victoria would be well advised 'to find a choice and firmly anchor herself to it'. In other words, an understanding with her cousin would be a safeguard against any attempts which might be made to force some unwelcome suitor on her. The Princess might discount the Orange boys, but Leopold knew they remained a danger and would be a popular choice, as a Coburg match would not. At the moment Conroy and the Duchess of Kent were all in favour of Albert, but Conroy might change his mind and his power over the Duchess remained as strong as ever, so strong indeed 'that it would once have been called witchcraft'.

Lehzen, obedient to instructions, talked the matter over with Victoria and the outcome was a letter from the Princess, written while Duke Ernest and his sons were still in London.

I must thank you, my beloved Uncle, for the prospect of *great* happiness you have contributed to give me in the person of dear Albert. Allow me, then, my dearest Uncle, to tell you how delighted I am with him, and how much I like him in every way. He possesses every quality that could be desired to render me perfectly happy . . . He has besides, the most pleasing and delightful exterior and appearance you can possibly see. I have only now to beg you, my dearest Uncle, to take care of the health of one, now *so dear* to me, and to take him under *your special* protection. I hope and trust that all will go on prosperously and well on this subject of so much importance to me.

Victoria at seventeen was all sensibility, as ready to go into ecstasies over a new parrot (Uncle Ernest had brought her a present of 'a most delightful *Lory*'), as over a new cousin, a new aunt or singing teacher. But under the *Schwärmerei*, the gushing enthusiasms and the ready tears lay a substratum of tough, unsentimental commonsense, admirably illustrated by the businesslike tone of her letter to Uncle Leopold. The Princess knew as well as anyone that her marriage must be a matter of arrangement and that her choice would be restricted to a small circle of not particularly inspiring Protestant royal cousinage. She was not in any sense in love with Prince Albert in 1836, but she approved of him, he would 'do' very well. Trusting Leopold's judgement as she did, she had accepted his implied assurance that Albert was the best she was likely to get (though it is noticeable that she made no definite promises), and having done this, appears to have dismissed the whole matter from her thoughts.

With the departure of the Coburgs, life went flat again. Victoria returned to the schoolroom, to Blackstone's *Commentaries* and Paley's *Political Philosophy*, and to the unrelieved society of the Conroys and Lady Flora Hastings. The season came to an end and with it the singing lessons from Lablache, and at the beginning of August the household moved down to Claremont.

The Duchess of Kent had received an invitation from the King asking her to bring the Princess to Windsor for the Queen's birthday on 13 August and stay on for the celebrations of his birthday on the 21st. The Duchess's own birthday – it would be her fiftieth – fell on the 17th and, once more exercising 'her remarkable talent for giving offence', she replied coldly that she preferred to spend that day at Claremont, took no notice of the Queen's birthday, but said she would come to Windsor on the 20th. Although this calculated piece of rudeness put the King 'in a fury', nothing was said, but the volcano of suppressed irritation which had been rumbling around in William's curiously shaped head for the past six years was about to erupt.

On 20 August he was in London for the prorogation of Parliament, and on his way back to Windsor something or, more likely, someone prompted him to make an unannounced inspection of Kensington Palace, where, of course, he discovered the Duchess of Kent's misappropriation of seventeen new rooms. William had put up with a good deal from his sister-in-law, her popularity hunting, her constant ostentatious receiving of loyal addresses, her open insolence to the Queen and himself, but this was definitely the last straw, and he arrived at the Castle late that evening in a royal Hanoverian rage.

Dinner was over and the company assembled in the drawing room when the King appeared.

He went up to the Princess Victoria, took hold of both her hands, and expressed his pleasure at seeing her there and his regret at not seeing her oftener. He then turned to the Duchess and made her a low bow, almost immediately after which he said that 'a most unwarrantable liberty had been taken with one of his palaces; that he had just come from Kensington, where he found apartments had been taken possession of not only without his consent, but contrary to his commands, and that he neither understood nor would endure conduct so disrespectful to him.'

This majestic rocket was delivered 'loudly, publicly, and in a tone of serious displeasure', but according to Charles Greville, whose informant was Adolphus FitzClarence, youngest of the *bâtards*, it was 'only the muttering of the storm which was to break next day'.

The next day, the King's birthday, was a Sunday and the celebrations were, therefore, 'what was called private'. However, Greville continues,

there were a hundred people at dinner, either belonging to the Court or from the neighbourhood. The Duchess of Kent sat on one side of the King and one of his sisters on the other, the Princess Victoria sat opposite. Adolphus FitzClarence sat two or three from the Duchess and heard every word of what passed. After dinner, by the Queen's desire, 'His Majesty's health and long life to him' was given, and as soon as it was drunk he made a very long speech, in the course of which he poured forth the following extraordinary and *foudroyant* tirade: 'I trust in God that my life may be spared for nine months longer. . . . I should then have the satisfaction of leaving the royal authority to the personal exercise of that young lady' (pointing to the Princess), 'the heiress presumptive of the Crown, and not in the hands of a person now near me, who is surrounded by evil advisers, and who is herself incompetent to act with propriety in the station in which she would be placed. I have no hesitation in saying that I have been insulted – grossly and continually insulted – by that person, but I am determined to endure no longer a course of behaviour so disrespectful to me. Amongst many other things, I have particularly to complain of the manner in which that young lady has been kept away from my Court; she has been repeatedly kept from my drawing rooms, at which she ought always to have been present, but I am fully resolved that this shall not happen again. I would have her know that I am King, and I am determined to make my authority respected, and for the future I shall insist and command that the Princess do upon all occasions appear at my Court, as it is her duty to do.' He terminated his speech by an allusion to the Princess and her future reign in a tone of paternal interest and affection, which was excellent in its way.

The King's 'awful philippic', uttered in a loud, excited manner, was received in stunned silence. 'The Queen looked in deep distress, the Princess burst into tears, and the whole company were aghast.' The Duchess of Kent said not a word, but immediately after the royal family rose and retired 'a terrible scene ensued', the Duchess calling for her carriage and announcing her immediate departure. Conscious of the appalling publicity this would create, various well-intentioned persons hastened to patch up 'a sort of reconciliation' and the outraged lady was prevailed on to stay until the following day. But the King himself was unrepentant. When Adolphus FitzClarence told him that, while most people agreed that the Duchess had fully deserved a rebuke, they thought it should not have been given at table before a hundred people, he replied that he did not care where he said it or before whom, that 'by God, he had been insulted by her in a measure that was past all endurance, and he would not stand it any longer.'

In Charles Greville's opinion, William had put himself irretrievably in the wrong by his outburst. Nothing could have been more reprehensible than the Duchess of Kent's behaviour towards him in the past, 'but such a gross and public insult offered to her at his own table, sitting by his side and in the presence of her daughter, admits of no excuse. It was an unparalleled outrage from a man to a woman, from a host to his guest, and to the last degree unbecoming the station they both of them fill.' In any case, as Greville pointed out, it was largely the King's own fault that the whole miserable situation had been allowed to develop in the first place. An early display of firmness and decision on his part would have prevented all these unseemly bickerings; making an exhibition of himself now would not impress the Duchess, but only have the effect of 'rendering their mutual relations (including that of the girl) more hopelessly disagreeable'.

'The girl's' inner feelings on this occasion were not revealed. Her public embarrassment had obviously been agonizing and acute, but privately she may well have agreed with most of her uncle's remarks. The experience of recent years had left her with plenty of reasons to doubt Mamma's competence 'to act with propriety' in a number of circumstances, and she had long ceased to have any doubt at all regarding the malignity of Mamma's closest adviser. The scene at Windsor was only the climax to a long succession of social embarrassments inflicted on her by their deliberate policy of baiting the King, but the knowledge that she would now more than ever be kept from taking her proper place at Court was a sadness, and a grievance she would not soon forget.

Chapter Eight
Little Vic

Such a little love of a Queen!

Countess Granville

There was no 'journey' in 1836, and after their unfortunate experience at Windsor the Duchess of Kent and her daughter went back to Claremont where, on 13 September, King Leopold joined them for another short private visit. To Victoria's disappointment Queen Louise was not with him this time – she was expecting a baby – but Leopold brought a present of dresses from Paris chosen by her, including one particularly delectable blue silk with a light blue satin bonnet.

Uncle and niece again enjoyed several 'important' conversations. 'He is *so* clever, *so* mild, *so* prudent,' wrote Victoria; '*he* alone can give me good advice on *every* thing. His advice is perfect. He is indeed "il mio secondo padre" or rather "solo padre!" for he is indeed like my real father, as I have none, and he is so kind and so good to me.' The Princess sat happily at Uncle's feet. His conversation was so enlightened and so clear. He spoke so mildly, yet firmly and impartially about Politics; in fact, to hear him speak on any subject was 'like reading a highly instructive book'.

By no means everybody shared these golden opinions, for Leopold, once sentimentalized as the handsome young husband and then the tragic widower of Princess Charlotte, had more than outstayed his welcome from the British taxpayer during the years when he continued to draw his annual £50,000. In political circles he was regarded at best as a bore and a humbug, at worst as a self-seeking intriguant, bent on extracting maximum advantage from his valuable connections; while ominous rumblings could also now be heard issuing from the ultra-Protestant Orange Lodges (Grand Master the Duke of Cumberland), who smelt a sulphurous taint of Popery spreading through the Coburg clan. One sister, Sophie Mensdorff-Pouilly, was married to a Catholic, the Kohary Coburgs were Catholics and Leopold himself, though he remained faithful to his Lutheran Protestantism, was ruling a predominantly Catholic country and had married a Catholic wife. Much to the annoyance of the King of the Belgians, his 1836 visit had provoked a fresh outburst of hostility in the press. 'I should like to know what harm the Coburg family has done to England', he wrote plaintively that November, but no amout of 'scurrilous abuse' would deter him from his duty, and letters of prudent, impartial advice continued to flow tirelessly from 'Dearest Uncle's' pen.

The rest of the year passed uneventfully for Princess Victoria. After the usual autumn holiday at Ramsgate, the household returned to Claremont. Victoria read Irish history with Lehzen and took a keen interest in the welfare of a gipsy family camped by the Portsmouth Road. A baby was born and the Duchess of Kent ordered broth and fuel to be sent every day until the mother had recovered. Other comforts were collected – blankets, some 'old flannel things' and 'a little worsted knit jacket for the poor baby' contributed by Lehzen.

I cannot say how happy I am that these poor creatures are assisted, [wrote the Princess on Christmas Day] for they are such a nice set of Gipsies, so quiet, so affectionate to one another, so discreet, not at all forward or importunate, and *so* grateful; so unlike the gossiping, fortune-telling race-gipsies; and this is such a peculiar and touching case. Their being assisted makes me quite merry and happy today, for yesterday night when I was safe and happy at home in that cold night and today when it snowed so and everything looked white, I felt quite unhappy and grieved to think that our poor gipsy friends should perish and shiver for want.

January passed, still at Claremont, and on 6 February 1837 she wrote to Uncle Leopold:

I do not know quite for certain when we leave this place, but I should think to-day week. You must be pleased, dear Uncle, I think, for we shall have been *six months* in the country next Thursday, as we left town on the 10th of August last . . . you may understand that my *Operatic* and *Terpsichorean* feelings are pretty strong, now that the season is returning, and I have been a very good child, not even *wishing* to come to town till now.

But when she did come back to town towards the end of the month, the Princess's life remained almost unnaturally quiet. On 14 March Uncle Leopold heard that 'we have been for these last three weeks immured within our old palace, and I longed sadly for some gaiety. After being so very long in the country I was preparing to go out in right earnest, whereas I have only been *twice* to the play since our return, which is marvellous!' There had, however, been one dinner party at which Victoria had enjoyed some pleasant and amusing conversation with the Foreign Secretary, Lord Palmerston – 'you know how agreeable he is' – and after Easter was hoping to 'make ample amends for all this solitariness'.

Meanwhile the schoolroom routine ground on much as usual. The Dean (Dr Davys) still came every morning and the Princess practised her music, filled more pages of her sketchbook, sat for her portrait to a Mr Lane, drove out with Lehzen and Lady Flora, and continued to endure the constant unwelcome society of the Conroy family. Early in April her half-brother, the Prince of Leiningen, arrived at Kensington with his wife and children. Charles Leiningen had been a regular visitor throughout Victoria's childhood and the Duchess of Kent was devoted to him, although he had not turned out very satisfactorily. A wild, hedonistic young man, he had married beneath him against the wishes of the family, sponged shamelessly off his mother and had formed a natural alliance with John Conroy. His arrival at this juncture therefore strengthened the Conroy faction at 'our old palace', where the lines were now being drawn for the last decisive round in the struggle for power.

There were now approximately six weeks to go before the Princess came of age and it seemed that the King, though ageing (he was 72) and suffering from asthma and heart trouble, was going to have the satisfaction of handing over directly to his successor. Conroy's future thus looked bleak. Unless he could somehow bully or cajole Victoria to bind herself to him in advance, his great gamble would have failed disastrously. The only card he had left to play was her youth and inexperience and Charles Leiningen was pressed into service to try and convince Uncle Leopold that Sir John was indispensible, that Victoria, 'a young lady of 18', would be incapable of ruling England unaided and, for everyone's sake, must be persuaded to ask for an extension of the regency period.

Leopold had his own ideas about Victoria's capacity to rule and his own ideas about who should guide her first steps in the grown-up world, but he was very anxious to avoid the appearance of a breach between the Princess and her mother. Any suggestion of filial ingratitude would, he knew, be extremely damaging – any insult to the sacred institutions of motherhood and widowhood would not soon be forgiven by sentimental, middle-class, middle England – but at the same time, Victoria should certainly be given some measure of independence after her birthday. It was a situation calling for exquisite tact and Leopold therefore intended to send the invaluable Baron Stockmar to England to support the Princess during the first months of her majority and, if possible, find a compromise which would satisfy John Conroy and the Duchess.

But before this carefully thought-out plan could be put into effect, King William had intervened with no tact at all and brought the battle of Kensington to a head. On 19 May the Lord Chamberlain, Lord Conyngham, arrived at the Palace bearing a letter from the King addressed to the Princess and with strict instructions to deliver it into her own hands. This he did, after running the gauntlet of both Conroy and the Duchess, and having accomplished his mission, made his bow and retired. There were no independent witnesses of the scene which followed, but some indication of its ferocity can be gathered from a memorandum dictated by the Princess herself about a fortnight later. The King had offered her an independent income of £10,000 a year to be administered by her own Privy Purse and the opportunity to set up her own establishment if she wished. In other words, complete emancipation from the day of her eighteenth birthday, a prospect which drove Conroy and the Duchess into paroxysms of alarm. fury and wounded feelings. According to her own account, the Princess suggested that her tutor, Dr Davys, should be named as her Privy Purse as a temporary measure. When this was refused, she asked if there might be a private consultation with the Prime Minister, Lord Melbourne. This was also rejected. The storm raged for the rest of the day until Victoria, feeling 'very miserable and agitated', retired to her room. She did not go down to dinner and went exhaustedly to bed at ten o'clock.

Next morning she was confronted with the draft of a letter to the King 'written by the Duchess of Kent on Sir John Conroy's advice', for her to copy and sign. All her attempts to modify it were shouted down and at last, 'as an answer must be sent', the letter was copied and sent off to Windsor. In it the Princess, after referring to 'her youth and inexperience', declared that she wished to remain as she was, in the care of her dear Mother, and requested that any additional money which might be necessary should be given to her dear Mother, who would use it on her behalf.

William was not deceived. 'Victoria has not written that letter', was his first comment. No one was in any doubt that the Duchess and 'King John' wanted money and were determined to keep control of any extra allowance granted to the Princess on her birthday, but the Duchess, for the moment at least, was in a strong position which would be difficult to attack without creating the sort of scandal everyone was anxious to avoid. Her ominous references, in a letter to the Prime Minister, to the confidence reposed in her by the country made it clear that she was quite ready to appeal to public sympathy and represent the King's offer as a deliberate attempt 'to wound every feeling that belongs to my maternal station', as a deliberate attempt, in fact, to separate a devoted, self-sacrificing mother from a tearful child who had, of her own free will, 'told the King that she desires nothing but to be left as heretofore with Her Mother.'

Lord Melbourne, leading an increasingly shaky Whig government, was frankly nervous of the capital his Tory opponents might make out of any fresh parade of royal family feuding. He knew nothing about the bullying going on behind the scenes at Kensington (if he had, he assured Victoria later, there would have been a 'blow up'), and was concerned solely to prevent any unnecessary rocking of the boat. With this end in view, he did his best to soothe the King, saying he thought it 'highly expedient' that the Princess should remain in her mother's care for the present, since 'the public feeling and the public interest both require it'. It was, however, agreed to make another approach to the Duchess of Kent, offering to split the £10,000 between her daughter and herself – £6,000 to the Duchess, £4,000 to the Princess – a compromise which the Duchess rejected out of hand.

In the middle of all this uproar the Princess came of age. 'Today is my 18th birthday!' she wrote on Wednesday, 24 May. 'How old! and yet how far am I from being what I should be. I shall from this day take the *firm* resolution to study with renewed assiduity, to keep my attention always well fixed on whatever I am about, and to strive to become every day less trifling and more fit for what, if Heaven wills it, I'm some day to be!' That afternoon she drove out with the Duchess, Charles Leiningen's wife and 'dear Lehzen' to receive a heartening welcome from the large crowds waiting to catch a glimpse of her. Kensington village was *en fête* with flowers and flags in honour of its most distinguished resident, and a silken banner bearing the name VICTORIA 'in letters of etherial blue' floated triumphantly over the Palace itself. 'The demonstrations of loyalty and affection from all the people were highly gratifying,' noted the object of all this interest. 'The Parks and streets were thronged and everything looked like a *Gala* day.' It was the same story that evening, driving to St James's for her birthday ball. 'The Courtyard and the streets were crammed . . . and the anxiety of the people to see poor stupid me was very great, and I must say I am quite touched by it, and feel proud which I always have done of my country and of the English Nation.'

But at Kensington the tensions had risen to a pitch where even some outsiders picked up the vibrations. Mr Potter, founder of the Cobden Club and a member of one of the many deputations presenting loyal addresses at the Palace to mark Princess Victoria's coming of age, thought that the Duchess of Kent, though resplendent in evening dress and 'a magnificent plumed hat', seemed anxious and harassed'. 'The Princess stood beside her', remembered Mr Potter, 'also in an evening dress and hat. She was pretty but her face, somehow, was not quite satisfactory. I cannot tell at this distance of time what was the matter with it; but I was less taken with her than with her mother . . . . The mother did not strike us as a woman of race or breeding, only as an excellent, rather handsome person, and a lady that would make a good mother-in-law.' (Whether this last slightly ambivalent remark was intended as a compliment or not remains unclear.) The Princess herself appeared very cool and collected, and quite grown-up 'but no height'. 'The addresses were read to *her*', Mr Potter went on, 'and were answered by her mother, who read with a German accent, but otherwise well.' The Duchess, of course, was seizing the opportunity to revive all the grievances of her early widowhood and to remind the public how, alone and friendless, she had selflessly given up home and kindred to devote herself to the task of bring up her daughter as an English child.

Confused sounds of strife were now reaching Uncle Leopold in Belgium, and on 25 May he wrote:

My Dearest Child, You have had some battles and difficulties of which I am completely in the dark . . . Two things seem necessary: not to be fettered by any establishment other than what will be *comfortable to you*, and then to avoid any breach with your mother. I have fully instructed Stockmar, and I must say he left me in such good disposition that I think he will be able to be of great use to you . . . Be steady, my good child, and *not* put out by *anything*; as long as I live *you will not want a faithful friend and supporter.*

Stockmar reached Kensington on 26 May to find Victoria still resolutely refusing to promise any appointment to John Conroy, despite the combined and constant pressure of Conroy himself, her mother and Charles Leiningen; but the strain was telling on her and she welcomed Stockmar thankfully. 'He is one of those few people who tell plain honest truth, don't flatter, give wholesome necessary advice, and strive to do good and smooth all dissensions.'

But the dissensions in the family at Kensington were now beyond even Stockmar's powers to smooth. He told Leopold that the Princess seemed 'extremely jealous of what she considers to be her rights and her future power', and determined not to allow Conroy to encroach on them. He continued:

> Her feelings seem, moreover, to have been deeply wounded by what she calls 'his impudent and insulting conduct' towards her. Her affection and esteem for her mother seem likewise to have suffered by Mamma having tamely allowed Conroy to insult the Princess in her presence, and by the Princess having been frequently a witness to insults which the poor Duchess tolerated herself in the presence of her daughter . . . . O'Hum [Stockmar's nickname for Conroy] continues the system of intimidation with the genius of a madman, and the Duchess carries out all that she is instructed to do with admirable docility and perseverance . . . . The Princess continues to refuse firmly to give her Mamma her promise that she will make O'Hum her confidential adviser. Whether she will hold out, Heaven only knows, for they plague her, every hour and every day.

As May turned into June, the situation acquired an added dimension of urgency from the King's failing health. He had not been well enough to attend Victoria's birthday ball, but on 2 June was said to be recovering. Then, on Wednesday the 7th, it was announced for the first time that he was seriously ill. A few days later Charles Greville ran into Adolphus FitzClarence at Ascot and heard a first hand account of the King's state, 'which was bad enough, though not for the moment alarming; no disease, but excessive weakness without power of rallying.'

Conroy was growing desperate and made his puppet Duchess write to Lord Melbourne, telling him that her daughter wanted the government to introduce a new Regency Bill into Parliament.

Fortunately for all concerned, Stockmar got to hear of this and wasted no time in putting the Prime Minister in the picture. According to Greville, who heard the story some years later, Melbourne was 'struck all of a heap' and promised to have nothing to do with the matter. On 13 June the poor silly Duchess of Kent also wrote one of her more tactless notes to Victoria. 'You are still very young, and all your success so far has been due to your *Mother's* reputation. Do not be *too sanguine* in *your* own *talents* and *understanding*.' Victoria ignored her – she was now barely speaking to Mamma – just as she ignored similar communications from Charles Leiningen, telling him to mind his own business.

As the King's life ebbed away, the political world seethed with speculation about the new reign. Robert Peel told Charles Greville that 'it was very desirable that the young Queen should appear as much as possible emancipated from all restraint', but concluded that 'King Leopold would be her great adviser.' 'If Leopold is prudent, however,' wrote Greville, 'he will not hurry over here at the very first moment, which would look like an impatience to establish his influence, and if he does, the first result will be every sort of jealousy and discord between him and the Duchess of Kent. The elements of intrigue do not seem wanting in this embryo Court.' Speculation and uncertainty were inevitable in the circumstances, arising as they did from

> the absolute ignorance of everybody, without exception, of the character, disposition, and capacity of the Princess. She has been kept in such jealous seclusion by her Mother . . . that not one of her acquaintance, none of the Attendants at Kensington, not even the Duchess of Northumberland, her Governess, have any idea what She is, or what She promises to be.

As it happened, the Princess, unknown to Greville, had already given a very definite sign of what she promised to be. On 15 June, in a last-ditch attempt to patch things up between mother and daughter, Lord Liverpool, an old and trusted friend, had been summoned to mediate at Kensington. He saw Conroy first, who told him that Victoria was mentally unstable, 'younger in intellect than in years', and would never be able to manage without a Private Secretary who knew her well enough to control and guide her. Liverpool replied that the Princess must have no Private Secretary, an appointment created solely for the convenience of her immediate predecessors, both elderly men and infirm. Instead he offered to suggest that Sir John should be made Keeper of the Privy Purse, without political power.

Lord Liverpool then went up to the Princess, seeing her alone, probably at Stockmar's insistence. This was Victoria's opportunity and she took it with both hands. In the course of 'a highly important conversation', she told Lord Liverpool that she realized she must continue to live with her mother, but intended to put herself unreservedly in the hands of Melbourne and his Ministers as soon as she came to the Throne. As far as Conroy was concerned, there could be no question of making him Keeper of the Privy Purse or anything else. Quite apart from the 'many slights and incivilities' she had suffered at his hands, she knew things of him which 'rendered it totally impossible for her to place him in any confidential situation', things which 'she knew of herself without any other person informing her'. She then produced a statement witnessed by Lehzen dissociating herself from any schemes being concocted by Conroy and repudiating in advance any promises which might be extorted from her under duress. Liverpool was impressed by her firmness and, like Stockmar, convinced of the discomfort of her present situation.

But in spite of every discouragement, Conroy and the Duchess of Kent pressed blindly on down their self-destructive path. On 16 June Stockmar reported that the battle between mother and daughter was still going on and that the Duchess was being urged by Conroy 'to bring matters to extremities and to force her Daughter to do her will by unkindness and severity'. Conroy, in fact, faced with the ruin of all his hopes, was rapidly losing the last shreds of control and common sense. He told the Duchess, in the presence of her son Charles, that if the Princess would not see reason, 'she must be coerced'. This was too much for Leiningen and, speaking in German so that Sir John would not understand, he earnestly warned his mother against doing anything of the sort. Conroy said later he had abandoned the idea because 'he did not credit the Duchess of Kent with enough strength for such a step', and Greville heard that 'the spirit of the daughter and the timidity of the mother prevented this plot taking effect', but the fact that it was even contemplated is a clear indication of the sort of atmosphere prevailing at Kensington.

The King's condition had continued to deteriorate and by the end of the first week of June it was plain that he was dying. The 18th was Waterloo Day, the twenty-second anniversary of the battle, and the old man rather pathetically asked his doctors if they could 'tinker him up to last over that day', as he should like to live to see the sun of Waterloo set. Leopold had written telling Victoria not to be alarmed 'at the prospect of becoming perhaps sooner than you expected Queen', but the Princess was not alarmed, anything would be better than the nightmare of the past few weeks, and although she was sorry for the King – 'poor man! he was always kind to me, and he *meant* it well I know' – she could not regret the prospect of freedom and was looking forward to the event 'with calmness and quietness'. She had not been out in public for nearly a fortnight and now all her lessons had been stopped, while she and Lehzen, 'the *dearest* friend I have', waited tensely for news.

Waterloo Day came and went and Monday, 19 June passed quietly. Victoria went for a drive in the morning with Lehzen, Mary Leiningen and the children. In the afternoon she saw her brother-in-law Ernest Hohenlohe, Feodore's husband and Queen Adelaide's cousin, who brought news from Windsor that 'the poor King was *so* ill that he could hardly live through the day'. Dinner was at seven and the Princess retired to bed soon after ten, reading Sir Walter Scott's *Life* while her hair was 'undoing'.

King William died during that night and the story of how the news reached Kensington is part of the nation's folklore – the carriage bearing the emissaries from Windsor clattering into the silent courtyard at five o'clock in the morning, a flustered maidservant protesting that the Princess was sleeping sweetly and could not be disturbed, the demand to see 'the Queen', and the final dramatic appearance of the childish figure in dressing-gown and slippers, her hair hanging loose on her shoulders. All this is — or, at any rate, used to be — programmed into the consciousness of every English schoolchild, along with Alfred burning the cakes, Drake playing bowls on Plymouth Hoe and King Charles hiding in the oak tree. Victoria's own account, as recorded in her Journal for 20 June, is tersely matter-of-fact.

I was awoke at 6 o'clock by Mamma, who told me that the Archbishop of Canterbury and Lord Conyngham were here, and wished to see me. I got out of bed and went into my sitting-room (only in my dressing-gown), and *alone*, and saw them. Lord Conyngham (the Lord Chamberlain) then acquainted me that my poor Uncle, the King, was no more, and had expired at 12 minutes p. 2 this morning, and consequently that I am *Queen*.

Writing to Uncle Leopold the previous day, she had told him that she was not afraid of what lay ahead, 'and yet I do not suppose myself quite equal to all; I trust, however, that with *good-will, honesty* and *courage* I shall not, at all events *fail.*' In the Journal, the new Queen wrote: 'Since it has pleased Providence to place me in this station, I shall do my utmost to fulfil my duty towards my country; I am very young and perhaps in many, though not in all things, inexperienced, but I am sure that very few have more real good will and more real desire to do what is fit and right than I have.' Thus, optimistic, touchingly innocent, a little priggish and magnificently unprepared, the eighteen-year-old Victoria embarked on her sixty glorious years.

There were few opportunities for introspection or stage fright on that momentous Tuesday. After breakfast, during which 'good faithful Stockmar came and talked to me', there were two hasty letters to be dashed off, one to dearest Uncle and the other to Feodore. At nine o'clock Lord Melbourne arrived 'whom I saw in my room, and of COURSE *quite* ALONE as I shall *always* do all my Ministers.' There was just time to write a kind note to the widowed Aunt Adelaide before Melbourne was back again, and at half-past eleven the Queen went downstairs to the Red Saloon to

hold her first Council meeting. 'I went in of course quite alone
. . . . I was not at all nervous and had the satisfaction of hearing
that people were satisfied with what I had done and how I had done
it.'

Satisfied is scarcely an adequate description of the reaction
which followed her performance. 'There was never anything like
the first impression She produced,' wrote Charles Greville, who
was present in his official capacity of Clerk to the Council.

It was very extraordinary, and something far beyond what was looked
for. Her extreme youth and inexperience, and the ignorance of the
world concerning her, naturally excited intense curiosity to see how
She would act on this trying occasion, and there was a considerable
assemblage at the Palace, notwithstanding the short notice which was
given.

This considerable and curious assemblage crowded into the
Red Saloon saw the doors thrown open to reveal a small, black-
clad personage waiting on the threshold as her uncles, the Dukes
of Cumberland and Sussex, those two bogeymen of her early
childhood, advanced to meet her. 'She bowed to the Lords, took
her seat, and then read her speech in a clear, distinct, and audible
voice, and without any appearance of fear or embarrassment.'

The Privy Councillors were then sworn, the two Royal Dukes
first;

and [Greville went on] as these two old men, her Uncles, knelt
before her, swearing allegiance and kissing her hand, I saw her blush up
to the eyes, as if She felt the contrast between their civil and their
natural relations, and this was the only sign of emotion which She
evinced . . . . She went through the whole ceremony (occasionally
looking at Melbourne for instruction when She had any doubt what to
do, which hardly ever occurred) and with perfect calmness and self-
possession, but at the same time with a graceful modesty and propriety
particularly interesting and ingratiating.

As soon as she had retired (and Greville could see that there was
nobody waiting in the adjoining room), an astonished 'chorus of
praise and admiration' broke out on every side, for this composed
and dignified young lady bore no resemblance to the weak,

childish creature depicted by the Conroy propaganda machine. Sir Robert Peel was amazed by the new sovereign's 'apparent deep sense of her situation, her modesty, and at the same time her firmness', while the Duke of Wellington remarked that 'if She had been his own daughter he could not have desired to see her perform her part better.'

The Queen spent the afternoon writing letters and giving audiences, 'all in my room and alone'. She saw Melbourne again, Lord John Russell, the Home Secretary, Lord Albemarle, Master of the Horse, the Archbishop of Canterbury, her old friend Dr Clark, whom she appointed as her Physician, and Ernest Hohenlohe, who brought her 'a kind and very feeling letter from the poor Queen [Adelaide].' Stockmar flitted in and out all day and Lehzen, of course, could not be forgotten. 'My *dear* Lehzen will ALWAYS remain with me as my friend but will take no situation about me, and I think she is right.' Two people, though, remained conspicuously absent from the Journal entry of 20 June – Mamma and John Conroy.

Victoria took her dinner 'upstairs and alone' before receiving Lord Melbourne for the third time for 'a very important and very *comfortable* conversation'. She was already charmed by her Prime Minister, 'every time I see him I feel more confidence in him; I find him very kind in his manner too.' Not until Melbourne had left, at nearly ten p.m. and after another quick word with Stockmar, did the Queen go downstairs to say good-night to Mamma. At some time during the day she had given orders that her bed was to be moved out of her mother's room and that night, for the first time in her life, she slept alone.

On the following morning she drove in state to St James's Palace to be present at her Proclamation and at twelve o'clock held another Council meeting, 'at which She presided with as much ease as if She had been doing nothing else all her life.' Charles Greville, who had apparently forgotten that he once described her as 'a short vulgar-looking child', thought 'She looked very well', and though 'without any pretension to beauty, the gracefulness of her manner and the good expression of her countenance give her on the whole a very agreeable appearance, and with her youth inspire an excessive interest in all who approach her, and which I can't help feeling myself.'

An upsurge of enthusiasm for 'little Vic' was a natural consequence of her novelty value. For as long as most people could remember the throne had been occupied by a succession of elderly men, all more or less eccentric, unappetizing in their habits and appearance, and capable of inspiring little but indifference, pity or ridicule, when they were not being actively execrated; but in spite of every discouragement, the nation had retained its deeply-rooted sentimental affection for the monarchy as an institution and was ready to be delighted with the romantic concept of a girl Queen.

Those who came into personal contact with the girl Queen continued to find plenty to delight and surprise them. True, she was no beauty, not with that sloping chin and birdlike profile, but at eighteen her physical attractions were by no means inconsiderable – an American visitor who had seen her at Ascot in 1835 had considered her 'quite unnecessarily pretty and interesting' for one destined to be sold in marriage for political purposes. It was an ephemeral prettiness of big blue eyes, clear pink and white complexion and smooth brushed dark blonde hair which reached its full bloom in that first halcyon summer of the reign and faded quickly, but Lord Holland, who came back from a visit to Kensington 'quite a courtier and a bit of a lover', thought her 'in person, in face, and especially in eyes and complexion, a very nice girl and quite such as might tempt.' Dorothea Lieven, that acute and seasoned observer, noticed the more lasting attributes of natural dignity and grace which contrasted so strikingly with the new-minted quality of the little Queen and she wrote to Lord Aberdeen in July: 'I have seen the Queen twice . . . She has an aplomb, an air of command, of dignity, which with her baby face, her tiny figure and her pretty smile, certainly make the most extraordinary effect it is possible to imagine.'

Victoria's diminutive size – she was just under five feet tall – added to her youthful appeal. Equally captivating were her hearty laugh, showing her gums, her hearty appetite, and the obvious, unaffected thrill she was getting out of her transformation.

Everything is new and delightful to her [wrote Greville]. She is surrounded with the most exciting and interesting enjoyments; her occupations, her pleasures, her business, her Court, all present an unceasing round of gratifications. With all her prudence and discretion She has great animal spirits, and enters into the magnificent novelties of her position with the zest and curiosity of a child.

Without question the Queen, revelling in her first exhilarating taste of liberty and personal success, was quite blissfully happy, and her letters to Uncle Leopold and the pages of her Journal bubble over with her delicious sense of self-importance. She had 'an *immense* deal of *business* to do' appointing her household, receiving her Ministers and signing papers, and was loving every minute of it. 'I *delight* in this work.'

On 26 June she drove down to Windsor and 'went instantly to the poor Queen's apartments'. Aunt Adelaide was 'wonderfully calm and composed' and 'gave us many painfully interesting details of the illness and last moments of my poor Uncle the late King.' Victoria was trying very hard to mourn poor old William. 'I have heard from all sides that he was really very fond of me', she wrote on the day of the funeral, 'and I shall *ever* retain a grateful sense of his kindness to me and shall never forget him.' At the same time, there was no denying that the late King's most valuable piece of kindness to his niece had been his death, and try as she would, cheerfulness kept breaking in.

Although genuinely fond of Aunt Adelaide, there may, in the circumstances, have been an element of guilt underlying the tender consideration which Victoria heaped on the Queen Dowager and which attracted much favourable comment; but it was clear from the outset that she appeared to feel little sense of obligation towards the other dowager in her life. It was not for nothing that the word 'alone' had appeared frequently and so emphatically in the Journal during those first few weeks and the Duchess of Kent, relegated literally overnight, was already sorrowfully reaping the bitter harvest of the past ten years. She had been present at St James's for the Proclamation, but 'was not prominent'. Lord Holland thought the 'poor woman' would count for little or nothing in the new Court, and Charles Greville soon heard that Mamma never appeared at Kensington these days and that 'her influence is very silently exercised, if at all'.

Sir John Conroy, too, had received his come-uppance, the Queen making it perfectly plain from the morning of her accession that she never wished to see or speak to him again. She remained impervious to emotional appeals from the Duchess to be allowed to take him, just this first day, to witness the Proclamation, and when Mamma unwisely tried to insist, she got a royal snub for her pains. As for Sir John, he wasted no time in seeking out Baron Stockmar to admit defeat and present a paper setting out his conditions for retirement from the arena; but when the Baron, in his customary role of intermediary, waylaid Lord Melbourne with the list of Conroy's demands: a peerage, the Grand Cross of the Bath, a pension of £3,000 a year and a seat on the Privy Council no less, the Prime Minister was aghast. 'This is really too bad!' he exclaimed, dropping the paper several times in his agitation. 'Have you ever heard such impudence!'

However, Stockmar, with his knowledge of past events, insisted that it was essential to buy Conroy off before the damaging coolness between the Queen and her mother could be brought to an end. Besides this, there was no denying that his eighteen years of service to the widowed Duchess gave him some claim on the Queen's generosity. Melbourne, therefore, reluctantly conceded the pension and added a baronetcy, following this up with the even more reluctant promise of an Irish peerage when one should become available, if he (Melbourne) was still in office at the time.

But Stockmar and Melbourne had seriously misjudged Conroy's staying power. He told Stockmar 'sneeringly' that he did not consider himself bound to fulfil his part of the bargain until the Queen had kept hers. Unhappily, Victoria had no power to dismiss him from her mother's household, and the Duchess herself, dependent as ever, clung stubbornly to her old friend. So he continued to lurk malevolently in the background like the bad fairy at a christening and, like the bad fairy, was to cause more mischief before he had finished.

But in July 1837 the Queen was not unduly concerned. She was taken up with preparations for moving into Buckingham Palace and writing to invite Leopold and dearest Aunt Louise to come and stay for 'a fortnight at *least*'. They could bring as many gentlemen, ladies, etc., etc., as they pleased and 'I should be too happy and proud to have you *under my own* roof.' Life was opening out before her in a glorious multicoloured vista of business and amusement, and Conroy and Mamma no longer had the power to dismay her.

Chapter Nine
Queen of Such a Nation

Poor little Queen! she is at an age at which a girl can hardly be trusted to choose a bonnet for herself; yet a task is laid upon her from which an archangel might shrink.

Thomas Carlyle

The Queen left Kensington for Buckingham Palace on 13 July.

Though I rejoice to *go* into B.P. for many reasons [she confided to her Journal], it is not without feelings of regret that I shall bid adieu *for ever* (that is to say *for ever* as a DWELLING), to this my birth-place, where I have been born and bred, and to which I am really attached! I have seen my dear sister married here, I have seen many of my dear relations here, I have had pleasant balls and *delicious* concerts here . . . . I have held my first Council here too! I have gone through painful and disagreeable scenes here, 'tis true, but still I am fond of the poor old Palace. . . . The poor rooms look so sad and deserted, everything being taken away.

Her new home was on a very different scale. Buckingham House, an unpretentious redbrick mansion, had originally been acquired by George III in 1762 as a convenient domestic annexe to St James's Palace and a dower house for Queen Charlotte. In 1825, George IV, with John Nash as his architect, embarked on an elaborate and expensive rebuilding programme, but the venture made heavy weather from the beginning. The King never really made up his mind whether he wanted a 'residence' or a palace. Nash was unhappy, feeling that he had not been allowed to do himself justice professionally. His designs were unpopular, the money ran out and in 1828 the whole project came under investigation by a parliamentary Select Committee. During the King's last illness work came to a standstill and after his death Nash was dismissed.

The unfinished palace had become something of a white elephant, and an uncommonly ugly one in most people's opinion, but in view of the huge sums already spent on it another architect, Edward Blore, was called in to complete the interior and at least make the place habitable. No one cared for the result. Mr Creevey thought there had never been 'such a specimen of wicked, vulgar profusion' and was revolted by the raspberry-coloured pillars and other evidence of costly bad taste, while homely Sailor William regarded the enormous, uncosy Palladian façade with undisguised loathing. When the Houses of Parliament were burnt down in 1834 he offered it as a permanent gift for the accommodation of the Lords and Commons, adding hopefully 'that it would be the finest thing in Europe'. His offer was rejected, but William and Adelaide never moved in themselves. In fact, Buckingham Palace was only just ready for occupation in July 1837.

A brand new Palace seemed just the thing for a brand new Queen, although, as shrewd old William had suspected, it was to prove neither comfortable nor convenient as a home. Bad smells rose from the basement kitchens and the chimneys smoked 'so abominably' that it was often impossible to light fires in many of the rooms. But the eighteen-year-old Victoria saw nothing amiss, not even with the raspberry-coloured pillars, and was uninterested in domestic details. She was 'much pleased' with her new rooms, which were 'high, pleasant and cheerful'. She spent a little time arranging her possessions and made the acquaintance of her two new Maids of Honour in waiting, before taking a walk round the gardens with Mamma, noting with satisfaction that 'dear Dashy' seemed quite happy in his new surroundings.

The days which followed the great move were crammed with still more delights, more thrills and new experiences. On 14 July the Queen drove to St James's in full dress and wearing the blue ribbon and star of the Garter. She received three Addresses and then held a chapter of the Garter. On Monday the 17th she went in state to the House of Lords to prorogue Parliament. On the 19th she received two more Addresses, gave audiences to various foreign ambassadors and then held a levée at which her hand was kissed 'nearly 3000 times!' It would have been an exhausting programme for the most seasoned monarch, but Victoria was undaunted and assured Uncle Leopold that she felt 'quite frisky' and not at all tired. Leopold, though considerably taken aback by the astonishing metamorphosis of demure little Princess into self-confident young Queen, was too tactful to let his surprise show. 'Your *spirit* in all these new and trying proceedings makes me *happy beyond expression*,' he wrote. 'Believe me, with courage and honesty, you will get on beautifully and successfully.'

A great deal of Victoria's initial success was, of course, due to Leopold's and Lehzen's early training in discretion and self-control, to her own common sense and the naturally ebullient temperament which had responded so enthusiastically to the challenges of her new life. But she had also been exceptionally fortunate in the personality of her first Prime Minister. William Lamb, second Viscount Melbourne, born into the exclusive inner circle of the Whig aristocracy, was a charmer and, at fifty-eight, still a strikingly handsome man. A cultivated, experienced man of the world, well-bred, sociable, easy-going and excellent company, he was uniquely qualified to guide the steps of a novice Queen.

The Queen herself certainly thought so. She had taken to her Premier at their first meeting – 'He is a very straightforward, honest, clever and good man' – and as the weeks passed and their friendship ripened, she grew more and more dependent on him. If Uncle Leopold had been her second father, Melbourne was rapidly becoming her third, and his comforting, supportive presence gave her the sense of security she craved. 'I feel *so safe* when he speaks to me and is with me.'

Charles Greville, watching from the sidelines, thought this very understandable.

No man is more formed to ingratiate himself with her than Melbourne [he commented]. He treats her with unbounded consideration and respect, he consults her tastes and wishes, and he puts her at her ease by his frank and natural manners, while He amuses her by the quaint, queer, epigrammatic turn of his mind, and his varied knowledge upon all subjects.

Victoria was entranced by Melbourne's 'stores of knowledge', hanging on his words and painstakingly collecting his wise and funny sayings. Melbourne, for his part, took his responsibilities with commendable seriousness, fully conscious that it had become his province 'to educate, instruct and form the most interesting mind and character in the world.' But although he talked to the Queen at length about the duties, rigours and limitations of her constitutional position and did his best to fill the yawning gaps in her political knowledge, their sessions were by no means all tutorial. They chatted endlessly about everything under the sun: about Shakespeare, about Christian names, bringing up children, euthanasia, horse racing, clothes, education, foreign affairs, the royal family, books, plays and people. Melbourne's conversation, his anecdotes, his sophisticated, often unconventional opinions, came as a revelation to Victoria, widening her horizons and helping to blow away the stuffiness of the Kensington schoolroom. She soon found that she could talk freely herself to this sympathetic listener, and it wasn't long before she was confiding to him all the details of her unhappy past.

Such a close association between Queen and Prime Minister was unusual enough to attract attention, the polite world deriving considerable amusement from the spectacle of free-spoken, lounging Melbourne on his best behaviour, carefully watching his language and sitting upright on a hard chair in the nursery atmosphere of the new Court, where evening pastimes commonly included the playing of round games and the putting together of 'dissected pictures' – a primitive form of jigsaw-puzzle – while the Duchess of Kent yawned over the whist table. But although there were a few gibes about 'Mrs Melbourne', the relationship was so plainly innocent that gossip found little to fasten on.

The gossip-mongers were, however, distinctly intrigued by the Queen's apparent estrangement from her Mamma. Victoria's public manners were irreproachable, but Mr Greville heard there was good reason to believe that 'She has no great affection for her mother. . . . She sees hardly anything of the Duchess, who never goes to see her without previously asking leave, and when the Queen gets messages or notes from her mother She frequently sends verbal answers that She is engaged and cannot receive her.' The total, 'almost contemptuous' banishment of Conroy had, of course, been noted with interest. 'He has never once been invited to the Palace or distinguished by the slightest mark of personal favour', wrote Greville, who considered that the contrast between the Queen's financial generosity to her mother's major domo and her ostentatious refusal to receive him or his family at Court presented 'a remarkable and rather mysterious appearance'. It was also, inevitably, reviving all the old suspicions about the exact nature of the Duchess of Kent's connection with her 'confidential servant'.

As well as the eclipse of Conroy and her own painful insignificance under the new dispensation, the unlucky Duchess was having to suffer the mortification of watching Lehzen's influence grow. The former governess, now respectfully referred to by all and sundry as the Baroness, had been given the ambiguous title of Lady Attendant and installed in apartments adjoining the Queen's. Lehzen, 'the person in the world She loves best', was in and out all day – no question of Victoria's ever being too busy to see *her* –and acted as unofficial personal secretary cum permanent lady-in-waiting.

Although she had brought so many of her present troubles on herself, it's difficult not to feel rather sorry for the Duchess, but she was typically not helping matters by irritating her daughter with constant complaints and, worse, broadcasting her overwhelming 'vexation and disappointment' to the world. When that well-known intelligencer Dorothea Lieven dined at the Palace at the end of July, the Queen, forewarned by the vigilant Uncle Leopold, was careful to talk 'of nothing but commonplaces', but Mamma seized the opportunity to unbosom herself. She told the fascinated Princess Lieven that she no longer counted for anything, 'that for eighteen years this child had been the sole object of her life, of all her thoughts and hopes, and now She was taken from her, and there was an end of all for which she had lived heretofore.' Madame de Lieven murmured tactfully that she would have thought her Royal Highness would be the happiest of mortals to see her child's prodigious success. Surely 'the praise and admiration of which she was universally the object' ought to be sufficient triumph and glory for any mother? But this was not at all what the Duchess wanted to hear. She shook her head, smiling sadly and indicating that the accomplishment of her wishes 'had only made her to the last degree unhappy.' 'King William is revenged', commented Charles Greville, 'and if his ghost is an ill-natured and vindictive shade, it may rejoice in the sight of this bitter disappointment of his enemy.'

Meanwhile, the child's triumph showed no signs of abating. 'Everyone continues to sing the Queen's praises,' wrote Lady Cowper, 'there is but one mind on that question . . . I have never heard anyone speak a single word in dispraise of her, or find fault with her in any way – this is indeed a rare happiness.' Victoria *was* very happy, radiantly so, in fact, the only shadows on her horizon being the tiresomeness of Mamma and slight anxiety over the outcome of the elections which had to follow a change of monarch. The Whigs had been losing ground steadily ever since the passing of the Great Reform Bill (which ironically had enfranchised some of the most conservative elements in the country), and the Queen made no secret of her partisanship – the defeat of dear Lord Melbourne was simply not to be thought of. However, all went well, or reasonably so, and Victoria was able to write to Leopold on 9 August: 'With respect to the Elections, they are, I'm thankful to say, rather favourable, though not quite so much so as we could wish. But upon the whole we shall have as good a House as we had, and *I* hope (as Lord Melbourne does also), a more moderate one than the last one.'

On 22 August the Court moved to Windsor. At first it all seemed strange and a little sad. 'I cannot help feeling as though *I* was not the Mistress of the House and as if I was to see the poor King and Queen.' But any initial sense of awkwardness soon wore off. The local people were 'remarkably friendly and civil', Lord Melbourne came to stay and a week after her arrival at the Castle, Victoria had 'the inexpressible *happiness and joy*' of welcoming *dearest most beloved* Uncle Leopold and Aunt Louise as guests in her *own* house.

The visit was a huge success, and the Queen rejoiced to see how well Uncle and Lord Melbourne got on together. 'Uncle and he perfectly agree in Politics too, which are the *best* there are.' She had several 'very interesting and highly important conversations' with them both and only wished she had time to take *minutes*, for 'the sound observations they make, and the impartial advice they give me would make a most interesting book.'

Victoria had taken up riding again for the first time since her illness at Ramsgate two years before, and the Household was out on horseback every day – cavalcades of up to thirty riders with the little Queen, pink-cheeked and bright-eyed in their midst. There were walks in the Park in glorious summer weather and in the evenings everyone was very merry, talking and laughing and playing draughts or spillikins or 'German Tactics' round a big mahogany table. Aunt Louise challenged her niece to a game of chess, but Lord Melbourne, Lord Palmerston and Sir John Hobhouse became so excited and offered so much contradictory advice that 'between them all, I got quite beat, and Aunt Louise triumphed over my Council of Ministers!' Meanwhile, Uncle Leopold was taking the opportunity to offer some advice to his sister, with the result, so Princess Lieven was informed, that the Duchess of Kent appeared in better spirits and was even talking of casting off her gentleman, 'which would be a wise step for her as for everyone else, for they say he bullies her incessantly.'

The days flew by – 'how quickly time passes when one is happy' – and the visitors departed. Victoria shed tears to see them go, *how* she would miss them, but cheered up again at the prospect of reviewing the Life Guards, the Grenadiers and a detachment of Lancers in the Home Park. Dressed in a habit of dark blue with red collar and cuffs – an adaptation of the Windsor Uniform 'which all my gentlemen wear' – she rode up to where a sergeant was stationed with the Colours, stopped and was saluted by the regiments. 'I saluted them by putting my hand to my cap like the officers do, and was much admired for my manner of doing so', she reported complacently. She then cantered up to inspect the lines, with the ladies and gentlemen of the household, including Lord Melbourne, following in carriages, before returning to her original position to watch the march past and manoeuvres, which included much firing and skirmishing. It all went off splendidly. Leopold, her mount, behaved 'most beautifully', even when the bands played right in his face, and the Queen, swelling with martial pride, 'felt for the first time like a man, as if I could fight myself at the head of my Troops.'

The enchanted summer was almost over now and on 3 October they went for a last, beautiful ride all round Virginia Water on a perfect evening, 'not a breath of air, and hotter coming home than going out'. Next morning the Court would be off to Brighton, but Victoria was '*very sorry* indeed' to be leaving Windsor. 'I passed such a very pleasant time here,' she wrote in her Journal that night;

the pleasantest summer I EVER passed in *my life*, and I shall never forget this first summer of my Reign. I have had the *great* happiness of having my beloved Uncle and Aunt here with me, I have had very pleasant people and kind friends staying with me, and I have had *delicious* rides which have done me the world of good. Lord Melbourne rode near .me the whole time. The more I see of him and the more I know of him, the more I like and appreciate his fine and honest character. I have seen a great deal of him, every day, these last 5 weeks, and I have always found him in good humour, kind, good, and most agreeable . . .. I am very fond of him.

The Queen did not care very much for Brighton. The Pavilion was 'a strange, odd Chinese looking thing both inside and out' and she could only see 'a little morsel of the sea' from her windows. But she was still ready to be pleased, and old Mr Creevey, who dined at the Pavilion on 12 October, found her quite delightful. There was a slight contretemps when he was presented. 'The poor little thing could not get her glove off. I was never so annoyed in my life; yet what could I do? But she blushed and laughed and pulled till the thing was done, and I kissed her hand.' At dinner he was placed next to the Duchess of Kent, who was 'agreeable and chatty', but Creevey could not take his eyes off 'Vic'.

A more homely little being you never beheld *when she is at her ease*, and she is evidently dying to be always more so. She laughs in real earnest, opening her mouth as wide as it can go . . .. She eats quite as heartily as she laughs, I think I may say she gobbles . . .. She blushes and laughs every instant in so natural a way as to disarm anybody. Her voice is perfect, and so is the expression of her face when she means to say or do a pretty thing.

At the beginning of November she was back at Buckingham Palace and on the 9th, dressed 'in *all my finery*', drove in state to the Guildhall for the Lord Mayor's banquet through 'the greatest concourse of people I ever witnessed' and preceded by 'all my suite, the Royal Family, etc.' After receiving an Address from the Recorder of London and replying to it, she knighted the Sheriffs, 'one of whom was Mr Montefiore, a Jew, an excellent man; and I was very glad that I was the first to do what *I* think quite right.'

Coming home, at about half-past eight,

the crowd was, if possible, greater than it had been when I went in the day; and they cheered me excessively as I came along. The streets were beautifully illuminated on all sides, and looked very brilliant and gay. . . . I cannot say HOW gratified, and HOW *touched* I am by the very brilliant, affectionate, cordial, enthusiastic and *unanimous* reception I met with in this the *greatest* Metropolis in the *World* . . . . I feel *deeply grateful* for this display of affection and unfeigned loyalty and *attachment* from my good people.

Victoria had scored another triumph. 'Our young Queen's reception in the City was magnificent', wrote Lady Cowper in a burst of patriotic fervour, 'loyalty, worship, applause . . . *and hardly a soldier anywhere*; this is the sort of thing that is only seen in England.' But while there was still nothing but loyalty and affection in public, the young Queen was once again having to contend with 'vexation' and unpleasantness at home. Any improvement effected by Uncle Leopold had been short-lived and the Duchess of Kent was back at her old tricks, making scenes and campaigning for the rehabilitation of Conroy. With almost pathological obtuseness she had nagged for permission to take him with her to the Guildhall.

I conjure you for the sake of your mother to relent in your line of conduct towards Sir John and his family [she wrote in one of her numerous notes to her daughter]. If you cannot like, at least forgive, and do not exclude and mark him . . .. The Queen should forget what displeased the Princess. Recollect I have the greatest regard for Sir John, I cannot forget what he has done for me and for you, although he had the misfortune to displease *you*.

Victoria would not relent. Not after Sir John's past conduct and especially after 'the unaccountable manner in which he behaved towards me a short while before I came to the Throne.' Nor would she listen to the Duchess's complaints about precedence, or her optimistic attempts to claim the rank of honorary Queen Mother. The Duchess (or, more likely Conroy) had dug up the dubious precedent of Lady Margaret Beaufort, mother of Henry vii, but Victoria was not impressed – it would do Mamma no good and undoubtedly give grave offence to the other royal ladies.

Trouble was brewing, too, over the Duchess's finances. It appeared that she was in debt to the tune of at least £55,000, and she and Conroy wanted the Queen to agree to settle more than half this amount out of her Privy Purse. But Lord Melbourne would not hear of such a thing – it was impossible and quite out of the question. After some bickering, it was decided to ask Parliament to increase the Duchess's allowance to £30,000 a year, on condition that she undertook to set aside an annual sum to pay off her debts; but Lord Melbourne told the Queen, 'with tears in his eyes', that the vote had only been carried 'out of respect and consideration for me'. A few months later, however, Victoria heard, to her consternation, that Mamma was in difficulties again and had been borrowing from the bank.

Doubts about Conroy's honesty and his management of the Duchess of Kent's affairs had already been raised in *The Times*, which wanted to know where 'a certain newly created baronet' had found the money to purchase a certain estate in Wales'. Although Conroy successfully sued the editor of *The Times* for libel, the doubts remained and were shared by the Queen and her Prime Minister, but, thanks to the stubborn loyalty of the Duchess of Kent, it was to be many years before the full extent of his peculations finally came to light. Meanwhile, there really seemed no solution to the problem. Stockmar and Lord Liverpool were inclined to blame Melbourne for his failure to get rid of Sir John, but unless and until O'Hum could be persuaded to resign his post in her household, or the Duchess herself took the initiative, there was little anyone could do, short of creating a first-class public row and risking an irreparable breach between mother and daughter.

The Queen's own financial affairs had been settled in December 1837, when Parliament voted her a Civil List of £385,000 a year for life. To Victoria, accustomed to ten pounds a month pocket money, this naturally seemed affluence beyond compare, but unlike her father and her uncles she was careful and sensible about money. At the same time, she showed a pleasing generosity. '*A propos* to our little Vic', wrote Thomas Creevey, 'we are all enchanted with her for her munificence to the FitzClarences. Besides their pensions out of the public pension list, they had nearly £10,000 a year given them by their father out of his privy purse, every farthing of which the Queen continues out of *her* privy purse, with quantities of other such things.' Queen Adelaide was touchingly grateful for this evidence of respect to King William's memory, and the *bâtards* themselves were surprised and delighted – as were the Duke of Kent's surviving creditors, when his daughter promptly set about the formidable task of paying off his debts.

Victoria's first Christmas as Queen was spent at Buckingham Palace and, apart from a short visit to Windsor in January, the Court stayed in Town through the winter. The Queen went occasionally to the theatre – she saw a performance of *Hamlet* at Covent Garden on 26 January – and read her first novel, Walter Scott's *The Bride of Lammermoor*. She had a new horse, 'a most *delightful* creature, called Tartar', and riding remained her favourite recreation. Early in March she went nearly as far as Harrow, 'where one could fancy oneself 2 or 300 miles from London', and back through Kilburn and down the Edgware Road. Towards the end of the month, the cavalcade made an ambitious excursion to Richmond Park and home over Wimbledon

Common and Vauxhall Bridge, 'having ridden 22 MILES!!! . . . It was as hot as summer, and *going* I thought I should have melted . . .. It was a heavenly day.'

She was still working hard learning her trade. Lord Palmerston shared the task of tutoring her, with special reference to foreign affairs, but although the Queen liked him and found him 'clever' and 'agreeable', Melbourne kept the first place in her affections. She had now heard an expurgated version of the tragic history of his marriage to the eccentric Caroline Ponsonby, 'the strangest person that ever lived, really half crazy, and quite so when she died', and how she had 'teazed that excellent Lord Melbourne in every way, dreadfully, and quite embittered his life.'

This knowledge added an extra romantic appeal to Lord Melbourne's glamour, but Victoria had apparently not been enlightened about the scandal of Caroline Lamb's notorious infatuation for Lord Byron, or she would scarcely have raised the subject of that interesting poet, asking about his appearance and 'countenance'. She continued to *delight* in Melbourne's conversation. 'He knows about everybody and everything; *who* they were and what they did; and he imparts all his knowledge in such a kind and agreeable manner; it does me a world of good, and his conversations always improve one greatly.' The constant daily companionship of her Prime Minister had, in fact, become essential to the Queen's comfort. 'He has something so fatherly, and so affectionate and kind in him that one must love him.' The relationship was by no means one-sided. 'I have no doubt that he [Melbourne] is passionately fond of her as He might be of his daughter if he had one', wrote Charles Greville, 'and the more because he is a man with a capacity for loving without having anything in the world to love.' Greville paid due tribute to Melbourne's 'discretion and purity', but at the same time could see dangers in 'a connexion of so close and affectionate a nature between the young Queen and her Minister; for whenever the Government, which hangs by a thread, shall be broken up, the parting will be painful, and their subsequent relations will not be without embarrassment to themselves, nor fail to be the cause of jealousy in others.'

These were prescient words and on 12 May, when a government defeat was threatened over the Irish Tithes Bill, the Queen, choked with tears, could scarcely find words to express 'HOW *low*, HOW *sad*' she felt when she thought of 'the POSSIBILITY of this excellent and truly kind man [Lord Melbourne] not *remaining* my Minister!' But the danger passed. '*We* had a majority of 19', and Queen and Minister could return to pleasanter topics, such as how did Lord M. like her hair done in plaits round her ears? 'He said, looking at me and making one of his funny faces, "It's pretty; isn't it rather curious – something new?" '

On 24 May Victoria entered her twentieth year, 'which I think *very* old!' Looking back over the past twelve months, she felt 'more grateful than I can express for ALL the VERY GREAT BLESSINGS I have received since my last birthday.' She grieved, quite sincerely, for the loss of one old friend – Mrs Louis, the housekeeper at Claremont who had so doted on the poor little fatherless princess, had died in April – but 'though I have *lost* a *dear* friend, I can never be *thankful* enough for the *true, faithful, honest, kind* one I've GAINED since last year, which is my *excellent* Lord Melbourne.' Typically, Queen Victoria saw nothing in the least incongruous in bracketing cousin Charlotte's old dresser with her Prime Minister.

She enjoyed every minute of her birthday ball, which, as so often in the past, she opened with her cousin George Cambridge, and didn't get to bed till five o'clock in broad daylight. 'I have spent the happiest birthday that I have had for years,' she told Uncle Leopold; 'oh *how* different to last year!'

Now the Coronation was almost upon her. In order to do justice to an event which, 'from the age and sex of the Sovereign, excited an extraordinary degree of interest among all classes', Parliament had voted a sum of £200,000 to be spent on the celebrations. Westminster Abbey was to be sumptuously decorated with swags of crimson and gold, a great two-day Fair with balloon ascents was to be held in Hyde Park and there were to be illuminations, firework displays and bands playing in all the royal parks. It had been decided not to revive the traditional coronation banquet, cut by William IV for reasons of economy, but to replace it by a state procession through the streets of Westminster, so that as many people as possible would get a sight of the Queen.

As the great day approached, London seethed with activity. The pavements along the processional route were obstructed with 'a vast line of scaffolding', and passers-by had to pick their way through piles of timber and run the risk of being stunned by falling fragments. The air resounded with hammering and knocking and the traffic jams were frightful.

> The uproar, the confusion, the crowd, the noise are indescribable [wrote Greville irritably]. . . . Not a mob here or there, but the town all mob, thronging, bustling, gaping and gazing at everything, at anything, or at nothing; the Park one vast encampment, with banners floating on the tops of the tents, and still the roads are covered, the railroads loaded with arriving multitudes . . . . In short, it is very curious, but uncommonly tiresome, and the sooner it is over the better.

On Wednesday, 27 June the Queen drove through all the exciting bustle and confusion to the Abbey to see the preparations and try the thrones she was to sit on next day – just as well, as they were both too low. No one got much sleep that night. Victoria was woken at four by the guns in the Park and couldn't get to sleep again for the noise going on outside. She was up at seven, 'feeling strong and well' and peeping out of the window at 'the crowds of people up to Constitution Hill, soldiers, bands etc.' She managed to swallow a few mouthfuls of breakfast while she dressed and by half-past nine was ready in the white satin petticoat, crimson velvet kirtle and diamond circlet she had worn for the prorogation of Parliament. Uncle Ernest, Charles Leiningen and Feodore came to see her before she set off, and punctually at ten o'clock she got into the State Coach with the Duchess of Sutherland, her Mistress of the Robes, and Lord Albemarle, Master of the Horse, and began her progress via Constitution Hill, Piccadilly, St James's Street, Pall Mall, Cockspur Street, Charing Cross, Whitehall and Parliament Street to the west door of the Abbey. 'It was a fine day', she wrote afterwards, 'and the crowds of people exceeded

what I have ever seen . . .. Their good humour and excessive
loyalty was beyond everything, and I really cannot say *how* proud I
feel to be the Queen of *such* a *Nation.*'

On arrival at the Abbey she was met by her eight young trainbearers, wearing dresses of white satin and silver tissue, with
wreaths of silver corn ears and pink rosebuds on their heads. The
Queen's mantle of velvet and ermine was arranged, and 'the
young ladies having properly got hold of it', the procession, led by
the great Officers of State bearing the regalia, moved off. As she
entered the nave Victoria was seen to falter momentarily, turn
pale and catch her breath, and certainly the scene which greeted
her was enough to take any nineteen-year-old girl's breath away –
the great grey church shimmering with crimson and gold, the gold
plate banked on the altar, the clergy in their gorgeous encrusted
copes, the massed ranks of the peeresses ablaze with diamonds,
the foreign dignitaries in their unfamiliar gaudy uniforms stiff
with gold lace and jewels. Prince Esterhazy, it was said, looked as
if he had been 'caught out in a rain of diamonds and come in
dripping'. Harriet Martineau, bluestocking and battleaxe,
recorded that 'about nine, the first gleams of the sun slanted into
the Abbey . . . I had never before seen the full effect of diamonds.
As the light travelled, every peeress shone like a rainbow. The
brightness, vastness, and dreamy magnificence of the scene
produced a strange effect.'

But if the little Queen was temporarily stunned, it was nothing
to the effect she produced on her audience. Her tiny, graceful
figure seemed to float in a cloud of white and silver, and her
poignantly childish appearance roused a wave of emotion almost
unbearable in its intensity. 'Everyone literally gasped for breath',
wrote one spectator, '. . . and the rails of the gallery trembled in
one's hands from the . . . trembling of the spectators. I never saw
anything like it. Tears would have been a relief.'

As the anthem 'I was glad' came to an end, the boys of
Westminster School exercised their historic privilege of chanting
the *Vivat* and the Queen moved to a chair in the carpeted space
known as 'the Theatre', kneeling for a moment of private prayer.
The Recognition followed, the Archbishop of Canterbury

presenting the new Sovereign to the four corners of the Abbey, and then the Acclamation – a great reverberating shout of 'God Save Queen Victoria'. The Litany was recited, the offerings made on the High Altar and, after a sermon preached by the Bishop of London, the Queen took the Coronation Oath. The choir sang *Veni Creator Spiritus* and the Queen retired to St Edward's Chapel, 'a small dark place immediately behind the Altar', where she exchanged her crimson robes for 'a singular sort of little gown of linen trimmed with lace' and the Supertunica of cloth of gold. She returned, bareheaded, to sit in St Edward's Chair, while four Knights of the Garter hoisted a canopy of cloth of gold over her and the Archbishop performed the Anointing: 'As Solomon was anointed king by Zadok the priest and Nathan the prophet, so be you anointed, blessed, and consecrated Queen over this people, whom the Lord Your God hath given you to rule and govern.'

Unfortunately, as the most solemn moments of the ceremony approached, the want of rehearsal among the officiating clergy had become painfully apparent. There was, according to Greville, 'continual difficulty and embarrassment' and the Queen was obliged to appeal to John Thynne, the Sub-Dean, 'Pray tell me what I am to do, for they don't know.' She was invested with the Dalmatic Robe, stiff with gold, and the Sceptre, but, despite her anguished protests, the Archbishop insisted on crushing the Ring on to the wrong finger. The Bishop of Durham gave her the Orb too soon and it was so heavy that she nearly dropped it, but the actual crowning was 'a most beautiful and impressive moment'. All the peers and peeresses put on their coronets, the trumpets brayed, the drums beat and the whole congregation cheered and shouted and waved hats and handkerchiefs, while, outside, the Tower and Park guns thundered in salute.

Consecrated, crowned and enthroned, the Queen now received the Homage. When it came to Lord Melbourne's turn to kneel and swear to become her liege man of life and limb and of earthly worship, 'he pressed my hand', wrote Victoria, 'and I grasped his with all my heart, at which he looked up with his eyes filled with tears and seemed much touched, as he was, I observed, throughout the whole ceremony.' A more critical observer – it

was the young Benjamin Disraeli – remarked that Melbourne
held the Sword of State 'like a butcher' and looked singularly
uncouth, with his robes under his feet and his coronet over his
nose. The Queen would not have been amused.

There was another 'most dear being present at this ceremony in
the box immediately above the Royal Box, and who witnessed all;
it was my dearly beloved Lehzen, whose eyes I caught when on the
Throne and we exchanged smiles.' Lehzen was sharing this
moment of supreme triumph with her old friend Baroness Späth,
who had come to London with Feodore.

There was, the Queen noted, a special round of applause for the
Duke of Wellington and for Lords Grey and Melbourne as they did
their homage, but the real sensation was reserved for old Lord
Rolle, '82 and dreadfully infirm', who fell and 'rolled quite down'
the steps of the Throne, but was fortunately not the least hurt.
'When he attempted to reascend them', wrote Victoria briskly, 'I
got up and advanced to the end of the steps, in order to prevent
another fall.' This pretty act of kindness made a great impression
on the congregation – at least among those members of it who
were not too busy fighting each other for the Coronation medals
being scattered by the Treasurer of the Household in the choir and
lower galleries.

When the Homage was over, the Queen removed her Crown
and took the Sacrament, another emotional moment. Then, once
more crowned and robed, she returned to the Throne, leaning on
Lord Melbourne's arm. Towards the end of the service the Bishop
of Bath and Wells inadvertently turned over two pages together
and told the Queen the ceremony was over. She withdrew to St
Edward's Chapel, but had to be hastily fetched back when the
mistake was discovered.

At last it *was* over. The Queen retired again to the Confessor's
Chapel, where a buffet had been laid out on the altar. Lord
Melbourne, worn out with lugging the heavy Sword of State
about, refreshed himself with a glass of wine and Victoria
thankfully took her Crown off for a few minutes. A special light-
weight crown had been made for her, but even so it weighed
nearly three pounds and hurt her a good deal. Finally, robed now

in purple velvet, with the Crown back in place, she took the Orb in her left hand and the Sceptre in her right, and 'thus *loaded* proceeded through the Abbey, which resounded with cheers'. In the Robing Room by the west door there was a delay while the Queen soaked her hand in iced water in order to remove the Ring, 'which I at last did with great pain', and at half-past four she re-entered the State Coach to return to Buckingham Palace through crowds which seemed, if possible, to have increased in size and enthusiasm.

After dinner on that long, dreamlike day – 'the *proudest* of my life' – the Queen sat on a sofa mulling it all over with Lord Melbourne, who thought everything had gone off *so* well. 'And you did it beautifully,' he said, 'every part of it, with so much taste; it's a thing that you can't give a person advice upon; it must be left to a person.' At about half-past ten Victoria began to think about bed. 'You may depend upon it, you are more tired than you think you are', said Lord Melbourne. But in the end she stayed out on Mamma's balcony till midnight, looking at the fireworks in Green Park 'which were quite beautiful'.

The Coronation was generally considered to have been a huge success. The foreign visitors had all been duly impressed – 'nothing can be seen like it in any other country' – and the vast crowds, estimated at between four and five hundred thousand, who had poured into London for the spectacle had been remarkably good-humoured and well-behaved. One unlucky individual was killed when a coping stone fell on his head during an unscheduled balloon descent in Marylebone Lane, but in general there seem to have been astonishingly few incidents. 'Indeed,' commented the *Annual Register*, 'the peaceable and orderly behaviour of hundreds of thousands of people in the middle and lower ranks of life, during a long day of excitement . . . was not the least striking characteristic of the proceedings, and drew forth the admiration of all the foreigners present.'

Certainly great efforts had been made to please the people. 'To amuse and interest *them* seems to have been the principal object', remarked Charles Greville rather sourly. The illuminations of streets and public buildings were magnificent, and, it was believed, grander than any previously seen in the metropolis, while the fireworks had also been provided 'on the most liberal scale'. The great Fair in Hyde Park – a paradise of theatres, taverns, booths, stalls and sideshows – went on for four days and was visited by the Queen herself on the Friday; and there were illuminations, fireworks, processions, public dinners and feasts for the poor in almost every town up and down the country. Cambridge, where no fewer than 13,000 persons were feasted on Parker's Piece, seems to have taken the prize for liberality.

It was an exceptionally brilliant season and the Coronation festivities went on well into July. There was a State Ball, a levée, a Coronation drawing-room and on the 9th a Review in Hyde Park in honour of Marshal Soult, Wellington's old adversary, who, in typically English fashion, had received the warmest welcome of all the foreign visitors. In view of the enormous crowds expected to be present, Melbourne and the military authorities insisted that the Queen must, on this occasion, be content to inspect her troops from an open carriage, and she had yielded, though bitterly disappointed 'not to have *ridden* and been in *my right* place as I ought'. She was, however, gratified to see the soldiers looking so handsome and doing so well, and to hear their praises from all the foreigners, 'particularly from Soult'. The crowd was immense and 'all so friendly and kind to me'. As Uncle Leopold wrote to her that month: 'the great thing is to be the *National* Sovereign of your *own* country', and in July 1838 Victoria could justly take pride both in her nationality and her popularity.

Chapter Ten
Grand Scompiglio

They wanted to deprive me of my Ladies, and I suppose they would deprive me next of my dresses and my housemaids; they wished to treat me like a girl, but I will show them that I am Queen of England.

Greville Memoirs

Despite the enormous popular success of the Coronation, the second summer of the reign somehow never quite recaptured the unclouded radiance of the first, and there were signs that the honeymoon period was coming to an end. The Queen, said some carping voices, was beginning to look 'bold' and discontented. She was losing her prettiness, they complained, and putting on weight. Lord Melbourne told her she ought to eat less and take more exercise, but Victoria retorted that she was always hungry and hated walking, she always got stones in her shoes. She was, in fact, feeling 'cross and low', suffering from frequent sick headaches and finding it difficult to control the nervous irritability which made her fly out at her maids and sometimes even, to her horror, at dear kind Lord Melbourne himself.

After the extraordinary series of strains and pressures to which she had been subjected during the past two years some kind of reaction was inevitable, and by the autumn of 1838 the Queen had fallen into a mood of lethargy and depression, making her prey to all kinds of vague anxieties. She was worried about her health, her weight, her appearance and, quite unnecessarily, her eyesight.

She worried about her shyness with strangers and lack of small talk. Lord Melbourne agreed that it was always better to say something, however trivial. The longer you stood thinking about it, the harder it got. She agonized over her youth, ignorance and general unfitness for her station, fearing that she was often inconsiderate and teased Lord Melbourne by asking so many silly questions. 'Oh! never,' he replied kindly. 'You *must* ask questions, it's your right, and it's my duty to answer you; pray don't ever think that.'

At the back of all this fretting, of course, lay Victoria's ever-present dread of losing Melbourne, and in October he felt obliged to warn her that he was afraid 'times of some trouble are approaching for which Your Majesty must hold yourself prepared; but', he went on carefully, 'Your Majesty is too well acquainted with the nature of human affairs, not to be well aware that they cannot very long go on even as quietly as they have done for the last sixteen months.' This was not very comforting to an over-wrought, apprehensive young woman who wanted nothing more than that affairs, human and political, should go on quietly for ever suiting her convenience.

The usual house party had assembled at Windsor in August and Uncle Leopold and Aunt Louise had come over for a brief visit in September, but relations between uncle and niece were no longer quite so loving as in the past.

There had been trouble earlier in the summer over broad hints dropped by Leopold regarding his claims to English support in the matter of Belgium's long-standing territorial dispute with Holland, now about to be settled at a conference of the great powers held in London. These hints Victoria had correctly, but irritatingly, ignored, passing Uncle's letters on to her Ministers and declining to bring politics into their delightful private correspondence. Much of Leopold's advice on such topics as the proper demeanour of a Queen, the advisability of sticking to regular hours for the transaction of business, and the wisdom of always refusing to be hurried into important decisions was to influence Victoria to the end of her life, but she made it clear that she would brook no interference, however well-intentioned, in the day-to-day conduct of her affairs. Dear Uncle was rather too inclined to believe 'that he must rule the roast [sic] everywhere'. Dear Uncle took offence, fearing that he had been put aside, 'as one does with a piece of furniture which is no longer wanted', and had to be soothed with renewed assurances of his niece's regard for himself and for Belgium, but a slight coolness remained.

Some differences of opinion had also arisen on the more delicate subject of Prince Albert. Victoria was relishing her hard-won personal independence far too much to be in any hurry to think about marriage, and Albert, she indicated, would have to await her pleasure. Baron Stockmar, noting with regret that the Queen had begun 'to take ill every piece of advice . . . which does not agree with her own opinion', counselled patience, and Leopold, disappointed but too intelligent to try and rush things, prepared to bide his time. Meanwhile, Stockmar set out for the Continent in order to accompany the Prince on the Italian tour which was to put the finishing touches to his education. Whatever the outcome, no pains would be spared in ensuring that Albert was groomed to the last hair before being finally presented for Victoria's approval.

At Buckingham Palace, the now festering problem of Mamma and Conroy was still refusing to go away. Conroy continued to haunt the place, a malignant presence, unseen but not unfelt, losing no opportunity to make mischief and spread malicious stories that the Duchess of Kent's health and spirit were being broken by the Queen's ungrateful and unnatural conduct. It must, one feels, have been at his instigation that the Duchess presented her daughter with a copy of *King Lear* on her nineteenth birthday, and the rift between them was, if anything, growing wider.

It is never pleasant to be hated, and there can be no question that John Conroy had come to hate the plump, smooth-faced little personage who had thwarted and rejected and cast him into outer darkness; or that he was pursuing her in what Stockmar described as 'a spirit of feminine revenge'. Feeling herself threatened, Victoria reacted by clinging more closely than ever to Lehzen, who loathed Conroy even more bitterly than she did, if that were possible, and to dear Lord M., her indispensible father figure. She had, in fact, got into the habit of referring to them both in her Journal as her Mother and Father, while 'my ANGELIC dearest Mother, *Lehzen*' had also been honoured with the pet name of Daisy.

Lehzen, of course, fed greedily on her darling's love, her 'half-anxious, smiling, fixed look' following the Queen wherever she went, her protective adoring presence never further than the next room. Melbourne, long experienced in the arts of gallantry, had always been careful to conciliate the Baroness and actually they got on rather well together, both being incorrigible gossips; but the ex-governess's inevitable underlying sense of insecurity was beginning to make her uncomfortably jealous and possessive. Victoria, too, was beginning to know the pangs of jealousy. She could hardly bear to let Melbourne out of her sight, resented the Duchess of Sutherland sitting next to him at dinner and taking his attention, and found it difficult to conceal her acute sense of deprivation on those evenings when he dined at Holland House.

It was not a healthy situation and Charles Greville, who was invited to spend a couple of nights at Windsor in December, again adverted to the dangers inherent in the intimacy existing between Queen and Premier. 'While She personally gives her orders to her various attendants', he commented, 'and does everything that is civil to all the inmates of the Castle . . . She really has nothing to do with anybody but Melbourne . . . . He is at her side for at least six hours every day – an hour in the morning, two on horseback, one at dinner and two in the evening.'

There was never the least hint of impropriety. 'His manner to her is perfect, always respectful, and never presuming upon the extraordinary distinction he enjoys; hers to him is simple and natural, indicative of the confidence She reposes in him, and of her lively taste for his society, but not marked by any unbecoming familiarity.' The Queen, as Greville had noted with approval on another occasion, 'never ceases to be a Queen.' All the same, so complete a monopoly was certainly not judicious; 'it is not altogether consistent with social usage, and it leads to an infraction of those rules of etiquette which it is better to observe with regularity at Court.' More importantly, thought Greville, it

was 'peculiarly inexpedient' from the point of view of the
Queen's future peace of mind, 'for if Melbourne should be
compelled to resign, her privation will be the more bitter on
account of the exclusiveness of her intimacy with him.'

On New Year's Day 1839 the Queen wrote in her Journal:
'Most fervently do I beseech Almighty God to preserve me and all
those dear to me through this year, and to grant that all may go on
as it has hitherto done, and to make me daily more fit for my
station.' There were few immediate signs of impending change.
On 2 January Lord Melbourne had on a green coat, which the
Queen remarked was a new colour for him. On the 3rd they
discussed, among other things, *The Beggar's Opera*, La Fontaine's
fables, the history of the House of Burgundy and the Queen's
having felt 'low and ill' at Windsor. She was convinced that the
place disagreed with her, which Lord Melbourne wouldn't allow.
'He said very funnily, "You have got some fixed fancies; Your
Majesty has settled in your mind certain things."' They discussed
Oliver Twist which Victoria found engrossing, although Mamma
had 'admonished' her for reading light books, and the miniatures
of the Queen worn by the Maids of Honour. A few days later they
were talking 'of Sedan Chairs and being carried in one, which
Lord M. said "is a very pleasant sensation." "My mother used
always to have her chair, and it was the usual mode of conveyance;
the Town is grown too large for it now." . . . Lord M. said there
used to be 300 Chairmen in London, all Irishmen, very strong and
very skilful.' They talked of clocks and Lord Melbourne's never
having one in his room. '"I always ask the servant what o'clock it
is; and then he tells me what he likes."' They talked about
vaccination, about sculptors and a new translation of *The Arabian
Nights*.

They also, to be fair, talked about the situation in Canada,
where the grievances of the colonists, both French and English,
had been giving cause for concern, and of 'the present clamour
about the Corn Laws'. Interests and opinions in the country, said
Lord Melbourne, were very much divided. 'Some think the
present system, which almost entirely excludes the Importation of
Foreign Corn, is very injurious to the Country; others just the

contrary.' Melbourne does not, however, appear to have made any effort to keep the Queen informed about the mounting agitation by those who regarded 'the present system' of imposing import duties on cheap foreign grain as an iniquitous form of protectionism, enabling aristocratic agriculturists to grow fat on the hunger of the poor. Nor does he seem to have gone out of his way to talk to her about the struggles of the infant Trade Union movement, or Chartism – brainchild of a group of disillusioned radical politicians, and so-called from the People's Charter, published in May 1838, which demanded amongst other things universal male suffrage, the removal of the property qualification for members of Parliament, the payment of members and a secret ballot.

Melbourne was not greatly interested in such matters except in so far as they might affect his government. He had never been troubled by a social conscience and, in any case, as his fondness for the Queen grew, he became increasingly reluctant to introduce topics from the harsh world outside which might distress or offend her. It was pleasanter to spend their time together chatting cosily about George IV's 'excessive high spirits and good humour' as a youth, about the theatre and whether the Queen should go to the play in state, or making her laugh with stories of his schooldays at Eton. Melbourne was all for a quiet life (understandably so perhaps after his stormy marriage), and would go to great lengths to avoid rows and ructions. But, unhappily, a row of particularly catastrophic dimensions was about to erupt within the precincts of the Palace and effectively destroy his and Victoria's brief, gentle idyll.

Lady Flora Hastings had recently come back into waiting on the Duchess of Kent, an occurrence which usually prompted the Queen to remind Lord Melbourne that they must be careful what they said in front of her, as she was 'a Spie of J.C.' Victoria had disliked and distrusted Lady Flora ever since the days at Kensington, when she had been a prominent member of the Conroy faction, but the Conroy interdict had not been extended to include her and on 10 January she dined at the Queen's table.

Lady Flora, it seemed, was not well and on that same day she had consulted Sir James Clark, the Duchess's and the Queen's physician, about a bowel disorder, a pain in her side and biliousness. Clark prescribed a course of rhubarb and ipecacuanha pills and a liniment containing camphor and opium, but it was his patient's shape rather than her symptoms which excited his attention. It was also exciting the attention of the Palace ladies and before the end of the month they were urging Lady Tavistock, one of the senior ladies of the bedchamber, to take steps to 'protect their purity'. Lady Tavistock discussed the matter with Lehzen and, with her agreement, approached Lord Melbourne to inform him of the general suspicion that Lady Flora was pregnant.

It would have been very much wiser, as well as being more courteous, to have gone first to the Duchess of Kent, or Lady Flora herself, but the hostility between the Queen and her mother had, of course, spread to their respective households. Sides had been taken and communication, on any but the most superficial level, had become virtually non-existent. Melbourne received Lady Tavistock's confidences with caution, advising her to keep her eyes open but say nothing for the moment, doctors, after all, had been known to make mistakes. He did, however, send for Clark, who told him that things looked bad for Lady Flora, though it was not yet possible to speak with any certainty; not, at any rate, without a proper examination.

It was agreed to wait and see, but the Queen and Lehzen had already made up their minds to think the worst, and on 2 February Victoria wrote dramatically in her Journal: 'We have no doubt that she is – to use the plain words – *with child!*' Nor did they doubt for a moment the identity of 'the horrid cause' of Lady Flora's misfortune. Who else but that 'Monster and Demon Incarnate' Sir John Conroy?

In justice to the Queen, it should be remembered that Lady Flora was, at this stage, not only exhibiting all the external appearances of pregnancy to more experienced eyes than hers, but also, it seems, 'the constitutional change usually attending that state.' There had, moreover, been talk before this about her friendship with Sir John, and it was known that they had travelled down from Scotland together unchaperoned in a post-chaise. In addition, Melbourne, on whose judgement the Queen relied so implicitly, foolishly fanned the flames by telling her that the Duchess of Kent was jealous of Lady Flora's intimacy with Conroy and, with sidelong looks, gave the impression that 'he *knew* more than he liked to *say.*'

Matters came to a head over the weekend of 16/17 February. Sir James Clark visited Lady Flora on the Saturday and asked her if she were privately married – this delicate method of conveying his suspicions having been devised by Lehzen. Lady Flora indignantly denied the imputation, pointing out that so far from increasing, her figure had recently begun to subside and she'd been able to have her dresses taken in. But Clark, a rugged fresh-air fiend who, even in an age of hit or miss medicine, seems to have behaved with unnecessary obtuseness and insensitivity, refused to listen. According to Lady Flora's own account, he urged her to 'confess' and told her brutally that no one could look at her and doubt her condition.

On Sunday the 17th Lady Portman, another of the senior Bedchamber ladies, at last saw the Duchess of Kent to explain that until the matter had been cleared up, it would be impossible for the Queen to admit Lady Flora to her presence. The Duchess was '*horror-struck*', but Lady Flora sensibly decided that the only possible course was to submit to an examination and named (confusingly) Sir Charles Clarke, an eminent doctor she had known from childhood. It so happened that Sir Charles was already in the Palace and the examination took place that same day in the presence of Lady Portman. The result was vindication for Lady Flora and a certificate was issued, signed by both doctors, which stated categorically that, despite an enlargement of the stomach, there were 'no grounds for suspicion that pregnancy does exist, or ever has existed'.

Lady Portman took the news to the Queen, who at once sent a message back, expressing her deep regret at what had happened and offering to see Lady Flora that evening, if she wished. But Lady Flora, after the upsetting experiences of the past two days, did not feel up to facing her Majesty and it was another week before they met.

During that week the situation became more complicated. In spite of the statement they had signed, the doctors, especially Sir Charles Clarke, were not entirely happy, and on Monday morning they called on Melbourne to tell him that although Lady Flora was technically a virgin and there were many reasons for believing that pregnancy did *not* exist, it was still possible. There was an enlargement in the womb 'like a child', and such things had been known to happen. This determination on the part of the medical men to cover themselves against all eventualities was to cause much unnecessary suffering for the wretched Lady Flora, since it had the inevitable effect of leaving Melbourne and the Queen in full possession of their prejudices, and thereafter neither of them really believed in her innocence.

Meanwhile, Lady Flora's brother, the Marquess of Hastings, had come storming up to Town, breathing vengeance and demanding apologies, reparations and heads on chargers. Melbourne murmured something soothing and hurriedly referred his lordship to the Duke of Wellington, universally accepted as the royal family's troubleshooter-in-chief.

Wellington had in the past successfully scotched a blackmail attempt by Princess Sophia's illegitimate son and personally superintended the destruction of George IV's compromising letter to Mrs Fitzherbert. Now he saw Lord Hastings and the Duchess of Kent, who was also up in arms on behalf of her injured friend, and advised them both to hush the matter up. For the sake of all concerned, not least 'the Young Lady Herself', every effort must be made 'to prevent the story going out of the four walls of the Palace'.

On 23 February the Queen finally saw Lady Flora, who 'was dreadfully agitated and looked very ill'. Victoria kissed her and took her hand, expressing sorrow at what had happened and a wish 'that all should be forgotten'. Lady Flora seemed satisfied. She thanked the Queen and said that for the Duchess's sake she was prepared to suppress her wounded feelings and 'would forget it etc.' The Queen now felt she had done everything that could reasonably be expected of her for a woman she disliked and still strongly suspected of being no better than she should be. But hopes that the affair was over, or could be kept within the four walls of the Palace, proved vain. Gossip, once started, was, as always, unstoppable and on 2 March Charles Greville reported that 'the whole town has been engrossed for some days with a scandalous story at Court.' Greville did not pretend to know how much truth there was in 'the various reports of what this or that person did or said', but, he went on, 'it is certain that the Court is plunged in shame and mortification at the exposure, that the Palace is full of bickering and heart-burnings, while the whole proceeding is looked upon by society at large as to the last degree disgusting and disgraceful.'

Greville was much inclined to blame the Prime Minister. 'There. may be objections to Melbourne's extraordinary domicilation in the Palace; but the compensation ought to be found in his good sense and experience preventing the possibility of such transactions and *tracasseries* as these.' Certainly Melbourne seems to have treated the whole, highly explosive situation with astonishing casualness. But then Melbourne, that relaxed and civilized Englishman, had never fully understood the rawness of the emotions generated by the feuds and jealousies of the Kensington snakepit; and quite failed to grasp that Conroy, presented with an opportunity of destroying his arch-enemy Lehzen and through her, perhaps, the Queen, would exploit it to the full. The Prime Minister also, and more surprisingly, seems to have failed to grasp that the Tory party (the Hastings family were all Tories) would naturally seek to make what political capital they could out of Lady Flora's wrongs.

But it was undoubtedly Conroy 'who was the prime mover of all the subsequent hubbub' caused by the Hastings scandal, and 'he it was who incited the Duchess and Lady Flora to *jeter feu et flamme*'. Lady Flora, an intelligent, outspoken and articulate woman, finding, so she said, that her name was being bandied 'in the Clubs', wrote a long and explicit account of her humiliation to her uncle, Mr Hamilton Fitzgerald (an account which he later published), stating she had no doubt that her original accuser had been 'a certain foreign lady'; and by the end of March the Hastings family and the Tory press were in full cry, determined to discover who had started the slander.

Lady Tavistock and Lady Portman were attacked, their families became involved, and

after a great deal of violence and much angry correspondence they [Hastings and his advisers] thought they had found out that Lady T.'s original informant was the Baroness, and they resolved to publish some letter or letters in which this would have been insinuated; but in point of fact it was not the Baroness, and when they found they were on a wrong scent they seem to have thought it best to draw off.

Nevertheless, broad hints were being dropped about snakes in the grass and the existence of a sinister 'foreign influence' at Court.

The whole affair [wrote Greville gloomily on 21 April] has done incredible harm, and has played the devil with the Queen's popularity and cast dreadful odium and discredit on the Court, especially in the country where a thousand exaggerated reports are rife . . . . The public takes it up (as it took Q. Caroline) on the principle of favouring an injured person, and one who appears to have obtained no reparation for the injuries inflicted on her.

The chief complaint against the Queen, of course, was that she had made no adequate apology or recompense to Lady Flora. The Duchess of Kent had dismissed Sir James Clark from her service immediately after the result of the medical examination was known, and why, it was asked, had the Queen not followed her mother's example? Why, after making such a shocking mistake, was Sir James still apparently enjoying her confidence and his post as Court physician? Why were Lady Tavistock and Lady Portman still at the Palace? How baneful was the influence of Baroness Lehzen? Was she the real cause of the Queen's estrangement from her Mamma?

The Queen reacted furiously to the criticism of herself and Melbourne. She could hardly bear to read the papers and wanted to hang the editor of the *Morning Post* and Lord Hastings with him, while inside the Palace the atmosphere was almost solid with hostility. The Duchess of Kent and Lady Flora cut Lady Tavistock, and the Queen retaliated by cutting Lady Flora, 'such a *nasty woman*'. A public politeness was still being grimly maintained between

Victoria and Mamma, but the Hastings affair was rapidly bringing the mother and daughter relationship to a crisis.

The Duchess of Kent had from the beginning sided openly with the Hastings family. 'The Duchess was perfect,' wrote Lady Flora. 'A mother could not have been kinder . . . and I love her better than ever. She is the most generous-souled woman possible, and such a heart!' The Duchess continued to watch tenderly over Lady Flora (who was, of course, dying of cancer but forcing herself to go about her duties in order to confound those still betting on when she would be obliged 'to bolt'), and made no secret of her opinion of Victoria's heartlessness. Victoria, on her side, had long since made up her mind that Mamma had never really loved her and was now scarcely bothering to conceal that she had 'neither a particle of affection nor of respect for her Mother'.

The Queen, in fact, quite frankly wanted to get rid of Mamma. If only she could be persuaded to go and live somewhere else! It was like having an Enemy in the House. That was all very well, but as Lord Melbourne pointed out, the Queen couldn't live unchaperoned by some lady of equivalent rank as long as she remained unmarried. This was unanswerable and brought Victoria face to face with the obvious solution to the problem of Mamma. It was not a solution she wanted to face, but on 18 April she 'mustered up courage' and told Lord M. that it was Uncle Leopold's great wish that she should marry her cousin Albert. 'How would that be with the Duchess?' asked Melbourne cautiously. If the Queen were to make 'such a connection' and her husband sided with Mamma, then her position would become worse than ever, but Victoria was able to reassure him that 'he need have no fear *whatever* on that score.'

Melbourne was still not very enthusiastic. 'He said ''Cousins are not very good things'' and ''Those Coburgs are not popular abroad; the Russians hate them.'' ' But who else was there? They enumerated the various Princes, not one of whom would do, and marrying a subject was out of the question – it made you so much their equal 'and brought you so in contact with the whole family'. Melbourne agreed, but still didn't think a foreigner would be popular. The Queen remarked that at present *her* feeling was quite against ever marrying. 'It's a great change in the situation,' admitted Melbourne. 'It's a very serious thing.'

Victoria said she thought Albert would be just the person, but of course she couldn't decide anything until she had seen him again. Apart from the means it offered of getting rid of Mamma – and certainly the present situation was dreadful – she would prefer not to marry at all for three or four years. Did Lord M. see the necessity? 'I said I dreaded the thought of marrying', confessed the Queen; 'that I was so accustomed to have my own way, that I thought it was 10 to 1 I shouldn't agree with anybody. Lord M. said "Oh! but you would have it still" (my own way). Lord M. asked if Prince Albert wasn't coming; I said, he would come with his elder brother in the autumn.'

There, for the moment, the matter rested and less than three weeks later the Queen was plunged into another crisis which drove all thoughts of marriage, and even of Mamma, temporarily out of her head. At 2.00 a.m. on Tuesday, 7 May, Lord Melbourne's tottering government finally tottered over the brink, and the Queen woke to the shattering news that 'we had only a majority of 5!' on the Jamaica Constitution Bill. There was to be a Cabinet meeting to decide what should be done, but during the morning a note arrived from Melbourne containing the dread information that he and his colleagues felt they had no alternative 'but to resign their offices into your Majesty's hands'. Lehzen, 'ever kind and good', was at hand to support her distraught Majesty, but Victoria was dissolved in tears and inconsolable. '*All, all* my happiness gone! That happy peaceful life destroyed, that dearest kind Lord Melbourne no more my minister.'

At ten minutes past twelve Melbourne arrived to see her.

It was some minutes before I could muster the courage to go in [wrote the Queen], and when I did, I really thought my heart would break. . . . I took that kind, dear hand of his, and sobbed and grasped his hand in both mine and looked at him and sobbed out, 'You will not forsake me'; I held his hand for a little while, unable to leave go; and he gave me such a look of kindness, pity and affection, and could hardly utter for tears, 'Oh! no', in such a touching voice. We then sat down as usual and I strove to calm myself.

She was not very successful, and when John Russell, the Home Secretary, called at three o'clock to tell her the result of the Cabinet meeting and confirm that the government 'could come to no other determination but to resign', she broke down again. Melbourne returned a little later, and, pulling a paper out of his pocket, said, 'I have written down what I think you should do.' The Queen must send, in the first instance, for the the Duke of Wellington, Grand Old Man of the Tory Party, but if, as seemed probable, the Duke advised her to turn to Sir Robert Peel, Tory leader in the Commons, then she must do so.

She must be prepared 'to place the fullest confidence' in the new administration but, at the same time, be vigilant that 'all measures and appointments are stated to your Majesty . . . and your Majesty's pleasure taken thereon previously to any instruments being drawn out for carrying them into effect.' Lord Melbourne was afraid that the 'extreme confidence' which her Majesty had been good enough to repose in him might have led to some carelessness over these most necessary preliminaries.

He also advised her Majesty to express the hope that none of her Household, except those engaged in politics, should be removed. 'I think you might ask him for that,' said Melbourne. 'I don't know who they'll put about you', he went on, and the Queen lamented that it was very hard to have people forced upon you whom you disliked. 'It is very hard', he agreed, 'but it can't be helped.' Victoria burst into tears again, and when Melbourne told her gently that he had better not come back that evening, she clung to his hand 'crying dreadfully'. The harassed Prime Minister finally tore himself away, promising to see her next morning before Wellington came. He kissed her hand, with *such* a kind look of grief and feeling, said 'God bless you, ma'am', and was gone.

The Queen's tears continued unabated and she spent the evening in her room, quite unable to face any dinner, finally going to bed about midnight, a little calmer but exhausted. In the morning '*all* this dreadful reality came back most forcibly' and so did the tears, but when Melbourne came at eleven, she was more composed. They spoke of the Duke of Wellington's being so deaf – the Queen must be sure he heard all she said – and about Sir

Robert Peel — the Queen must try and conquer her dislike of him. 'He's a close, stiff man', said Melbourne. He tried again to make her understand that he could not come and dine while the new government was being formed, and repeated his warning not to show her dislikes so openly, 'for that's repeated and creates such bitter enemies.' 'They'll not touch your ladies', were his parting words, and the Queen replied sharply that she would not allow it.

She saw the Duke of Wellington at one o'clock and, as anticipated, the old hero (he had just had his seventieth birthday) declined the offer of the Premiership, advising the Queen to send for Sir Robert Peel, in whom she could place every confidence 'as a gentleman and a man of honour and integrity'. Wellington quite understood her distress at parting from Melbourne and was 'excessively pleased with her behaviour and frankness'. She promised to send a note to Peel, and that afternoon Sir Robert, in full Court dress, presented himself at the Palace ready to receive his sovereign's commands to form a new government.

The interview was inevitably a difficult one for them both. Robert Peel was, as Wellington had said, a man of honour and integrity. He also possessed a much better brain than Melbourne's and was a far more skilful politician, but he had few social graces and was apt to conceal his shyness beneath a reserved, off-putting manner. On this occasion, too, he was at a distinct disadvantage, knowing he could not hope to compete with his predecessor in the little Queen's resentful, tear-swollen eyes. But the Queen, making a heroic effort to conceal her antipathy, received him more graciously than he expected. (She afterwards described herself as being 'very much collected, civil and high'.)

She thought Peel seemed 'embarrassed and put out' and not at all sanguine. He said that forming a minority government was very difficult and was far from exulting at what had happened. The Queen spoke of her great friendship for, and gratitude to, Lord Melbourne, in which Peel agreed, 'but he is such a cold, odd man she can't make out what he means.' She also raised the subject of her Household, 'to which he at present would give no answer', but he promised nothing should be done 'without my knowledge and approbation'.

After about twenty minutes Sir Robert departed, not dissatisfied by the way things had gone, and the Queen once more gave way to tears, before hurrying to her desk to write a detailed account of the afternoon's events to Melbourne. Peel was to come back at one o'clock next day to report progress in the formation of his government, but Victoria had the decided impression that he was neither *happy* nor sanguine, and 'the Queen don't like his manner after — oh! how different, how dreadfully different, to that frank, open, natural and most kind, warm manner of Lord Melbourne.'

Thursday the 9th began with still more tears and wretchedness, but the Queen was slightly cheered to receive 'such a kind delightful long letter' from Melbourne during the morning, in which he advised her 'to urge this question of the Household strongly as a matter due to yourself and your own wishes.' He did, however, add a caveat: 'if Sir Robert is unable to concede it, it will not do to refuse and to put off the negotiation upon it.' Anything would be better than to run the risk of getting into a situation, as in France, 'of no party being able to form a Government and conduct the affairs of the country.' And Melbourne ended with another earnest entreaty to her Majesty not to be put off by Peel's manner. 'Depend upon it, there is no personal hostility to Lord Melbourne nor any bitter feelings against him. Sir Robert is the most cautious and reserved of mankind . . . but he is not therefore deceitful or dishonest'.

More notes flew to and fro that morning, and in one of them Melbourne suggested that 'if Sir Robert Peel presses for the dismissal of those of your Household who are not in Parliament, you may observe that in so doing he is pressing your Majesty more hardly than any Minister ever pressed a Sovereign before. . . . If this is put to him by your Majesty, Lord Melbourne does not see how he can resist it.'

When Peel arrived, the audience began smoothly enough. He announced several ministerial appointments, and although two were of men whom the Queen had special reason to dislike, she accepted them without argument. On the question of the

Household, she mentioned a wish to have her old friend Lord Liverpool, and Peel at once promised to offer him the Lord Stewardship. 'Now, ma'am,' said Sir Robert, 'about the ladies . . .' and was stopped in his tracks by her Majesty, who declared that she had no intention of giving up *any* of her Ladies and had never imagined such a thing would be required of her. Did she mean to keep them *all*, enquired Sir Robert nervously. '*All*', came the reply. 'The Mistress of the Robes and the Ladies of the Bedchamber?' '*All.*'

In vain Peel tried to explain that these would be the wives of prominent opponents of his government, and that some changes in her exclusively Whig circle were necessary as an outward and visible sign of the Queen's confidence in the new administration. The Queen was unimpressed. She never talked politics with her Ladies, and in any case quite a number of the Bedchamber women and Maids of Honour were related to Tories. Oh, he didn't mean *all* the Bedchamber women or the Maids of Honour, interposed Peel hastily, just the Mistress of the Robes and the Ladies of the Bedchamber. *They* were the most important, retorted the Queen, deliberately missing the point. She would not consent and such a thing had never been done before. But she was a Queen Regnant, said Peel, and that made the difference. 'Not here', insisted the Queen Regnant, all four foot eleven of her, her Ladies were *entirely* her own affair and nothing to do with the government. Peel retreated, baffled. He would have to consult the Duke of Wellington upon such an important matter. By all means! The Queen would like to see the Duke as well, and would expect them both to wait on her again that afternoon.

The moment Peel had gone, she bounced to her desk to dash off another note to Melbourne.

The Queen writes one line to prepare Lord Melbourne for what *may* happen in a very few hours. Sir Robert Peel has behaved very ill, and has insisted on my giving up my Ladies, to which I replied that I never would consent, and I never saw a man so frightened . . . I was calm but very decided, and I think you would have been pleased to see my composure and great firmness; the Queen of England will not submit to such trickery. Keep yourself in readiness, for you may soon be wanted.

Wellington appeared at half-past two. 'Well, I am very sorry to find there is a difficulty', he opened cautiously. 'Oh, *He* began it and not me', said the Queen with a schoolgirlish naïveté which imperfectly concealed her rising excitement and absolute determination to exploit her advantage. Was Sir Robert so weak that *even* the Ladies must be of his opinion, she enquired sarcastically, thrilled by her own cleverness. The *opinions* of the Ladies were nothing, replied the Duke. It was the principle of the thing which mattered. The Queen could make as many objections as she liked about details, and every possible consideration would be shown to her feelings, but she could not fight her Prime Minister on principles without creating 'insuperable difficulties'. When she snapped that it was offensive to suppose that she gossiped with her Ladies about public affairs, he said, keeping his temper, 'I know you do not. I am quite certain you do not; but the public does not know this, and it is on account of the impression necessarily to be produced on the public mind . . . that the proposal is made to you.'

It was no good. As Wellington remarked, 'I have no small talk and Peel has no manners', and they could make no dent in the royal obstinacy. Peel went away again for more consultations and the Queen seized her pen to scribble another report to Melbourne. He must not think the Queen had been rash, but she felt 'this was an attempt to see whether she could be led and managed like a child', and if it led to Sir Robert's refusing to form a government, which would be absurd and make him 'cut a sorry figure indeed', the Queen would feel satisfied that she had only been defending her rights. 'I should like to know if they mean to give the *Ladies* seats in Parliament?' she finished triumphantly.

Peel was back at five o'clock. He had discussed the matter 'with those who were to have been his colleagues' and, bearing in mind that they would be in a minority in the Commons, they had agreed they could not go on, 'unless there was *some* (*all* the Officers of State and Lords I gave up) demonstration of my confidence, and if I retained all my ladies this would not be.' The Queen replied that although she felt certain she would not change her mind, she would do nothing hastily but communicate her decision within twenty-four hours, and in the mean time Peel 'would suspend all further proceedings'. 'What an admission of weakness! What a blessed and unexpected escape!' she wrote in her Journal.

Now at last she could summon Melbourne, who came at half-past six. 'Now you can tell me all', he said cosily as they sat down. But while Lord M. quite saw that her Majesty could not have done otherwise, he felt bound to warn her that her spirited defence of her 'rights' might have 'very serious consequences'. 'I must summon the Cabinet', he said, and the Queen begged him to let her know the result that night. She sat up in her room after dinner waiting anxiously, and at a quarter to two received a note from the Prime Minister. All was well, and the Cabinet, with one or two waverers, was ready to carry on. Most of them, in fact, were already regretting their somewhat precipitate decision to resign, which had surprised the political observers, and when Melbourne read out the Queen's letters of Thursday afternoon, the general feeling was that it would be impossible 'to abandon such a queen and such a woman', a chivalrous resolve strengthened by the knowledge that the Radicals, whose defection on 7 May had caused the crisis in the first place, were now scurrying back into the fold.

At nine o'clock on Friday morning a letter went to Sir Robert Peel from the Palace, informing him that 'the Queen, having considered the proposal made to her . . . to remove the Ladies of her Bedchamber, cannot consent to adopt a course which she conceives to be contrary to usage, and which is repugnant to her feelings.' Later that day Peel resigned his commission and the unfortunate 'Scompiglio', as Greville called it, appeared to be over. Melbourne had scrambled back into the saddle, where, against all odds, he was to remain for another two years, and the Queen gave a ball.

One of the more bizarre features of the Bedchamber crisis, as it rapidly became known, was that it took place against a background of rising popular unrest (there were serious Chartist riots in Birmingham that July) and the hectic social whirl of the London season. On the evening of Friday, 10 May the Queen entertained the Russian Grand Duke Alexander at a State Ball at Buckingham Palace, which she enjoyed very much. All her friends were very kind, she recorded complacently, and it was after three when she left the ballroom 'much pleased, as my mind felt happy'.

Chapter Eleven
I and Albert Alone

My mind is quite made up – and I told Albert this morning of it . . . He seems *perfection*, and I think that I have the prospect of very great happiness before me.

Queen Victoria to King Leopold

The repercussions of the Bedchamber crisis rumbled on for some weeks. 'Nothing', wrote Greville on 11 May, 'could surpass the excitement and amazement that prevailed. The indignant Tories exclaimed against intrigue and preconcerted plans . . . while the Whigs cried out against harshness and dictatorial demands.'

It is usually said that her fear of finding herself surrounded by hostile Tory ladies who supported Flora Hastings, together with a belief that Lehzen's position was being threatened, lay behind the Queen's headstrong behaviour, and certainly the Hastings scandal and the Bedchamber fracas were closely linked. But Queen Victoria, even at nineteen, could have dealt with any number of Tory ladies, and Peel had no power to dislodge Lehzen, who held no official post, even if he had wanted to. Charles Greville was almost certainly right when he observed: 'The simple truth in this case is that the Queen could not endure the thought of parting with Melbourne, who is everything to her. Her feelings which are *sexual* though She does not know it, and are probably not very well defined to herself, are of a strength sufficient to bear down all prudential considerations and to predominate in her mind with irresistible force.' During the course of the negotiations she thought she saw an opportunity of getting Melbourne back, and, exhibiting 'the talent of a clever but rather thoughtless' girl, had 'boldly and stubbornly availed herself of the opening which was presented to her.'

The constitutional issue on which the battle had been fought – whether or not the Prime Minister had the power to dictate the political complexion of the non-political appointments to the Sovereign's Household – had, perhaps fortunately, been clouded by some genuine misunderstandings and confusion over how the rules applied to a Queen Regnant. But, in the circumstances, Peel was undoubtedly within his rights when he asked her Majesty to agree to change some (and not *all*, as she insisted) of her senior ladies. A more disturbing aspect of the crisis was its highlighting of the Queen's immaturity, her violent partisanship, her obstinacy and apparently wilful refusal to put her constitutional responsibilities before her private inclinations. Little Vic's ingenuous whiggery had, in fact, ceased to be amusing.

As more details of the story came out and it became clear that there had been no attempt to strip the Queen of all her friends, or 'to destroy her social comfort' – Peel had even told her he would not object to her continuing friendship with Lord Melbourne – Greville grew more indignant. 'It is a high trial of our institutions when the caprice of a girl of nineteen can over turn a great Ministerial combination', he scolded. Still more shocking was the spectacle of 'this mere baby of a Queen' setting herself in opposition to the Duke of Wellington, the great man 'to whom her Predecessors had ever been accustomed to look up with unlimited confidence as their surest and wisest Councillor in all times of difficulty and danger.'

Melbourne, too, had been slightly shaken by his recent glimpse of the Queen on the rampage, and made a conscientious attempt to soften her attitude towards Peel. 'You must remember that he is a man who is not accustomed to talk to Kings,' said his lordship superbly. 'It's not like me; I've been brought up with Kings and Princes. I know the whole Family, and know exactly what to say to them; now he has not that ease, and probably you were not at your ease.

Victoria herself was outwardly unrepentant and did not fail to mention in her Journal that she was 'loudly cheered' on her way to and from the Chapel Royal on Sunday the 12th. But the frequency with which Peel's name and his various enormities came up in conversation over the next few weeks seems to indicate that her conscience was not entirely clear, and she threw herself into the gaieties of the Season with a vigour which contained more than a hint of defiance.

Her birthday came and went – 'this day I *go out of my* TEENS and become 20!' – and she indulged in a little mildly daring flirtation with the Grand Duke Alexander. On 27 May there was an informal ball at Windsor. They danced a mazurka and the Grand Duke asked the Queen 'to take a turn'. She had never tried it before, but found it an exhilarating experience. 'The Grand Duke is so very strong, that in running round, you must follow quickly, and after that you are whisked round like in a Valse, which is very pleasant. . . . I never enjoyed myself more,' she went on. 'We were all so merry; I got to bed by a ¼ to 3, but could not sleep till 5.' Two days later the Russians departed and Victoria 'felt so sad to take leave of this dear amiable young man, whom I really think (talking jokingly) I was a little in love with.'

All this excitement did her good, she told Melbourne. 'But you may suffer afterwards,' he said warningly, and added, 'you must take care of your health . . . . You lead rather an unnatural life for a young person, it's the life of a man.' She did feel it sometimes, admitted the Queen and certainly everything went sadly flat without the Grand Duke and his sweet smile and fine manly figure. She talked to Lord M. about it, and of its being so seldom that she had young people of her own rank with her. 'A young person like me must *sometimes* have young people to laugh with,' she said rather wistfully. 'Nothing so natural', replied Lord M. with tears in his eyes.

There was to be precious little to laugh about during June, though the month opened with an astonishing piece of news. 'They have got rid of Conroy,' wrote Charles Greville, 'he has resigned his place about the Duchess of Kent and is going abroad.' Just why Conroy had chosen this particular moment to throw in his hand is not entirely clear. The Duke of Wellington had been working away in the background for several months, patiently cajoling, flattering and representing to Sir John 'that his conduct in retiring would not only be gratifying to the Duchess's family but be honorable to himself, and appreciated by the public; and by honied words like these he prevailed on him at last to go.' But, according to Greville, Conroy's 'primary motive' for retiring was 'the unanimous opposition which he met with from the Coburg family'.

The family – which included Dukes Ernest and Ferdinand of Saxe-Coburg, Charles Leiningen (who had long since abandoned his old crony), and Feodore and her husband – had begun to gang up on Sir John. They complained that he used 'insolently' to come and invade their private sitting-room at the Palace and asked Wellington if he could be formally warned off. This the Duke would not allow. The Duchess of Kent was 'a great Princess', independent and with an undoubted right to choose her own attendants. It would be 'an outrage' to prohibit her officer from entering her apartments. However, he spoke 'pretty roundly' to the Duchess on the subject and Conroy's position was becoming steadily more untenable. It was obvious by now that the Queen's implacable hostility would never alter and he may also have been afraid that more awkward questions were about to be asked concerning his management of the Duchess's financial affairs. On 10 June it became known that he had dismissed his servants and shortly afterwards he left for Italy.

His departure did not result in any dramatic reconciliation between mother and daughter. Victoria took the news coolly, saying it was a matter of indifference to her and she could not get on with her mother anyway. Besides, although Conroy had gone, the tragedy of Lady Flora Hastings was not yet over. 'Violent and libellous' articles in the *Morning Post* and the unappeased wrath of the Hastings family had been keeping the indignation of society alive, and the Queen was hissed from the stands when she attended Ascot races.

Early in June Lady Flora had entered the terminal stage of her illness. She was reported to be very sick. ' "Sick" ' said Lord M.

with a significant laugh' – he and Victoria *still* seem to have believed the dying women was pregnant. A few days later the reports were still bad. The invalid had continued fever and could keep nothing on her stomach. After 'much gulping' the Queen sent to make kind enquiries and agreed to postpone a forthcoming ball at the Palace at the Duchess of Kent's urgent entreaty, though she told Melbourne she didn't believe Lady Flora was so very ill. 'As you say, ma'am', said Lord M., 'it would be very awkward if that woman were to die.' Charles Greville was more forthright. 'They are in a great fright lest Lady Flora should die', he wrote; 'because she is very ill, and if She should die the public will certainly hold an inquest on her body and bring in a verdict of wilful murder against Buckingham Palace.'

On 20 June, the second anniversary of the Queen's accession, Dr Chambers, who had succeeded Sir James Clark as the Duchess of Kent's doctor, thought Lady Flora was in very great danger, she was growing weaker and could digest nothing. But though the Queen had invited her sister, Lady Sophia, to stay at the Palace (an invitation which was refused by the Hastings family), her Majesty did not allow the invalid's worsening condition to interfere with her social round more than she could help. That evening she attended a ball given by Lord and Lady Westminster which was '*so* gay and pretty', and enjoyed herself excessively.

A week later it was clear that Lady Flora was sinking fast and Victoria at last overcame her aversion and offered to go and see her. 'I went in alone,' she wrote;

I found poor Lady Flora stretched on a couch looking as thin as anybody can be who is still alive; literally a skeleton, but the body *very* much swollen like a person who is with child; a searching look in her eyes, a look rather like a person who is dying . . . she was friendly, said she was very comfortable, and was very grateful for all I had done for her, and that she was glad to see me looking well. I said to her, I hoped to see her again when she was better, upon which she grasped my hand as if to say ''I shall not see you again.'' '

On the morning of Friday, 5 July, the Queen was told that Lady Flora had died during the night. 'The poor thing died without a struggle and only just raised her hands and gave one gasp.' The immediate consequence was a fresh onslaught against the Palace. The *Morning Post* rose to new heights of venom and attacked the Queen daily 'with the most revolting virulence and indecency'. A post-mortem revealed that Lady Flora had a tumour on the liver, but her friends and 'the faction who had made an instrument of her' did not hesitate to say she had died of a broken heart and that the Queen had broken it. 'There is no doubt that an effect very prejudicial to H.M. has been produced', wrote Greville, 'and the public, the women particularly, have taken up the Cause of Lady Flora with a vehemence which is not the less active because it is so senseless.' 'Scandal and malignity always go down,' he added; 'it is the food the public loves to batten on.' The press, of course, was only too pleased to be able to provide its readers with their favourite fare and Lord Liverpool was afraid that some hostile demonstration was being planned for the day of the funeral. The Queen, however, insisted on sending a carriage and nothing worse than a few stones were thrown. The scandal and malignity continued in some quarters throughout the summer before finally dying a natural death from lack of further sustenance, but it left an unpleasant taste and went a long way towards destroying the image of the gay, innocent little Queen.

By no means all the reproach hurled at her was justified; Lady Flora herself had not been entirely blameless and the Tory extremists had unquestionably made full use of her sufferings for their own ends. Nevertheless, it has to be admitted that neither Melbourne nor Victoria came very well out of the whole squalid little episode. Melbourne, whose mental indolence and cheap cynicism had allowed the scandal to get out of hand in the first place, must, in the circumstances, shoulder most of the responsibility; but the Queen had displayed an intolerance and lack of compassion which not even her youth and inexperience or the poisoning effect of old resentments can entirely excuse.

Although she kept up a defiant front, telling Melbourne that she felt *no* remorse and did not consider herself in any way to blame for Lady Flora's death, she was not happy or pleased with herself. All the fun and excitement of being Queen seemed to have gone sour. She was tired and bored – bored with the prospect of another sojourn at Windsor, but bored at the thought of staying in London, which would be just as dull when the opera season came to an end. In short, she felt 'disgusted with everything' and was in a distinctly fractious mood when the approaching visit of the Coburg princes cropped up in one of her daily sessions with Lord M. early in July. 'Talked of my Cousins Ernest and Albert coming over, – my having no great wish to see Albert, as the whole subject was an odious one, and one which I hated to decide about.' Lord M. agreed soothingly that it was disagreeable. Better wait for a year or two, he said; 'it's a very serious question.' The Queen remarked pettishly that she would rather never marry at all. 'I don't know about *that*', said Lord M.

On 15 July Victoria wrote discouragingly to Uncle Leopold, more than hinting that she would prefer the cousins' visit to be postponed indefinitely. She asked if Albert was aware of the plans being made for him (in fact, she knew he was), and if he realized that 'there is *no engagement* between us.' She could make *no final promise this year*, 'for, at the *very earliest*, any such event could not take place till *two or three years hence.*' Apart from her youth and '*great* repugnance' at the thought of changing her present position, there appeared to be no public anxiety for her marriage, and the Queen was of the opinion that it would be more prudent to wait till 'some such demonstration is shown.'

Though all the reports of Albert are most favourable [she went on], and though I have little doubt I shall like him, still one can never answer beforehand for *feelings*, and I may not have the *feeling* for him which is requisite to ensure happiness. I *may* like him as a friend, and as a *cousin*, and as a *brother*, but not *more*; and should this be the case (which is not likely), I am *very* anxious that it should be understood that I am *not* guilty of any breach of promise, for *I never gave any*. I am sure you will understand my anxiety, for I should otherwise, were this not completely understood, be in a very painful position. As it is, I am rather nervous about the visit, for the subject I allude to is not an agreeable one to me.

All the same, reading between the lines of this agitated communication, Uncle Leopold was probably not too depressed and wisely refrained from comment. But he had no intention of allowing Victoria to put off renewing her acquaintance with Prince Albert, being reasonably confident that nature would then take its course.

The Queen continued to feel depressed and out of sorts, but the Duchess of Kent was really suffering. She missed the Conroy family bitterly. They had, after all, been her constant companions for more than twenty years and their going left an aching void. She was also genuinely stricken by the death of Flora Hastings. She had nursed her friend devotedly during the last month of her life, withdrawing almost completely from the ordinary round of Court routine and showed little inclination to return. Fortunately, the Duke of Wellington, that indispensible confidant and peacemaker, was on hand to intervene. Throughout the unhappy events of the past few months he had 'kept his eyes steadfastly fixed on the two great objects of saving the character of the Queen, and putting her and her mother upon decently amicable terms', and it was through him that Victoria, who confessed to feeling quite callous about Mamma, had been persuaded to write a kind letter to the Duchess after Conroy's departure. Wellington also went to work on the Duchess, urging her 'to resume her place in the Court circle', and telling her sternly that she must be conciliatory and affectionate to the Queen and civil to all the persons in attendance on her, even Lehzen, the Duchess's particular *bête noire*.

The poor Duchess, receptive as always to the nearest advice-giving male, took this with docility. On 17 August the Court migrated to Windsor, where it was joined by the Kohary or Ferdinand Coburgs. The arrival of this jolly party of relations – Duke Ferdinand, his daughter Victoire, Augustus, who had once looked at albums and read his newspaper in Princess Victoria's sitting-room at Kensington, another son, Leopold, and yet another cousin, Alexander Mensdorff-Pouilly – helped to ease the Duchess of Kent's return to the family circle and also raised the Queen's drooping spirits. She danced and giggled and played silly games with her cousins, though she was afraid it must be very tiresome for Lord M. to hear so much unintelligible German always spoken before him. 'I said to Lord M. I was very childish with all my Cousins. "That's a very good thing," he said kindly. I added I often forgot I *was* young. "That's a capital thing to be reminded of," he said *so* kindly.'

In September the holidays came to an end with the usual tears and regrets. King Leopold had also been spending a few days at the Castle, putting the final touches to the arrangements for Albert's visit, and when he had gone, Victoria's nervous malaise returned. She dreaded the future but yet was dissatisfied with the present. Buttressed by Lehzen and Melbourne she felt 'safe', always an essential requirement, but although she wouldn't admit it, Lord M.'s companionship no longer filled her every need. Melbourne was beginning to feel his age and the strain of dancing constant attendance on a demanding young mistress. He couldn't always keep up the endless flow of entertaining conversation (his stock of anecdotes was running out), or stave off the sleepiness which threatened to overwhelm him after dinner. He was also becoming increasingly disturbed by Victoria's violent and freely expressed antipathy to all things Tory, and finding her increasingly difficult to control. She was no longer so willing to be guided and instructed or gently teased out of her more unreasonable prejudices. Even with Lord M., 'this *dear excellent* man who is kindness and forbearance itself', her temper was liable to flare dangerously at times, and Lord M. found himself having to choose his words with care. For all the Queen's protestations, it was time for a change.

Although Victoria admitted that she heard Albert's praises on all sides, and that he was very handsome, she really knew very little about her intended husband. There had been virtually no contact between them since that brief visit of three years ago, and the Queen would have been shocked and surprised had she known that Albert, too, was dreading their forthcoming meeting. A prim, serious-minded young man, he listened with alarm to stories that Victoria was said to be 'incredibly stubborn', that she delighted in court ceremonies, etiquette and trivial formalities. 'These are gloomy prospects,' he wrote to his old tutor. 'She is said not to take the slightest interest in Nature, to enjoy sitting up at night and sleeping late into the day.'

Gloomy prospects indeed to one who liked to get up at five and fell asleep over his supper, and took an earnest interest in the beauties of Nature.

Nor was the Prince prepared to wait his cousin's pleasure indefinitely. He would wait a little longer for marriage if necessary, but Victoria must make up her mind now. If, at the end of another two or three years, she were finally to reject him, he would not merely have wasted a lot of valuable time, but have been made to look ridiculous into the bargain. Victoria, with her usual honesty, had accepted this condition, put to her by Uncle Leopold, as reasonable, but it inevitably increased the tensions of the waiting period.

The waiting period ended at half-past seven on the evening of Thursday, 10 October, when the Queen stood at the top of the staircase at Windsor to greet her two dear cousins, Ernest and Albert. 'It was with some emotion that I beheld Albert – who is *beautiful*.' Nature, just as Leopold had hoped, was already beginning to take its course. 'Albert really is quite charming', wrote Victoria in her Journal on Friday the 11th, 'and so excessively handsome, such beautiful blue eyes, an exquisite nose, and such a pretty mouth with delicate moustachios and slight but very slight whiskers; a beautiful figure, broad in the shoulders and a fine waist.' There was dancing that evening, and it was 'quite a pleasure to look at Albert when he gallops and valses, he does it so beautifully.' On Sunday evening, she told Melbourne that seeing her cousins had a good deal changed her opinion about marrying, but she must decide soon, 'which was a difficult thing'. 'You could take another week', said Lord M. and agreed that Prince Albert was 'certainly a very fine young man, very good-looking.'

Next day, while the cousins were out shooting, the Queen broke the news to Lord M. that she had now made up her mind to marry 'dearest Albert'. Lord M. privately thought dearest Albert was a bit of a stick, but knew better than to say so. 'I think it is a very good thing', he said tactfully, 'and you'll be much more comfortable; for a woman cannot stand alone for long, in whatever situation she is.' 'He was *so* kind, *so fatherly* about all this,' wrote Victoria. 'I felt *very* happy.'

Albert now had to be informed of his good fortune – rather a blush-making business for the Queen, as 'in general such things were done the other way'. However, at about half-past twelve on Tuesday, she nerved herself to send for him. 'He came to the Closet where I was alone, and after a few minutes I said to him that I thought he must be aware *why* I wished them to come here, – and that it would make me *too happy* if he would consent to what I wished (to marry me). We embraced each other, and he was *so* kind, *so* affectionate . . .. I really felt it was the happiest brightest moment of my life.'

No one was to know just yet, except darling Daisy, of course, and Uncle Leopold (naturally) and Stockmar, not even Mamma, who would never be able to keep her mouth shut – though some people might be allowed to guess. The weeks which followed were blissful ones. Prince Ernest had helpfully succumbed to a bilious attack, so the lovers were able to enjoy many cosy hours alone together in the Blue Closet getting to know one another. They talked, played the piano and sang duets, exchanged kisses and rings and locks of hair. Albert sat beside the Queen while she wrote letters and scratched out her mistakes and blotted her signature on papers and warrants, etc. He clasped her in his arms, and kissed her again and again, calling her *Vortrefflichste* (matchless). 'Oh! what happiness is this! How I *do adore* him!!' It seemed too good to be true. 'Oh! how *blessed*, how happy I am to think he is *really* mine; I can scarcely believe myself *so blessed* . . . He is such an Angel, such a *very* great Angel!'

The wedding date had been fixed for 10 February and the Prince, who wanted to have two months at home first was to leave on 14 November. On the 10th Mamma was at last let into the secret, and took her daughter in her arms and cried and 'seemed delighted' – though she was later to complain, with some justification, that even the servants had known before she did.

Albert was teaching the Queen to waltz – in her station she had never been able to allow any man to put his arm round her waist before – and on the 12th they had a dance, Victoria's last 'as an *unmarried girl*'. Two days later he had to leave. The young couple gazed tenderly into each other's eyes and the Queen kissed her fiancé's 'dear soft cheek, fresh and pink like a rose'. But although she cried, she was able to control the floods of grief which usually drowned her at any parting.

On 23 November the Queen went up to London to make a formal declaration of her intended marriage to the Privy Council. It was an emotional occasion and she was understandably nervous. Charles Greville, watching her at the Council meeting, noticed that her hands were trembling so much she could hardly hold her script. However, fortified by Albert's picture, worn in a bracelet, she got through it triumphantly.

I cannot describe to you with what a mixture of self possession and feminine delicacy she read the paper [wrote John Wilson Croker to Lady Hardwicke]. Her voice, which is naturally beautiful, was clear and untroubled; and her eye was bright and calm, neither bold nor downcast, but firm and soft. There was a blush on her cheek which made her look both handsomer and more interesting; and certainly she *did* look as interesting and as handsome as any young lady I ever saw.

Unhappily, now that the secret was out, the Queen made the painful discovery that not everyone shared her rose-tinted view of beloved Albert. On the contrary, there was a pretty general feeling that the 'lucky Coburgs' had been lucky once too often, and a marked lack of enthusiasm at the prospect of having to provide for another penniless German princeling. Admittedly, it was an unpropitious moment to be asking for money. At the beginning of the Hungry Forties there was bitter hardship and discontent among the 'labouring poor', both in the agricultural south and the industrial north; and equally bitter anger and frustration among the politically aware over the failure of the 1832 Reform Bill to enfranchise the working class.

Nevertheless, when, in January 1840, John Russell rose in the House of Commons to propose that an annual income £50,000 should be granted to Prince Albert out of the Consolidated Fund, the government was only following well-established precedent. £50,000 had been recognized as a suitable allowance for the sovereign's consort, male or female, for more than a century, and the row which followed was very largely the result of Victoria's alienation of the Tories, the penalty of making herself 'the Queen of a party'.

In fairness to the Queen, it should be remembered that in her rabid whiggery, she, too, was only following tradition. Her immediate predecessors had been equally rabid Tories, and the ideal of the impartial monarch was one which did not begin to emerge until later in the reign, the consequence, ironically enough, of Albert's sobering influence. But there are ways and ways of showing partisanship, and the young Queen Victoria had made some quite unnecessary enemies by her intemperate, undisguised hatred and social ostracism 'of everything in the shape of a Tory'. 'Her Court', observed Greville, 'is a scene of party and family favouritism, a few chosen individuals being her constant guests, to the almost total exclusion of everyone however distinguished or respectable of the opposite side.'

The Tories, naturally enough, seized the opportunity to get their own back, and voted to a man against Albert's £50,000 (Peel, 'nasty wretch', actually *spoke* against it). The Radicals and even some Whigs joined them, and the government had to accept defeat and a Tory amendment fixing the Prince's income at a beggarly £30,000, thus, to the Queen's unspeakable indignation, valuing her angel at £20,000 a year less than George of Denmark, Queen Anne's 'stupid and insignificant husband'.

Worse was to follow. Victoria had set her heart on giving Albert precedence after herself over all the English royal family. This meant canvassing her uncles, and Sussex and Cambridge (both of whom wanted 'some additions to their incomes') were ready to agree, but Cumberland, now installed as King of Hanover, would not. He contemptuously refused to give place to a 'paper Royal Highness' and bullied his brothers into withdrawing their consent. The Duke of Wellington, who had taken 'one of his very stiffest crotchets' into his head, opposed the idea strongly in the House of Lords, and further complications arose when it was realized that if the Queen got her way, Prince Albert would also take precedence over his eldest son, the Heir Apparent. Charles Greville, an expert in such matters, eventually solved the problem by decreeing that the Queen, by exercise of the royal prerogative, could confer whatever precedence she chose on her husband by Letters Patent; but the Bill for the Prince's naturalization had to go through Parliament with his status still unsettled.

Greville thought the Conservatives had behaved with unnecessary churlishness over the precedence question, and the Queen's white-hot fury with the 'vile, confounded, infernal Tories' seared the pages of her Journal. 'May they be well punished for this outrageous insult', she fumed. 'Poor dear Albert, how cruelly they are ill-using that dearest Angel! Monsters! You Tories shall be punished. Revenge! Revenge!' Wellington, 'this wicked foolish old Duke', came in for special execration and she threatened to refuse to invite him to the wedding, until Melbourne was obliged to point out, gently but firmly, that there were certain things the Queen of England couldn't do, and that to insult England's senior hero was one of them. 'I hear that our Gracious is very much out of Temper', remarked the senior hero himself.

Other matters, too, were combining to put her Majesty out of temper. Persistent, ill-informed rumours that Albert had 'papistical leanings' had to be firmly squashed and Mamma was being difficult again, showing ominous signs of wanting to stay on at the Palace with the newly-weds which, of course, would never do, and complaining that her daughter was planning to turn her out of the house. Even Albert was being a little tiresome over the appointment of his Household. The Prince, well aware that his position was going to be an exceedingly delicate one, was anxious to appear above party faction from the start and also, naturally, wanted his staff to include at least a few of his own compatriots and friends. At all events, he wanted to pick them himself, and early in December Victoria found herself having to put him in his place. 'As to your wish about your gentlemen, my dear Albert, I must tell you quite honestly that it will not do. You may entirely rely upon me that the people who will be about you will be absolutely pleasant people, of high standing and good character . . . .. Lord Melbourne has already mentioned several to me who would be very suitable.'

From what he knew of Lord Melbourne, Albert had grave doubts as to whether that nonchalant individual's standards of good character and suitability would match his own, and was alarmed to discover that he was being expected to take over Melbourne's own Private Secretary. If that did not mark him down as a partisan of the Whig interest, what would? 'Think of my position, dear Victoria', he wrote piteously; 'I am leaving my home with all its old associations, all my bosom friends, and going to a country in which everything is new and strange to me . . .. Except yourself I have no one to confide in. And is it not even to be conceded to me that the two or three persons who are to have the charge of my private affairs should be persons who already command my confidence?'

There were no concessions. For his own good, the Prince's people would be chosen for him by the Queen and Lord Melbourne, a 'very clever, very honest, and very impartial man'. 'I am distressed to tell you what I fear you do not like, but it is necessary, my dearest, most excellent Albert. Once more I tell you that you can perfectly rely on me in these matters.'

This exchange revived all the Prince's former misgivings and he suffered another defeat over the question of the honeymoon. His hopeful suggestion that he and his bride should retire from the public eye for at least a fortnight was smartly snubbed. He had not at all understood the matter. 'You forget, my dearest love, that I am the Sovereign, and that business can stop and wait for nothing. Parliament is sitting, and something occurs almost every day, for which I may be required . . . therefore two or three days is already a long time to be absent.'

In the circumstances it was scarcely surprising that the Prince should have reached Brussels on his way to his wedding 'rather exasperated about various things, and pretty full of grievances'. Not, King Leopold hastened to assure Victoria, that Albert was inclined to be sulky, 'but I think that he may be rendered a little melancholy if he thinks himself unfairly or unjustly treated.'

The Queen had had a bad cold and was feeling 'a little agitated and nervous'. 'Most natural', said Lord M. 'How could it be otherwise?' However, she was relieved to get 'a delightful letter' from dearest Albert from Dover on Friday, 7 February. He had suffered 'most dreadfully' during an appalling sea-crossing and arrived with a face 'the colour of a wax candle', but had been greatly heartened by the warmth of his reception. 'He must take care not to be intoxicated by that', warned Lord M.

That Friday evening Victoria and Melbourne sat together chatting tête-à-tête for the last time.

Lord M. was so warm, so kind, and so affectionate, the whole evening, and so much touched in speaking of me and my affairs. Talked of my former resolution of never marrying. 'Depend upon it, it's right to marry,' he said earnestly; '. . . it's in human nature, it's natural to marry; the other is a very unnatural state of things; it's a great change – it has its inconveniences; everybody does their best, and depend upon it you've done well . . .. After all,' he continued, much affected, 'how anybody in your situation can have a moment's tranquillity! – a young person cast in this situation is very unnatural.' . . . Talked of Albert's being a little like me; of the Addresses and dinners A. would be plagued with; of my taking him to the Play soon. 'There'll be an immense flow of popularity now,' Lord M. said.

At half-past four the next afternoon the Queen stood at 'the very door' of Buckingham Palace to welcome her betrothed who looked, she thought, in spite of his seasickness, 'beautiful and so well'. Uncle Leopold had felt sure that once the lovers were reunited all the little misunderstandings of the past two months would quickly melt away, and so indeed it proved. 'Seeing his dear dear face again put me at rest about everything.' On the Sunday they had a talk about the thorny question of the Household and Albert, as Uncle had promised, showed himself 'open to conviction if good arguments are brought forward', and only wishing 'to have it proved that he misunderstands the case, to give it up without ill-humour.' During the evening they read over the Marriage Service together 'and tried how to manage the ring.'

Victoria had won a victory over Lord M. and Mamma, who had both had doubts about the propriety of the engaged couple sleeping under the same roof, scruples which the Queen had dismissed as 'foolish nonsense'. She had also got her way about not appearing publicly at church on the day before the wedding, and a service was held inside the Palace with the Bishop of London preaching 'a very fine sermon'.

The wedding day itself dawned wild, wet and windy, but the Queen was undismayed and wrote a cheerful little note to Albert on waking. 'Dearest . . .. How are you today, and have you slept well? I have rested very well, and feel very comfortable today. What weather! I believe, however, the rain will cease. Send one word when you, my most dearly loved bridegroom, will be ready. Thy ever-faithful, Victoria R.'

She had breakfast and a visit from Mamma, who brought her a nosegay of orange flowers. 'Dearest kindest Lehzen' gave her a dear little ring, and she again defied tradition by seeing Albert 'for the *last* time *alone*, as my Bridegroom.' At half-past twelve she was ready to leave for the Chapel Royal, accompanied by Mamma and the Duchess of Sutherland, dressed in 'a white satin gown with a very deep flounce of Honiton lace, imitation of old'. She had a wreath of orange blossom on her head and wore a diamond necklace and earrings, with Albert's wedding present of 'a beautiful sapphire brooch'.

It was still raining, but nevertheless 'a countless multitude thronged the park, and was scattered over the town.' The Tories and prosperous upper classes might not think much of the Queen's choice, but the ordinary Londoners were generously pleased about her romance and sympathetically inclined towards a young, good-looking Prince.

Arrived at St James's, Victoria went into the dressing-room to be greeted by her trainbearers, twelve young ladies 'dressed all in white with white roses', and waited until dearest Albert's procession had moved into the Chapel. Her own procession then formed up in the Throne Room, Lord Melbourne, in a fine new dresscoat, again carrying the Sword of State. As the Queen entered the Chapel there was a flourish of trumpets and the organ began to play, 'which had a beautiful effect.' Albert, resplendent in the uniform of a British Field Marshal and wearing the Order of the Garter, stood at the Altar flanked by the rest of the royal family: Mamma, Uncle Sussex in his invariable black skull cap, who sobbed audibly throughout the ceremony, the Cambridges, old Aunt Augusta, Aunt Adelaide in purple velvet, Princess Sophia Matilda of Gloucester and, watching their nurselings anxiously from the shadows, Baroness Lehzen and Baron Stockmar.

The body of the Chapel was filled with an almost exclusively Whig congregation. The Queen, lamented Charles Greville, 'had been as wilful, obstinate and wrongheaded as usual about her invitations.' 'Nothing could be more improper and foolish than to make this a mere Whig party', he grumbled, but Victoria was unrepentant and, with the exception of the Duke of Wellington, Lord Liverpool and one or two others, she had once again successfully kept the Tories out. This was, as she pointed out, HER marriage and she meant to have only those present who could sympathize with her.

It was three hundred years since a Queen Regnant of England had been married and, as Queen Mary Tudor's wedding had followed the Catholic rite, it was not much help as a precedent. It had therefore been decided to use George III's and Queen Charlotte's marriage service as a pattern.

The Ceremony was very imposing [recorded the Queen], and fine and simple, and I think OUGHT to make an everlasting impression on every one who promises at the Altar to *keep* what he or she promises. Dearest Albert repeated everything very distinctly. I felt so happy when the ring was put on, and by Albert. As soon as the Service was over, the Procession returned as it came, with the exception that my beloved Albert led me out.

After signing the Register, Victoria returned to Buckingham Palace alone with Albert. The crowd was again immense and 'they cheered us really most warmly and heartily.' Back at the Palace the newly married couple had a quiet half-hour alone together before the wedding breakfast, at which the Queen sat between her husband and Uncle Sussex. Healths were drunk and 'Albert and I drank a glass of wine with Lord Melbourne, who seemed much affected by the whole.'

Victoria went upstairs to change into 'a white silk gown trimmed with swansdown and a white bonnet with orange flowers', and saw Lord M. for ten minutes. 'I shook hands with him and he kissed my hand. Talked of how well everything had gone off. "Nothing could have gone off better", he said, and of the people being in such good humour.' Then it was time to go. 'I pressed his hand once more, and he said "God bless you, Ma'am", most kindly and with such a kind look. Dearest Albert came up and fetched me downstairs, where we took leave of Mamma and drove off at near 4; I and Albert alone which was *so delightful.*'

Greville, who seemed determined to find fault, thought they went off 'in a very poor and shabby style. Instead of the new chariot in which most married persons are accustomed to dash along, they were in one of the old travelling coaches, the postillions in undressed liveries, and with a small escort.' However he admitted that they were 'pretty well received' and the Queen wrote that the crowds 'never ceased until we reached Windsor Castle. Our reception was most enthusiastic and hearty and gratifying in every way; the people quite deafening us; and horsemen and gigs etc. driving along with us.'

That first evening, alone with Albert, was a revelation. Victoria had such a sick headache that she couldn't eat any dinner and was obliged to lie down on the sofa, but headache or not, she had *never, never* spent such an evening.

My *dearest dearest dear* Albert sat on a footstool by my side, and his excessive love and affection gave me feelings of heavenly love and happiness I never could have *hoped* to have felt before! . . . Really how can I ever be thankful enough to have such a *Husband*! . . . to be called by names of tenderness I have never yet heard used to me before – was bliss beyond belief! Oh! this was the happiest day of my life! – May God help me to do my duty as I ought and be worthy of such blessings!

The Victoria and Albert idyll had begun.

Postscript

As Lord Melbourne had sagely remarked, marriage was 'a great *change*' and from the day of her marriage the Queen's old life began, slowly but inexorably, to fade around her. Melbourne remained in office for another eighteen months or so, but when his government finally fell in the late summer of 1841 Victoria was entering the seventh month of her second pregnancy, she had other interests, other preoccupations, and Albert was at hand to ease the parting.

She still felt it, of course. 'I am still bewildered, and can't believe that my excellent Lord Melbourne is no longer my Minister,' she wrote to King Leopold. '. . . After seeing him for four years, with very few exceptions – *daily* – you may imagine that I *must* feel the change; and the longer the time gets since we parted, the *more* I feel it.' But this time there were no tempests of tears, no tantrums and no foot-stamping. The Queen's conduct at the Council when the new Cabinet was sworn in was exemplary, and Charles Greville was quite touched. 'She looked very much flushed, and her heart was evidently brim full, but she was composed and throughout the whole of the proceedings . . . preserved complete self-possession, composure and dignity. . . . Peel told me she had behaved perfectly to him.'

Thanks to Albert's tactful stage-management, the threat of a repetition of the Bedchamber crisis had been averted – two senior ladies being persuaded to resign – and, guided by Albert, Victoria began gradually to perceive Sir Robert's many sterling qualities.

The new Prime Minister was, in fact, to become a valued and respected friend of the royal couple.

As for Melbourne, once the first wrench was over, it was he who suffered most from the separation. He had grown more dependent than he had realized on his daily contact with the Queen, and away from her he became a lonely, pathetic old man. His health began to fail – he suffered a slight stroke in October 1842 and from then on aged rapidly. When he died six years later at the age of sixty-nine, the bulky image of Lord M. with his kind, fatherly looks, his ready tears and loud hooting laugh had already melted, ghostlike, into the Queen's past, and Albert's influence was paramount. She mourned her old friend with gentle melancholy, conscientiously dedicating twenty-four hours to his memory, but she had by this time rather come to regret her once intense affection for him, feeling that, as Albert said, she had worked herself up 'to what really became at last, quite foolish'.

The other victim of change, of course, was Lehzen, and the first two years of the Queen's marriage were darkened by storms caused by the raging jealousy between Albert and 'darling Daisy'. Lehzen's shrewdness seems to have deserted her in her dealings with the Prince. Possibly her period of ascendancy at the Palace had made her over-confident. Possibly she had convinced herself that the newcomer, a shy boy of twenty, could, with a little firmness, be kept in his place as a plaything and nonentity. At all events, she misread the situation disasterously and embarked on a battle to which there could be only one outcome. By the autumn of 1842 Albert had succeeded where John Conroy had failed, and Lehzen, who in over twenty years had never taken a day's holiday, departed to make her home with her sister in Bückeburg with what inner heartbreak we can only guess at. Selfless to the end where her beloved was concerned, she slipped away without saying goodbye in order to spare Victoria the distress of a farewell scene, leaving the Queen feeling sad but agreeing with dearest Albert that perhaps it was 'for our and her best'. They continued to correspond and met occasionally on the royal visits to Germany. 'Saw my poor old Lehzen,' wrote the Queen in 1862.

'She is grown so old. We were both much moved.' Lehzen lived on for another eight years, dying in 1870 at the age of eighty-six, the last survivor of those who could remember the little Princess at Kensington Palace.

For the Duchess of Kent, on the other hand, her daughter's marriage meant release from the outer darkness into which she had been so unceremoniously thrust in June 1837. The Coburg bond was always a strong one, and from the beginning relations between Prince Albert and his aunt cum mother-in-law were warmly affectionate. The birth of the Princess Royal in November 1840 helped to draw the family closer together, and the disappearance of Lehzen removed the last barrier to a reconciliation between mother and daughter. Assured now, for the first time since her arrival in England, of a secure and honoured place in the royal circle, the Duchess was finally relieved of the need to assert herself which had been the cause of so many of her troubles. She could relax and become once again the affectionate, cheerful, outgoing, rather simple-minded soul who had captivated the Duke of Kent at Amorbach so many years ago. When she died in March 1861 the unhappy past had long been buried, and the Queen, going through her mother's papers, was almost unbearably moved to discover 'how very very much she and my beloved Father *loved* each other. *Such* love and affection. I hardly knew it was *to that extent*. Then her love for *me*. It is too touching; I have found little books with the accounts of my babyhood, and they show *such* unbounded tenderness!'

For Victoria herself marriage brought the greatest change of all, and was undoubtedly the most important influence of her long life. During that lifetime, as the world changed around her at a speed unknown to previous generations, several Victorias had been presented to the public eye. There had been Lehzen's Victoria, the withdrawn, enigmatic Princess; Melbourne's Victoria, the exuberant, headstrong little Queen; Albert's Victoria, the adoring, submissive wife; and, finally, England's Victoria, the formidable matriarch, grandmother of Europe and Regina Imperatrix who gave her name to an age.

Hers was a complex, contradictory character – she could be

shrewd yet sentimental, devious yet outspokenly honest, hysterical yet icily composed, charmingly naive yet terrifyingly regal – but beneath all the contradictions, the paradoxes and the different personas there remained, quite recognizably, to the end the strong-willed, emotional, hot-tempered, incurably truthful, loving, insecure child who had ridden in her donkey carriage in Kensington Gardens and played on the sands at Ramsgate.

Genealogical
Tables

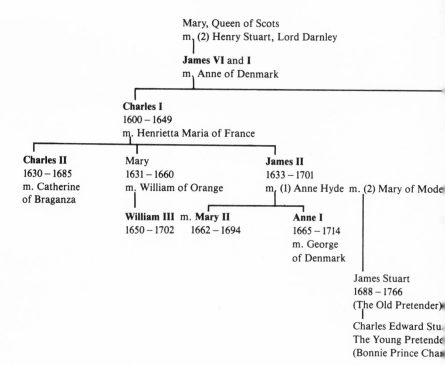

Mary, Queen of Scots
m (2) Henry Stuart, Lord Darnley

James VI and **I**
m Anne of Denmark

Charles I
1600 – 1649
m. Henrietta Maria of France

Charles II
1630 – 1685
m. Catherine
of Braganza

Mary
1631 – 1660
m. William of Orange

James II
1633 – 1701
m (1) Anne Hyde m. (2) Mary of Mode

William III m. **Mary II**
1650 – 1702   1662 – 1694

Anne I
1665 – 1714
m. George
of Denmark

James Stuart
1688 – 1766
(The Old Pretender)

Charles Edward Stu
The Young Pretende
(Bonnie Prince Cha

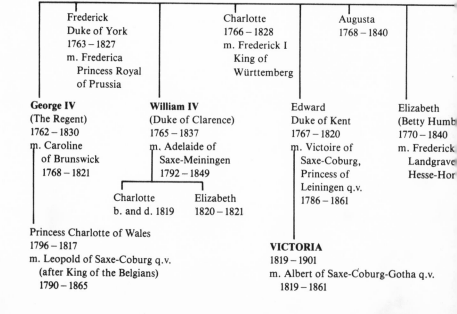

Frederick
Duke of York
1763 – 1827
m. Frederica
Princess Royal
of Prussia

Charlotte
1766 – 1828
m. Frederick I
King of
Württemberg

Augusta
1768 – 1840

George IV
(The Regent)
1762 – 1830
m. Caroline
of Brunswick
1768 – 1821

William IV
(Duke of Clarence)
1765 – 1837
m. Adelaide of
Saxe-Meiningen
1792 – 1849

Edward
Duke of Kent
1767 – 1820
m. Victoire of
Saxe-Coburg,
Princess of
Leiningen q.v.
1786 – 1861

Elizabeth
(Betty Humb
1770 – 1840
m. Frederick
Landgrave
Hesse-Hor

Charlotte
b. and d. 1819

Elizabeth
1820 – 1821

Princess Charlotte of Wales
1796 – 1817
m. Leopold of Saxe-Coburg q.v.
(after King of the Belgians)
1790 – 1865

VICTORIA
1819 – 1901
m. Albert of Saxe-Coburg-Gotha q.v.
1819 – 1861

Queen Victoria's Descent from the House of Stuart

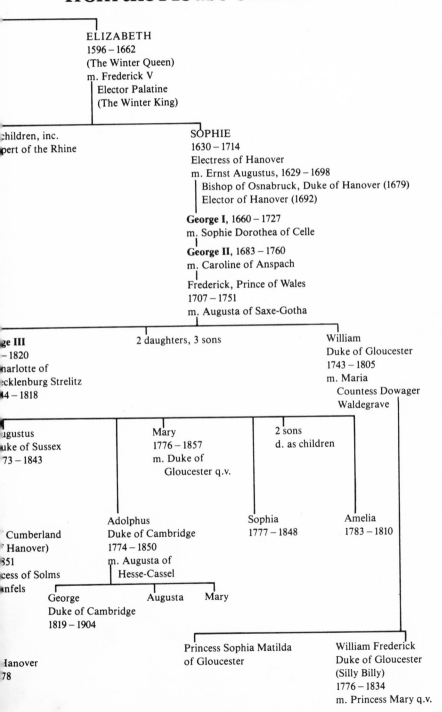

ELIZABETH
1596 – 1662
(The Winter Queen)
m. Frederick V
  Elector Palatine
  (The Winter King)

:hildren, inc.
pert of the Rhine

SOPHIE
1630 – 1714
Electress of Hanover
m. Ernst Augustus, 1629 – 1698
  Bishop of Osnabruck, Duke of Hanover (1679)
  Elector of Hanover (1692)

George I, 1660 – 1727
m. Sophie Dorothea of Celle

George II, 1683 – 1760
m. Caroline of Anspach

Frederick, Prince of Wales
1707 – 1751
m. Augusta of Saxe-Gotha

ge III
– 1820
narlotte of
:cklenburg Strelitz
4 – 1818

2 daughters, 3 sons

William
Duke of Gloucester
1743 – 1805
m. Maria
  Countess Dowager
  Waldegrave

ugustus
uke of Sussex
73 – 1843

Mary
1776 – 1857
m. Duke of
  Gloucester q.v.

2 sons
d. as children

Cumberland
Hanover)
351
cess of Solms
infels

Adolphus
Duke of Cambridge
1774 – 1850
m. Augusta of
  Hesse-Cassel

Sophia
1777 – 1848

Amelia
1783 – 1810

George
Duke of Cambridge
1819 – 1904

Augusta

Mary

Ianover
78

Princess Sophia Matilda
of Gloucester

William Frederick
Duke of Gloucester
(Silly Billy)
1776 – 1834
m. Princess Mary q.v.

Queen Victoria's Maternal Relations

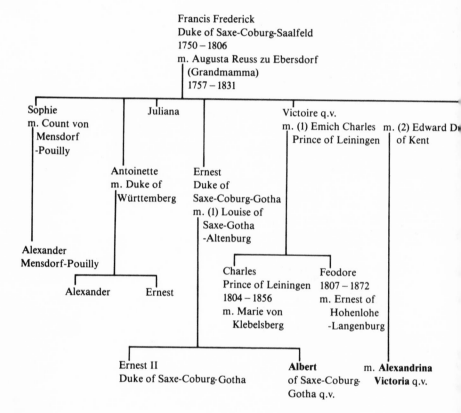

Francis Frederick
Duke of Saxe-Coburg-Saalfeld
1750 – 1806
m. Augusta Reuss zu Ebersdorf
(Grandmamma)
1757 – 1831

Sophie
m. Count von
Mensdorf
-Pouilly

Juliana

Victoire q.v.
m. (1) Emich Charles   m. (2) Edward D
Prince of Leiningen   of Kent

Antoinette
m. Duke of
Württemberg

Ernest
Duke of
Saxe-Coburg-Gotha
m. (1) Louise of
Saxe-Gotha
-Altenburg

Alexander
Mensdorf-Pouilly

Alexander   Ernest

Charles
Prince of Leiningen
1804 – 1856
m. Marie von
Klebelsberg

Feodore
1807 – 1872
m. Ernest of
Hohenlohe
-Langenburg

Ernest II
Duke of Saxe-Coburg-Gotha

Albert   m. Alexandrina
of Saxe-Coburg-   Victoria q.v.
Gotha q.v.

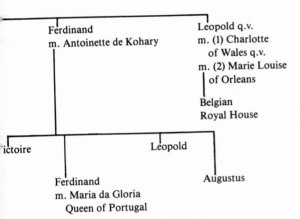

Ferdinand
m. Antoinette de Kohary

Leopold q.v.
m. (1) Charlotte
  of Wales q.v.
m. (2) Marie Louise
  of Orleans

Belgian
Royal House

ictoire

Leopold

Ferdinand
m. Maria da Gloria
  Queen of Portugal

Augustus

Bibliography

Albermarle, Lord, *Fifty Years of my Life*, vol. II (London, 1877)

Anecdotes, Personal Traits and Characteristic Sketches of Victoria I . . . by a Lady (London, 1840)

Annual Register of World Events, 1819, 1838

Arbuthnot, *The Journal of Mrs, 1820–1832*, vol. II, ed. Francis Bamford and the Duke of Wellington (London, Macmillan, 1930)

Ashdown, Dulcie, *Queen Victoria's Mother* (London, Robert Hale, 1974)

Brougham, The Life and Times of Henry, Lord, written by himself (London, 1871)

Burghersh, Correspondence of Lady, with the Duke of Wellington, ed. R. Weigall (London, 1903)

Bury, Lady Charlotte, The Diary of a Lady in Waiting, ed. A. F. Steward (London, 1908) .

Cathcart, Helen, *Royal Bedside Book* (London, W. H. Allen, 1969)

Colchester, Diaries and Correspondence of Charles Abbot, Lord (London, 1861)

Creevey Papers, The, ed. Herbert Marshall (London, 1904), ed. John Gore (London, John Murray, 1948)

Creston, Dormer, *The Regent and his Daughter* (London, Eyre & Spottiswoode, 1947)

Creston, Dormer, *The Youthful Queen Victoria* (London, Macmillan, 1952)

Croker Papers, 1808–1857, The, vol. I, ed. L. J. Jennings (London, 1884–1885)

Duff, David, *Edward of Kent* (London, Stanley Paul, 1938)

Esher, Viscount (ed.), The Girlhood of Queen Victoria, vols. I & II (London, 1912)

Fulford, Roger, *The Royal Dukes* (London, Duckworth, 1933; new edition Collins, 1973)

Gillen, Mollie, *The Prince and his Lady* (London, Sidgwick & Jackson, 1970)

Granville, Letters of Harriet, Countess, 1810–1845. ed. F. Leveson Gower (London, 1894)

Greville Diary, The ed. Philip Whitwell Wilson (London, Heinemann, 1927); *Greville Memoirs, The,* ed. Roger Fulford and Lytton Strachey (London, Macmillan, 1938)

Grey, C., *The Early Years of the Prince Consort* (London, 1867)

Harcourt Papers, The, ed. E. W. Harcourt (London, 1881)

Hibbert, Christopher, *George IV* (London, Allen Lane, 1973)

Hunt, Leigh, *The Old Court Suburb*, vol. II (London, 1855)

Jerningham Papers, vol. II, ed. Egerton Castle

Knight, Charles, *Passages of a Working Life*, vol. II (London, 1864)

Lee, Sidney, *Queen Victoria* (London, 1902)

Lieven, Letters of Dorothea, Princess, 1812–1834, ed. L. G. Robinson (London, 1902)

Lieven, The Private Letters of Princess, to Prince Metternich, 1820–1826, ed. P. Quennell and D. Powell (London, John Murray, 1937)

London Gazette, The, May 1819

Longford, Elizabeth, *Victoria, R. I.* (London, Weidenfeld & Nicolson, 1964)

Longford, Elizabeth, *Wellington, Pillar of State* (London, Weidenfeld & Nicolson, 1972)

Martineau, Harriet, *Harriet Martineau's Autobiography* (London, 1877)

Neale, Erskine, *Life of Edward, Duke of Kent* (London, 1850)

Newton, The Diary of Benjamin, ed. C. P. Fendall and E. A. Crutchley (London, 1933)

Saxe-Coburg-Saalfeld, Augusta, Dowager Duchess of, *In Napoleonic Days*, extracts from the diary of, ed. H.R.H. Princess Beatrice (London, John Murray, 1941.)

Stanley, Life and Correspondence of Arthur Penrhyn, 2 vols, ed. R. E. Prothero (London, 1893)

Stockmar, The Memoirs of Baron, ed. Baron E. von Stockmar, trans. G.A.M. (London, 1872)

Stuart, D. M., *Daughter of England* (London, Macmillan, 1951)

Sudley, Lord (ed.), *The Lieven-Palmerston Correspondence, 1828–1856* (London, John Murray, 1943)

Victoria, Letters of Queen, 1837–1861, ed. A. C. Benson and Viscount Esher (London, John Murray, 1907)

Walmsley, Robert, *Peterloo, The Case Reopened* (Manchester, U.P., 1969)

Wharncliffe and her Family, The First Lady, vol. ii, ed. Caroline Grosvenor and Charles Belby. (London, Heinemann, 1927)

Woodham-Smith, Cecil, *Queen Victoria, 1819–1861* (London, Hamish Hamilton, 1973)

Index